HISTORY
and
GASTRONOMY
in
SICILY

Franco Campo

Ordering Information:

Prime Seven Media
518 Landmann St.
Tomah City, WI 54660

Printed in the United States of America

NOTES OF HISTORY AND GASTRONOMY IN THE SICILIAN TERRITORY

AUTORE: **FRANCO CAMPO**

E-mail: camporotondo1947@gmail.com

DEDICATION

I would like to express special thanks of gratitude to Mr. Hassan Nazer, movie director of World Film Production, for his support in making my dream a reality.

Special thanks to Mrs. Toktam Mazhari and all the staff of Harmony Cafe' in Aberdeen, for their invaluable encouragement and support toward my feelings.

My thoughts are for Barbara, my long-time partner and our Sophie baby, who have been the source for the success and for the unsuccess of my life.

Last but not least, I want to dedicate my book to Donna Carmela Campo (1928-2023) la mia meravigliosa mamma per avermi dato la vita e la passione.

CAPITOLO PRIMO: MISERIA E NOBILTA'

PARAGRAFO I - LA CUCINA DEI RICCHI E LA CUCINA DEI POVERI

PARAGRAFO II - A CONVIVIO CON I RICCHI E L'OSPITALITÀ CASALINGA

PARAGRAFO III - LE COTTATE DI FAVE ED IL VINO DELLE TAVERNE

PARAGRAFO IV - LE TEORIE UMORALI - LE ANIME - LE RICORRENZE

PARAGRAFO V - I MONSÙ E LA CUCINA DEL GATTOPARDO

PARAGRAFO VI - EFFETTO MONSÙ NELLA CUCINA SICILIANA

LA CUCINA DEI RICCHI E LA CUCINA DEI POVERI

GASTAREA: *È la decima musa.*
Essa presiede ai piaceri del gusto.

Da: Fisiologia del Gusto, Pensieri Trascendentali
Autore: A. BRILLAT-SAVARIN, 1755-1826
Giurista e Gastronomo Francese

Already in the Middle Ages it was possible to draw a brief distinction between *poor cuisine and rich cuisine.*
In the poor kitchen the absolute protagonist was *hunger* or fear of the same; it was therefore considered a necessity to proceed with the setting aside and preservation of food as abundance could, inevitably, follow moments of famine and the consequent specter of hunger.

Hence the need and observance to proceed with the transformation of everything that was fresh into something that could be preserved with the purpose and in order to last over time.
Apart from certain foodstuffs of a non-perishable nature such as cereals and legumes; the idea and the need were to transform, for example: milk into cheese, meat into cured meats and sausages, the preservation of food in oil or pickled, transforming fruit into jams, proceeding to salting and smoking fish and meat. All this was invented by the poor, peasants to create supplies of available foods.

Another feature of poor cuisine would be home fantasies; that is, the fictions of imagining what was in a dish; when in reality this thing is missing.
So we can eat: *A fake broth, a fake sauce, fake tripe, escaped birds, mountain fish and so on.*
It is said that: *A good housewife would be able to draw blood from a turnip or you could put a boot in the pot, instead of capons,* as *Charlie Chaplin* did.
It is precisely from the shortage that masterpieces can be born, these are not counterfeit foods, the kitchen turns into an illusion of taste, replacing expensive ingredients with others at low prices; without diminishing the happiness of tastes.

In the rich cuisine or of the rich or of the fat people, since Roman, medieval and Renaissance times, fresh foods, meat and fish in particular, were made and cooked with the artifice that is: giving them different flavors that are clearly conferred by the wise use of spices and condiments.

Another factor that determines the rich cuisine would be the presentation or rather the ostentation of the foods, which gourmets define: *Food Style.*

One of the purposes of the kitchen, using a large number of condiments, was to make the guests to understand how rich the master was. The ostentatious preparations and presentations of food in the tables of the rich also referred to the individual conditions and positions, to the social hierarchies of the host, his bride and the children begotten.
There was no lack in the cuisine of the nobles, the parvenu or those who wanted to fit well into the privileged caste, the tendency to pleasure for the exotic, for the exclusive; that is, the use of particular dishes that contributed to assign a social *status.*

Such a Piemontese doctor, at the service of the Princes of Savoy in the eighteenth century, recommended to the nobles and wealthy of those districts, to refrain from heavy soups such as those of legumes; in turn the poor should abstain from chosen and refined foods as their gross stomach would hardly be able to assimilate or fully appreciate them.

Someone, in the distinction between rich and poor cuisine, said that the difference would also consist in the fact that the rich are endowed, compared to the poor, with higher tastes; as the culinary art, good food, the philosophies of food, conviviality and commensality;these are disciplines that impinge tastes.

The gastronomes say: Everything is entrusted to our oral organ as taste is a sensory process linked to the recognition, judgment, identification of foods such as food and drinks that generates, with annexes and connected, the art of cooking and the imagination of gastronomy.
The study of tastes, in modern disciplines, is called: Gastrosophy.

A father of gastronomy in the nineteenth century, the French lawyer Brillat-Savarin in its composition: *The Physiology of Taste,* states that our God ordered us to eat to live, and to this end, he compensated us humans with appetite.

From these statements it is easy to deduce and attribute taste to the rich and appetite to the poor.

I think that the food wisdom of our farmer is closer to the affirmation of appetites. It is not possible to combine the tastes of the people but it can be said, without a shadow of a doubt, that our farmers did not lack appetite in the past and is not lacking nowadays.

In my opinion and with all due respect to gastrosophy,good food and the related conviviality; not necessarily the rich must be endowed with higher tastes; our taste buds do not depend on wealth or poverty or on the basis of people's social class; the food divergences between rich and poor cuisine depend not on sensory vehicles but on the economic possibilities of the subjects.

Philosophers, gastronomes and lovers of good living have asked themselves and imposed the question rebus on us:

IF, you live to eat – or – IF, you eat to live.
In other words, it is up to us to decide the Hamlet: IF – *In this case the doubter is a must -*

In nutrition, understood as the need for survival, material and cultural factors play a decisive role:

1. The material factors are represented by the orographic nature of the soils, by the climatic conditioning, by the morphological qualities of the soils; the means and methods of finding agricultural commodities and the way in which the processes of breeding, fishing and harvesting are managed.
2. Cultural factors are represented by the development of historical events, the provision of migratory flows, the influence of religious dictates, the alternation of fashions and food choices.

A worthy answer to the question might be that the rich:
They live to eat.
The minute people, contrary to the philosophical commandments:
Eat for a living

The pro-gastronomic creed of the farmer was:

- *U Picca N'avasta, u Magnu N'Assupercia.*

The little is enough for us. Too much overwhelms us

Or to quote another saying:

- *Carni e pisci e a casa si finisci.*

This was the favorite saying of my grandmother *Ciccina*, a native of Scicli, which meant that the excessive use of expensive foods led, irreparably, to the disintegration and ruin of the fragile domestic economy.

From these popular sayings it is clear how parca had been the peasant cuisine in general, contrary to food waste; affixing the title of – *Manciatari* or Eaters – for those who made use, disuse and waste of expensive foods.

My grandfather *Franco* told me that, from the beginning of the last century and clearly in the times before it; there were friars preachers in the city streets, called *Cucuzzuna* because their heads were shaved and bold.

These friars, in their spiritual exercise, addressed congregations of the people such as workers and peasants, vehemently invoking parsimony in food, abstention from gluttony:

Pi' La Panza si và All'Unfiernu.
The Belly symbolized the goodies that led souls to the kingdom of Lucifer .

The religious friar, thus cursing, in the grip of hysterical convulsions, dissolved the chain he carried attached to his hips and began to whip himself without any pain, causing himself dents and bruises of various kinds.

In the religious spirit of those times the purity of the soul was preached, which had to survive on the weakness of the bodily flesh; inasm the religious ordinances or precepts condemned - The *Sins of Gluttony.*
The same throat from mere expression of pleasure or eccentric exhibition of wealth; it became a capital sin, an unclean vice: one that distances man from God and from eternal salvation.

Therefore, the Christian doctrines, whose task was to take us all to Heaven and the narrow economy that, even after the war, was based, almost exclusively, on a non-mechanized agriculture; they have certainly influenced eating patterns in the Sicilian countryside.

Our farmers:
Eat to live
and he had no other choices.

Comparing the two terms, it would be healthier to: Eat to live, than to live to eat; examples are food diets for people who are obese or suffering from food dysfunction such as diabetics.

The Hyblaean peasant cuisine, in the strict sense of the word, cannot be defined -*Poor* - because even if the farmer was not rich, he had at his disposal: the sowing in the fields, the vegetables in the garden, fruits that hung from the trees; the farm animals that produced eggs, from which they plucked the milk; the whole thing, honestly, it wasn't a trivial matter.

The gastronomic autarchy of the peasants made use and still makes use of those foods that are typical of the Mediterranean diet: Bread, pasta, vegetables, cereals, fruit, oil, vinegar and wine.
Certainly and until the second post-war period there were needy people suffering from poverty; those who did not have a sheet of earth or a job or an art that could, in a certain way, provide the food necessary for survival.

The Hyblaean peasants or the vast majority of them did not refuse to any poor needy a piece of bread, a bowl of ricotta or a semblance of it, or seasoned macaroni pasta, or a plate of beans or everything that would have been enough to hold a human being vertically instead of horizontally.

A CONVIVIO CON I RICCHI E L'OSPITALITÀ CASALINGA

Vuoi una ricetta per la tua vacanza?
Scegli un paesaggio unico,
aggiungi tanto sole ed una splendida natura,
sport e benessere a volontà,
mescola con ottimo vino e cucina autentica
e, infine, servi il tutto con il calore dell'ospitalità.
Il risultato è garantito.
Dallo scritto: Cucina Orale e Cucina scritta di Angelo Longo

In our area, when you have guests, for Christmas dinners or to celebrate an important event, the table is laid with tablecloths finely embroidered by grandmothers, sparkling utensils are placed on it, bottles filled with precious nectar, dishes with drawings are exposed and the desco is adorned with fragrant wild flowers.

The hosts dressed up for the party and with a joyful soul receive the family members, the guests, the foreigner.

All this happens not for ostentation on the part of those who give hospitality, but for that respect that distinguishes true expressions of reception towards our guests who sit at our table.

* * *

In the receptions of the rich, guests must assume a strict composure. The label or the *Bon Ton* imposed: the torso erected, compact legs boxed under the table; the face had to take on an expression of almost rigor, the chin had to be held up, the neck stiff and at most it would be allowed to give the bystanders a smile more melancholic than benevolent.

The party hall is pervaded by animate whispers that should denote the collective conviviality, the exchange of compliments, the personal reports of academic achievements, which are followed by interposed purposes and social paranoia; as if the table were a place where you feed not on food but *on verbum.*

Here the curtain opens with the bevy of gloved servants who have to lay down those insecure cups containing restricted broths, which in French cuisine is called *Consommè,* paying attention not to harass the contents in the jackets of the guests.

The ingestion of this broth, by the guests, without emitting lip noises or without pouring a stealthy drop into the exuberant ties or lace shirts, must be carried out with a rhythmic cadence; eight tablespoons of broth should be consumed in eight minutes.

The clearing by the waiters must be rapid, who has consumed or not consumed the broth makes no difference; as for a certain time, not a minute more and not a minute less, the landlord must take the floor, recently awarded the title of *Commendatore* with a certificate signed by the President of the Republic; who must offer the warm greeting and thanks to the special guest who, in turn, he renounced further valuable commitments to do honor, with his presence, to the table of the host lord.

En Suite is served the *Tournedos with Bernese Sauce* and side dish of *Ratatuille Brasata,*and as an accompaniment; the *Sommelier* uncorkes a classic Chateau De *Saint Germain* barricaded for at least seven years and appropriately decantated in garaffe of transparent glass to make it oxygenate: poor wine after seven years of *lockdown* will have the right to take a breath of air.

Here is the speach of the special guest, mentioned above, possibly a Senator of Palazzo Madama: *We who eat like caimans, who sleep like hippos, who drink like elephants. While in Africa children perish from disease and malnutrition.*

At the end of the agitated oratory, applause erupts from the distinguished presents, the landlord stands up to better be noticed and confirm his support for the underlying cause.
The ladies, because of the heartfelt appeal, in dismay look for that fatal handkerchief, to dry the tergiversante tear on the rosy cheeks, real or fake that it had been.

Certainly the dinner does not end here, there will be the *Gateau Sant'Honorè, the Chateau Margot champagne or the vintage Veuve Cliquot Ponsardin;* and dinner finally becomes a lavish feast.

Food worries, the urgent medical care that African children so much need, have been forgotten or set aside: if ever, they will be discussed again in a future banquet or in a future party.

* * *

More frank are the lunches or dinners in the home or in the peasant tenends regarding the afore mentioned Sicilian hospitality.

These are shabby festivals in which the *Champagne of Reims* is missed but certainly the joy of the table is not lacking.

The housewife who bowls those *Macaroni à Ciazzisa* - geographical reference to the charming town of Piazza Armerina - impregnated by that sweet and dense tomato ragout sauce to which the flakes of the savory and seasoned cheese are added.

Previously it was served an appetizer of gelatin seasoned with red chillie and with the pikles of the *Jardiniere.*

This main course is followed by large pork rib steacks, that in Sicilian dialect are called: *Sciurnatu.* These are the same meats that have produced, due to the long cooking, the savory seasoning for macaroni: greased and dripping from the permanence of tomato extracts; still keep attached, in the sides, that natural fat that when it crosses the oral cavity will release the soft sensations that will have the power to masturbate the taste buds.

These are the various tastes of Sicilian culinary traditions that enclose centuries of history.

How can one remain silent in front of the magnificence of the table, in front of the goodness of that glass filled with sincere wine; how can we not thank the one who hosted us and made a gift of these foods.

Because we are not in a restaurant where in the end we have to pay a high bill, we are welcome guests; our payment must not be made in cash or debit card but in gratitude to those who have shared and freely given their food and wines.

How can we not have gratitude to the priestess of the house who dedicated herself, early in the morning, to the various preparations, to the frying, to the cooking of the meat, to the drafting of the stews; to the complex making of homemade desserts.

I had almost forgotten to include in our Sicilian table the pastries stuffed with fig jam, the marzipan biscuits, the *cotomelle,* a soft ricotta dough enriched with Hyblaean honey and cinnamon powders or the scents of cassata pastry filled with soft ricotta mixed with sugar and lemon peel .

From these vibrant sensations of taste, from the exhalations of smells comes the joy of the table that generates amazement, smiles that will turn into laughter as a result of the stories; everyone will have a joke or push joke to tell, to share with the bystanders.

Let's stop time for a moment and photograph what hovers in that familiar desco, such as the instantaneous sensations of the subjects, their fleeting thoughts, the moments of reflection:

- The wife, pleased with the success of the party, looks at the guests to verify that they are at ease.
- the elderly grandfather who turns around and sees the generations of his offspring united in a desco.
- The father who looks at his young daughter who continues to grow in beauty.

- The anxious parent notices the sadness of the older daughter who broke up with her boy friend; so she decided, for her future, to continue her studies abroad, possibly to find an occasional job to relieve the family from excessive university expenses.

When the farewell arrives, it will be the most touching moment, we hold each other tightly in the embrace, we wish each other the most beautiful things and we renew our regard for the indissoluble bonds of kinship.

With the guests the sacredness of relationships is established that is expressed in friendship, in coming together in mutual help: *Do not hesitate to call me if you need anything.*

Among all the hope of future meetings is born, to be able once again to be together to revive moments like these, which will have the magical power to procrastinate the worries to the following day.

*   *   *

Giving food means creating solidarity, most of the food traditions, since the times of *Magna Grecia civilasition*, on the offering of food as a ritual gift and even spiritual sacrifice towards the Gods.

This is the Sicilian table that in the social aspect is common to all the tables of this planet but Sicilian cuisine is a dextrous cuisine, hovering between past and future, opulence and poverty.

It is the goodness of food that generates feelings, loves and modesty, which cause feelings of value towards the family, the society to which we belong, towards the nature that surrounds us.

The peasant society has played a predominant role in the various structures of nutrition, which have influenced the symbolic values of food as well as influenced the behaviors and customs of the Sicilian people.

Nutrition, apart from physiological needs, gives us life and creates the conditions to continue living and sometimes leads us to healing from fears, affective gaps and discomforts to which we are subjected to daily stresses.

To be alive, to be active, means to be present and our presence is required as an integral part of this earthly humanity and by the heterogeneous societies that compose it.

Black Lives Matter is the slogan of this time for protest against racism present and past; to which one could add, to the presence of a Pandemic Virus that is reaping victims all over the globe: The life of everyone *matter,* our existence and the existence of every single human being is important because the wealth of a nation depends on the people who are part of it.

LE COTTATE DI FAVE ED IL VINO DELLE TAVERNE

Da: Le Parità Morali dei nostri Villani:

- *Se tutti fossimo ricchi, Addio Fave.*

Il mondo dei poveri non potrebbe sussistere.

- *Il ricco ha 100 mila malanni:*

Reuma, Gotta, Calvizie e tante altre diavolerie;

mentre il Villano è sempre vegeto e sano

anche se si trova esposto ai venti, alla neve, ai solleoni.

- *Come se non bastasse il Ricco ha una infinità di grattacapi;*

ed il Villano è senza pensieri o ha un solo pensiero

di come meglio frodare i padroni.

Serafino Amabile Guastella, 1819-1899

Scrittore ed Antropologo di Chiaramonte Gulfi

Our Sicilian compatriots, not surprisingly, call us : *Sciusciamaccu - Those who blow on the macco of beans.*

We are the ones who, before starting to eat a plate of broad or fava beans with macco; blow on it: it will be a mere act to cool the soup or there may be other ritual reasons that can, in a certain way, provide a worthy justification for this gesture.

The breath could be compared to a kiss; a kiss of love towards those products that our land, mother and stepmother, has lavishly offered to their children?

In our kitchen there are arcane gestures, semiologies, invocations and evocations, religious rites such as those of performing yourself with the cross or self-blessing.

Well could therefore also a breath be a symbol of these wonders.

The breath, in the dialect of Ragusa is pronounced *Ciatu;* it makes me think of Sicilian mothers, when cuddling their child they exclaimed - *Ciatu, ciatuzzu miu* - irrefutable sign of maternal love: *You are my breath .... You are my life.*

Blowing then on food is a snob, the one who blows on cold dishes; while making a useless gesture, it wants to mean that he takes care of his person, making sure that the food does not damage but magnify his fine palate.

The human being is an animal endowed with a culture that is also outlined in its eating behavior; in the act of eating, man transmits his own identity: the ways, gestures, words that are put into action are endowed with a symbolic and ritual value.

The cottate or soups of fava beans, in the Hyblaean countryside, are the dish of the peasants or if we want to call them *viddani* or rather it would be to say *Contadini* those who manually worked the land with hoes, scythes, tridents and plows.

I don't see anything transcendental about being a farmer, it's a decent job that involves intelligence, physical strength, dedication, sweat in front and elbow grease.

On the other hand, it is also a useful job for nature; because trees are pruned, weeds are cleared from gardens; then the farmer milks the cows, cleans the stables, collects the olives, plows the fields, reaps the crops

Once a Lady with whom we had had a disagreement, on a virtual kitchen portal, about the drafting of a recipe, configured me with the joke: *Arms taken away from agriculture.*
To which I felt the duty to answer that my arms have always been dedicated to agriculture: you cannot love cooking if you do not love agriculture, the two functions are closely and inextricably linked; because gastronomy is not a science for its own sake but open to the horizons of human knowledge.

*   *   *

From what could derive the fact of placing these beans as a symbol of a category, or what would be the merits, characteristics, intrinsic properties of these legumes to be indicated, counted as a dish at the level, not only local, but well known in the cuisines of different countries.
To validate what has been said, the term *Macco* does not find translations in any other language, in the gastronomic magazines of international cuisine, whatever the language used: English, Arabic, African, Indian or Cantonese; the macco is pronounced, read and written: *Macco, at most, Maccu.*

The LEGUMES in question are the fruit of the *FAVA Vicia or Vulgaris* plant that was sown in the late-autumn season on clayey soils, to then be able to obtain the pods in the spring months.

Seedlings in the favata sprouted after 15 days after planting; when these reached 20 centimeters it was considered appropriate to proceed with the topping to accelerate fruiting and prevent attacks of aphids. The plants of fava did not require special fertilization but it was necessary to proceed with the mouvement of the soil to protect the plants from the cold and from weeds and plant pests.

Among these weeds, for the peasants, the most dangerous was considered the *Lupa* which was a fungus against the vegetation of the plants.

I remember that my dad sent me through the rows of favata to eradicate this: *Lupa mashroom* .

To get dry broad beans you need to leave the pods in the plants, for a couple of months, until the fruits harden.

Subsequently, the plants are eradicated, accumulate forming bundles that will be arranged in a closed place to be subsequently beaten and shaken, so that the product, that is the beans, can be collected and stored in wide and high baskets composed of intertwined reeds; bottomless and without lid. Which were called: *Cannizzi* in Sicilian dialect.

In the Hyblaean soils are cultivated the fava beans called *Cottoie* which, compared to the other varieties, have a thinner skin that facilitates cooking.

The peasants claimed that the fava to be edible had to be *Cucivuli that is Cottoie and San Pantaleo*. Although I inquired what San Pantaleo has to do with the fava beans and if there was ever a San Pantaleo; I have been unable to find the sources.

The non-sewable beans are smaller in size so they are called *Favetto* and are used as feed for farm animals.

It seems that at the beginning the size of the broad beans were actually smaller; before they had been domesticated in the soils.

From the protein point of view it was claimed that the fava vicia beans contained *Iron,* which would provide the human body with energy and vigor that the peasants needed for hard work in the fields.

The beliefs of farmers have not been disproved by food chemistry: *Beans are rich in protein, iron, fiber and mineral salts.*

For these characteristics, hyblaean fava beans have been a fundamental and basic food to combat hunger and famine caused by the wars of the last century; moreover, the cultivation in hyblaean soils is considered optimal for the chemical-physical characteristics of the soil and for the microclimate of the areas.

The Greek playwright Aristophanes tells us that Hercules fed himself with a plate of beans, from which he drew strength and courage, before embarking on the extraordinary twelve labors.

Giuseppe Parini, in the eighteenth-century poem *Il Giorno,* expresses in the verse: *Soave, as the taste of Hyblaean beans.*

* * *

In my not short existence I remember having once eaten, in the company of friends, an authentic dish of broad beans in the *Taverna Candiano* in that of Modica, where there was a long table so that all the diners could sit together and in the large dining room where placed majestic wine barrels.

Cottata of beans, fresh homemade bread and red wine tapped directly from the barrels: Guys, what more do you hope for from life?

Then in the taverns after having dined abundantly with soups and boiled beef, due to the drinkng of several reeds of wine, - *Drink You that I drink too* - it was customary to sing loudly.

One of the most popular hymns, sung by the Ragusan tavern guest 'Nzinu Belfiore, was - U *Jadduzzu* - that is: the anxieties of a farmer in search of a bold cockerel escaped from the chicken coop.

The melodious Bellfiore sang the verses and the members of the brigade sang the choir, which recited:

Haimè.... Persi u jadduzzu e non sacciu un'è.

I was a member of these choirs; for the avoidance of doubt, I am not referring to the Coro dei Lombardi – *Miseri ed Assetati* – sung at the La Scala theater in Milan; but to the choral screams of the Gaudentes ragusani - *Appanati and Avvinazzati* - in the Taverne Modicane.

At the Taverna Vita Eterna; it was the motto of the place managed by Michele Nicastro in Modica Alta, where the cuisine was an authentic expression of genuine artistic-gastronomic identity of the Baroque County.

I used to go there with friends for lunch on weekdays, so that there were not so many people and Michele made us taste the most genuine things like that sausage twisted in an axis suspended between two chairs for the drying process that was slowly carried out in the shadows of the room, exposed to the beneficial airs of the soft winds.

Certainly other Taverns, in that arcane Baroque of Modica, were not outdone.

* * *

Returning to the cottata I will try to describe the elements that make this soup on the bases of my memories of the culinary techniques learned from my mother Carmela, who in the kitchen was and still is, despite the venerable age of 93 years old: *A Myth .. the Myth* and *My Myth*.

I confess that I am afraid to cook traditional Ragusan foods because my culinary skills are far inferior to those of our mothers, of which I hope I had inherited at least a hair.

Driven by a curious search I did a *surfing* on the internet to visit the countless images of broad bean soup in which everyone mentions the macco.
If you cook the fava beans, for example, they are boiled and then passed to the blender: We have not obtained a macco, we have at most a velvety soup.
If in the soup instead of dried fava beans we use the pods of green beans: We have not obtained a Macco, we have a wonderful soup but different from the traditional cottata.

Macco di Fave means the thick liquid, released and obtained by boiling dried broad beans in salted or slightly salted water; whose color, must be dark, not green and not yellow.

As a result I will stick only to the recipe of cottata di fave ragusana or modicana of peasant style; not to other recipes indicated in various blogs by self-styled gastronomes.

Despite the fact that it is said that the beans named *Cottoie* do not need to soak in water; in my opinion it is better to make this soak for at least two or three hours.

Before soaking, the beans must be cleaned of that black stripe located on the surface of the legume; that my mother called: *the nose;* otherwise, during cooking, the beans drink water swelling until it bursts.

These noses can be eliminated from the beans using a mall knife, by engraving the side from where this strip begins, making sure to pull it away.

The housewives of Ragusa carried out this work with their teeth; they put the bean in the mouth and pinching the black strip with incisor teeth detached it from the body of the legume.
So the various strips remained attached to the teeth and when they had collected, in the oral cavity, more or less twenty strips; these were bluffed out: then these strips from the mouth went to arrange themselves in the black garments of the housewives.

15 or 20 percent of the available fava beans were cleaned of the skins, these bare beans will give the future macco a greater thickening.

One of the characteristics of the peasant cottata, unlike modern soups, was that most of the peels were not eliminated, but were part of the context.
A general principle would be that in foods the less you throw away the better; or that the skins could in a certain way give more protein to the soup, also improve the tastes and factivity of the macco.

* * *

The beans, as well as to compose soups, were also used by farmers as a delicious pastime.

Nowadays, while watching a movie, you eat popcorn; our farmers, in moments of relaxation – which in truth were few – spent the time with the : *Favi Caliati*.

The beans were cleaned of the skins and divided into two parts: which was not a difficult operation, as in the middle of the beans there was a natural crack; it was therefore enough to enlarge the tips of the beans with a small knife and this was divided into two parts.
At this point the half beans were arranged in a *dashboard,* with a pinch of sea salt, and baked, over gentle heat, until they appeared with a beautiful blond color.

The toastwed beans were crunchy and pleasant on the palate, a real panacea, they can be classified as things that enjoying them soothe the soul and lead it towards the joke: A *babbiata*.

Peasants and housewives used to praise these pastimes: *La bellezza de favi caliati:*

> *Chi t'arrivuordi quenn'erumu ziti*
> *ca ni manciaumu i favi caliati;*
> *now, ca siemu married,*
> *cauci, pugna and timpulati.*

*   *   *

So let's see the elements to create this fava cottoia soup, assuming we have to feed a team of ten workers who have come, in our countryside farm, to carry out the harvest in a wheat field *that I do not know ...*

After the farmer gave the seed the last tanning, called *Conza ri Maiu*, in the following month of June the wheat is harvested, mowing the stems of the seedlings that contained the ears in which the wheat seeds were settled.

This work began when the sun came out, the head of the crew - *called the Corporal* - designated the point from which to start the harvest, that is, from the highest part of the field, proceeding downwards and going against the wind.

Each reaper wear an apron and a leather bracelet on his wrist, and slips into the left hand fingers the cane to protect his limbs from the blade of the sickle.

The work lasted until sunset – *a cuddata ro suli*.
During the day there were clearly stops or intervals, to rest the limbs and to be able to take a few bites: *U Muzzicuni*.

In the reapers' saddlery – called *Viettili or Usazzi: depending on whether he lives in the ups or downs of Ragusa* – there will be homemade bread, a piece of *tomaccio cheese*, a fresh tomato, sliced cucumber, cutted onions, salt and fantasy.
By *fantasy* we meant everything that was materially missed and we imagined that there was: *Bread, knife and fantasy.*

For the lunch the reapers all keep seated in a circle, the farmer wife will provide some milk biscuits, the container with fresh well water and the red wine, and everyone start eating what he has available. For good manners any single reaper turn to his companions and showing the foods he has in his saddlery, invites all those present: *To Favor or to share the foods.*

The *carratello* was a cherry wood barrel with oval shapes, which contained three or five liters of wine, equipped with a main opening at the top and a hole on the sides from which you could suck the wine.

Na Vasata or Carrateiddu - It meant sipping from the hole of the barrel a sip of: *Vinu ro Pilarinu - Cà era bellu e finu.*

Pedalino is a village, suited to viticulture, between the municipalities of Comiso and Chiaramonte, whose wine produced would enter the area and the denomination of: *Cerasuolo di Vittoria*

This sip of wine was considered a prodigious remedy according to the dictates of the Salerno Medical School, founded in the ninth century, according to the treatise *Regimen Sanitatis Salernitanum.*

Wine, if moderately drunk, comforts and increases natural body heat, expels yellow bile with sweat and urine, softens the stiffened and hardened limbs from fatigue and tiredness, removes exhaustion, restores strength, fattens the body, strengthens energy and appetite.

Peasant wisdom is also expressed in the sayings: *Wine makes good blood – Wine is the milk of the old - wine prolongs life – In Vino Veritas... Etc.*

Allow me to explain some recent discoveries of biochemical science that confirm the aforementioned adages: wine is a support to digestion due to the presence of tartaric, malic and citric acid; performs antiseptic activities exerted by tannins and also, validating the indications of the father of medicine – Hippocrates – the wine has a diuretic action due to the presence of potassium and magnesium.

*   *   *

Mrs. Massaia, can we make this cottata of broad fava beans?
We then have the dressed beans to which we have removed the noses, we have proceeded to soak, we have the bare beans; it is time to light the fire.

Our housewife cook or *Massaia* must have at her disposal:

- Foodstuffs: The Beans, as prepared above. *A Junta ad personam.*
  For Junta we mean the beans contained in the two hands joined in.
- Meat: *A lard taffuni ad personam.*
  It is pork lard with the skin attached that has been stored in salt to be preserved. This lard was cut into square shape from the side of about 3 cm.
- Vegetables: For ten people: Onions 5, Garlic 10 teeth, *Celery* 2 heads, Carrots 3, Large ripe tomatoes 3
- Pasta: Dough with flour, salt and water. Composition of long macaroni twisted on themselves, called: *Lolli or manicu di fauci.*
- Spices: Fennel seeds and dried oregano. Salt. Black pepper.
  Chili flakes
- Olive oil. It must be used at the beginning, in the middle and at the end of cooking. Recommended quantities: *Ad Libitum*

Preparations

Finely cut the onions into strips, the garlic teeth into strips and the diced carrots, fry them with olive oil in a large pot .

Season the sauté with black pepper and arrange the lard squares.

Brown the sauté without burning the onions or other contents: in case spray the contents with red wine, to revive them.

Put the fava beans inside the pot, cover everything with cold water and proceed to salting.
Bring the contents to a boil and proceed over medium low heat for 30 minutes, making sure that the liquids move simmering.

Chop the two heads of celery, leaves included, add the tomatoes cut into bruschetta with the seeds and juices; incorporate these vegetables with the beans into the cooking liquids, give the context a generous turn of thick olive oil.

Continue cooking and proceed to the preparation of *the lolli* – which, in international cuisine, are called: *Dumplings*.
The latter are often used in the cottate of beans, in particular, when you have several guests; in the harvests in particular they are called: *Manicu di fauci;* to symbolize the scythes used in the work of the reapers.

Compose a dough with flour, a intake of salt and warm water .

Work the dough and compose a roll as long and thick as a breadstick that must be cut into segments of five. Gently roll these segments into the surfaces of the table to adjust their shapes.

These *lolli* should be inserted into the cottata in the last 15 minutes of cooking; which in total should last about 90 minutes from the moment of boiling.

It would be advisable, before inserting the dumplings,to check on the progress of cooking in order to verify the state of the beans; which skins should be soft and savory to taste; the macco must present itself in dense compactness; as a cream of bright dark gray color and the flavors must be transcendental: The sweetness of the carrots, the hints of celery and the juices of fats will certainly have given to our macco the required flavors.

Now the cottata needs aromas and here are the seeds of fennel, perhaps combined with oregano, the flakes of red chillie *and the last but not the least,*a further turn of that dense oil that should never be missed in these compositions.

Here, once the cooking is completed, the pot is placed on the table and we proceed to the partition.

* * *

The Massaia, with transient movements, using a lidle, lays the contents of broad beans, macco, lard and dumplings in the bowls that are brought by the workers; which, for the occasion, will present a captivating smile that wants to signify a due tribute to those who have made available and dedicated to the workers the magnificence of the evening food that will allow them to rest serenely in the haystacks, made available by the massaro; not without first having once again sipped the wine mixed with bubbling water.

The fact of mixing wine with water, even if now it is perhaps in disuse, was a practice that dates back to Roman times that to make their meetings last longer,without necessarily going into excandescences.

In the post-war Hyblaean peasant cuisine usually wine, during meals, was mixed with hydrolytin water, which they called: *Dancing Water,* because of the bubbles.

This Hydrolytin was composed of two sachets, which were poured, one at a time, into a liter of fresh water: in the first sachet there were bicarbonates and subsequently, with the second sachet, tartaric acid that hydrolyzed the carbonate ion; releasing -CO_2- the effervescence of carbon dioxide.

I remember the commercial of the hydrolytin of Cav. Gazzoni in the television commercial break:

> *Said the innkeeper to the Wine*
> *You become old to me*
> *I want to marry you with the water of my bucket.*
> *Answered the wine to the innkeeper*
> *Prepare publications*
> *groom the hydrolytin of Cav. Gazzoni*

In taverns the wine was usually mixed with the gaseous limonade.

The rural scents, carbon dioxide and sugars of the gaseous were well combined with wine; which even if it had been a bit rough wine, not really the flower of the grape must, it came out a mix not despicable but agreable to palate.

Then we must not forget that water, gaseous limonade or hydrolytin actually diluted the ethyl alcohol of wine, often avoiding, in taverns, inebriation: not everyone, in a state of drunkenness or suffering from acute ethylism, knew or were able to control their instincts with other people or with the family ...

Dulcis in Fundo - It was used, in the tables of Sicily, in *Spunsata;* when at the end of the meal the biscuits of almond pastry were dipped in Marsala wine; a purely Sicilian custom; that only in Sicily because of our sweet palates, of our sometimes fiery nature, could take place this indescribable sweetness, this combination between the unmistakable flavor of almonds and marzipan; conjugated with the voluptuousness of wine.

＊　＊　＊

Excuse me: *Tender is the night,*but our workers must go to rest because tomorrow they have to be on the field and our massaia has to prepare another cottata or maybe she will make a gastronomic surprise: *Le Lasagne cacate.*
Do not be horrified, this is a wide-brimmed home pasta filled with fresh ricotta cheese.

The dough for a peasant lasagna can be composed with the same dough as *the lolli or dumplings.*

LE TEORIE UMORALI - LE ANIME - LE RICORRENZE

Fa che il cibo sia la tua medicina
e la medicina il tuo cibo
Ippocrate, 460 a.C.- Medico e Padre della Medicina

We have seen the fava beans as food, *Staple food,* of a peasant cuisine; we will see now, going back in the centuries, a bit of history, mystery, shadows and superstitions that cloak or blend around this legume.

According to ancient traditions, the fava broad beans were a means of direct communication with the dead.
What could have led the ancient Egyptians, Greeks and Romans to reach these dramatic and arcane conclusions?

A first consideration may be the black color of the stripes on the surface of the legume; that we called *nasi* - if that were not enough, there would also be the color of the flower of the fava vicia that is white with macules of black, a color that is quite rare among the flowers of vegetables.

Black as we know has always been a sign of mourning, linked to the world of the dead, a symbol of mystery and the afterlife.

As if that were not enough, the ancient Greeks analyzing the flower of the fava beans discovered that these black spots, seemed to be arranged in the shape of T *or TAU* with which one would identify the term - *Thanatos* - which would indicate: the: *Death.*

*   *   *

Socrates' trilogy: *Men are mortal, Socrates is a man;* it is deduced that: *Socrates is mortal.*

It seems that the late philosopher liked the decoction of poisoned hemlock offered to him, with the tributes of the oligarchic government; who condemned Socrates for impiety, not tolerating that the young Athenians were more erudite to the virtues than to a sophistic philosophy of that time.
Even his wife *Santippe, as a good housewit,* considered her husband a loser, who spent time speaking in the square instead of going to work the fields.

A follower of Socrates was the Siciliota Empedocles as he was born in Akragas, acropolis of Magna Graecia – today Agrigento – in 494 BC.C. and died 60 years later, probably committing suicide, inside one of the craters of Mount Etna or *Mungibieddu.*

The philosopher Empedocles identified the roots of existence, which were later called *Elements: <u>Fire</u> - <u>Air</u> - <u>Earth</u> - <u>Water</u>.*

In philosophical thought: the union of such roots determines the birth of things, and their separation produces the end or death of things; but life and death are apparent in the sense that the roots or elements mentioned are not created or destroyed; it is only a continuous phase of transformation.

In a modern conception supported by the English scholar *Mattew Arnolds* in 1826, the theories of Empedocles can be traced back to the concept that: *Everything returns to the elements from which we come* or Nothing is born and *nothing dies.*

The philosopher Empedocles, throwing his body into the crater, wanted to prove his own theory:

- *Our bodies to the earth*
- *Our blood in the water*
- *Heat to the fire*
- *Breathing in the air.*

According to the physician Hippocrates, 460 a.C., to the elements expressed by Empedocles, corresponded the *Humors of our body:*

- *Yellow Bile / Fire*
- *Blood / Air*
- *Black Bile / Earth*
- *Phlegm / Water*

The theory of the four humors offered a basis on which to work in medicine; because, according to Hippocrates, many treatments for diseases would consist in modifying the diet of patients; so that by ingesting certain foods, their humoral levels were balanced.

Subsequently, the theory of the four humors was taken up by *Galieno of Pergamon* in the second century, who lived in Rome in 162 d.c. practicing the profession of doctor, becoming official physician of the emperor Marcus Aurelius.

Galieno asserted that imbalances in the quantities of moods would affect the way mankind thinks and acts; Precisely: *The expressions of melancholy, sadness, temperament, happiness,* would depend on the levels and combinations of moods present in the human body.

- *Happy and optimistic people* – blessed are they – would correspond to the element of *Blood*
- *Melancholics would be characterized by the amount of Black Bile present in their body*
- *The Flemma mood would clearly correspond to people with a cold and rational temperament.*
- *The temperament correlated with the Yellow Bile, would be expressed in people: passionate, energetic and even angry.*

The humoral theory of temperaments: Sanguine, Phlegmatic, Choleric and Melancholic; it enjoyed new fortune in the Renaissance, as it was further developed and implemented by the Swiss physician and alchemist, known by the name of: *Paracelsus.*

The theory of Hippocrates and Galieno was interpreted and put into practice by the Persian physician *Avicenna Ibn Sina – 980 d.C.* – according to which: *Many diseases depend exclusively on the continuous errors in the regime of diets.*

According to the current practices of Parsi cuisine and Levantine cuisine, in a broad sense, a relationship must coexist between *Sardi and Garmi,* that is, between foods defined as cold and foods defined as hot.

For example, rice, in Pilaf dishes, is served warm because in its nature, it is considered *Sardi;* consequently the pilaf dishes are consumed with Garmi foods *of meats and sauces* or with the presence of spices that produce heat, such as saffron.

Another example, remaining in the Parsi kitchen, can be found in appetizers in which olives and walnut kernels, which are considered hot elements – that is *Garmi* – are joined with seeds or pomegranate molasses, which is considered the cold element; that is, *Sardi.*
For the record, the dish in question would be called: *Zeytoon Parvardeh.*

From these combinations of *Sardi and Garmi* one can arrive at the theory that garmi foods are used in the cold and winter seasons to keep the body warm; while Sardi foods will be consumed in the summer seasons to prevent health problems related to hot climates.

* * *

The problem of the fava beans was highlighted by Pythagoras.
Pythagoras was a vegetarian; the Greek author Porphyry, in the third century reports, the diet of Pythagoras:

- Honey for breakfast
- Oat bread for lunch

- Boiled or raw vegetables for dinner
- Abstinence from meat, abstinence from legumes. Porphyry does not tell us if Pythagoras ever ate fish or fish products.

At this point scholars, since the times of ancient Rome, have asked themselves the question: Pythagoras excludes meat from his diet because he is a vegetarian; what would be the reason for abstinence from legumes such as fava beans?

Another question that arose was: why even the disciples of Pythagoras were forbidden, by their master, to eat broad beans or to walk through the fields of favate.

The Greek historian Herodotus - 430 a.C. - considered the father of ancient history, reported that although fava beans were regularly grown in ancient Egypt, these legumes were considered - *Unclean* - by the priests of the temples: an unclean food for the body and spirit of souls.

From these observations one came to the belief or superstition that: the souls of the dead transmigrated into the tissues of the fava beans.

This story was also confirmed by the Greek writer *Diogenes Laertius* or *Laertius* who lived in third century: who expressed himself in one of his writings: The fava beans contain substances of animate matter from which the souls of the dead are *particles*.

This association between fava beans and death has not remained, in ancient customs, an isolated event; so much is proof that the fava vicia beans were eaten, in ancient Rome and not only in those parts, during the practices of funeral festivals.

In the month of May of each year the *Ceremonies of the Lemurs* were then celebrated, to exorcise the spirits of the dead; called precisely: *Lemurs.*

Tradition had it that these anniversaries had been instituted by Romulus, the first King of Rome, to appease the spirit of his twin brother Remus, killed by him in a duel.

The rituals provided that the head of the family – *Pater Familias* – would get up at midnight to throw behind him some black beans, for a symbolic number of nine times; reciting, in the meantime, propitiatory formulas: *Redimo meque, meosque fabis.*

The fava beans, therefore, constituted a sort of unconscious communion between the living and the dead; almost a material exchange between the earthly world and the realm of the dead.

A plausible reason why Pythagoras does not mention fava beans in his diet and the prohibition on followers eating or dealing with these legumes, could derive from the fact that: Pythagoras personally had been affected by *Favism.*

Favism would be a form of food intolerance, a disease that seems to have been genetic and hereditary; causing a form of poisoning that may affect people, fortunately only a smaller percentage, who turn out to be susceptible to the ingestion of these beans or to the breathing of the pollen, during spring blooms.

The consequences of the disease, in these subjects, are immediately revealed in the difficulty of breathing, leading to symptoms of anemia and jaundice and a strong metabolic reaction can lead to serious problems such as a cardio-respiratory collapse.

Another inherent problem, to which I have personally been subjected, would be that dried beans in particular when they are bagged or stored in silos can cause reactions even for those who are not affected by favism.

It is, in this case, contact dermatitis of the body to a substance that can be allergenic.

The effects of this dermatitis are immediate, generating urgent sensations of itching and urticaria in all parts of the body and consequently inconveniences burning, redness, heat and swelling of the skin.

In particular, these swellings of the skin were called by peasants – *Roccie* – when these occurred, caused by the constant itching, an immediate remedy was: undress and take a bath.
In all confidence, in the Hiblean countryside, the sanitation left much to be desired in the past years and the poor farmer affected by a looming itch; had no other immediate solution than to dive, with all the clothes, into a container full of cold water, called: *Scifo*

This *Scifo* was a boulder of living stone dug in an oval shape that was located near the wells, so that they could easily be filled with water to quench the thirst of cows, horses or other animals.
Sometimes, this scifo was used as a sink by the housewife to do the laundry that is to wash the dirty clothes that, as the saying goes: it was advisable to carry out this work away from prying eyes.

Therefore, all these inconveniences may have caused in the ancient peoples fears, superstitions and even the *Animate Matter,* reported by Diogenes Laertius, could cruelly be connected with the fact that the ingestion of the fava beans invariably involves flatulence, in some cases even abdominal spasms .

*   *   *

In the Christian tradition, precisely in the tenth century, the Day of the Dead was officially placed on the date of November 2, merging practically with the first of November which in the year 853 was declared, by the Catholic Church, the feast of All Saints.

Among the people the belief was maintained that, in those days, the dead could return to the living or even could visit relatives still alive; so it was used for dinner to leave an extra place at the table, reserved for the deceased with the necessary accessories to eat: Bread, water and wine.

In Sicily there was the custom of preparing gifts and sweets for children; who were told that these were gifts brought and given by deceased relatives.

Tradition had it that on the morning of November 2, a gift was hidden in the house that parents told their children that it had been brought by the souls of the deceased.

In this regard there would be the wonderful story of an eight-year-old boy who, on the morning of the Day of the Dead, looked for where his late grandfather had placed the wicker basket with gifts and delicacies intended for his grandson. When he managed to find the mystical basket he was pervaded by so much joy that he even became feverish. The boy in question was the late writer and author from Agrigento: *Andrea Camilleri.*

Before moving on to the review of sweets on the occasion of the feasts of the dead, allow me for a moment to return to the fava beans: Following a fortuitous meeting I had, several years ago, with Mr. Campo, undertaker - no *relation* - we spoke, causally, of Hyblaean fava beans; my interlocutor confided to me that the best, tastiest and most *sewable* fava beans, in the city of Ragusa, they were located in Contrada *Curtuliddu.*

At my request where this suitable place was located: He confided to me that the land with the most famous favate fields has always been located near the cemeteries.

From these affirmations I was again the doubt of the arcane mystery.

*   *   *

One of the sweets linked to the recurrences of the dead is undoubtedly the so-called *Frutta Martorana.*

The *Monastery of Noble Lords of the Order of St. Benedict,* was founded by the noble woman *Eloisa* and the gentleman *Goffredo Martorana,* in the city of Palermo, in the year of grace 1194.

The pious nuns, who ruled the monastery, were therefore linked to the religious rules of *St.* Benedict and were called: *Benedictine Sisters.*

All things that are destined to endure over the centuries have a legend; in fact, it is said that these sweets were invented on the occasion of a royal visit, during the winter, to the Benedictine monastery.
Then the nuns came up with the idea of hanging these almond paste fruits from the bare branches of the trees, as decoration; made with their own hands and so well painted that they look real.

The real visitor then picked up, from one of these trees, a minute but shiny lemon and was surprised by the fact that this lemon did not smell of orange blossom, but of almond.

What mystery is this? The guest exclaimed, somewhat suspicious.
Taste it, Your Majesty – Said the Mother Superior in a persying voice.

The guest then - according to the story of Maria Oliveri in her book: *The Secrets of the Kiosk* - affects with his teeth the crunchy surface, under which there is a soft and sweet heart.
The visitor was amazed, incredulous, overwhelmed by the sweet deception.

The mother superior, pleased, expresses herself: *These fruits of almond and honey were made in your honor.*
The answer, from the guest, was not long in coming: *They are sweets worthy of a King, let's call them: Pasta Reale Martorana.*

Thus the name of the noblewoman Eloisa Martorana will be remembered in the centuries to come and will be imperishably linked to these sweets made by the skilled hands of the Benedictine Sisters.

I do not remember if martorana fruit was packaged at home; they were inevitable sweets at the time of the dead and now they are inevitable sweets in every part of the year; but they go to buy in pastry shops because they would need plaster molds and colors suitable for food; as well as a great deal of time and dedication to be able to make the shades of colors and arabic gum to make the polishes of these delicious desserts.

The technique would be to prepare sugar syrup, called: *Gileppo;* which consists of 800 grams of sugar and 600 ml of water. Prepare a kilo of sweet almonds and some bitter almonds, scald them in boiling water, then remove the skins and chop them finely.

Cook the *gileppo,* boil it and when the sugar begins to *spin,* that is, mix; turn off the heat and pour the chopped almonds, in one fell swoop, into the *gileppo.*

Cool the mixture in a pastry board and when it is cold you can proceed to shape the dough into the desired shapes.

*　*　*

A dessert that was used for the dead celebrations and nowdays for Christmas and Easter ricourrence, would be the: *Mucatoli or Nucatoli.*
There are different versions of these biscuits and every Sicilian city or town boasts the rights: Syracuse, Ragusa, Modica, Vizzini, Nicosia and certainly the capital of Palermo.

A confectionery specialty of ancient Rome that comes closest to today's nougat was mentioned in the treatise by Marco Gavio Apicio: *De Re Culinaria et Art Coquinaria – I or II century d.C. -* in which appears the recipe for a dessert prepared with nuts, honey and egg white; called, in Latin: *Nuca*

What was stated by the learned Apicius, would not exclude that the Roman source of nougat, had been found from Syria or Mesopotamia or Persia; because in those Middle Eastern areas were in use, from illo tempore, confectionery crosses between dried fruit and honey.
There would in fact be the Arabic term: *Naqal* with which dried fruit would be indicte.

The Sicilian historian Michele Amari in his treatise: *History of the Muslims in Sicily* which dates back to 1854; raises the exception that the Latin term, expressed by Apicius - Nucatum or Nucatus - referred to the use of walnuts.
The illustrious Amari, Count of St. Hadrian and Master of the Kingdom of the Two Sicilies, concluded that since walnuts are not present in the *Sicilian Mucatola,* the source would not be that of Apicius but would derive from a Turkish-Arabic term: *Nukl.*

Comparing the Palermo recipe of Mucatoli with that of Syracuse; we have that in the first walnuts are not used; instead, in the Syracusan one, despite the prevalent presence of almonds, walnuts are also used.

Apart from the historical sources, Roman or oriental that could be; it is possible to notice the discordance of the elements that make up the fillings and, as if that were not enough, there are also manifest aesthetic differences regarding the shapes of the mucatoli.

The mucatoli in Eastern Sicily are stuffed biscuits, long *S-shaped;* those of North-Western Sicily are in the shape of *a handkerchief or sheet* with folded corners.

From these exceptions it can be said that the Palermo mucatoli are sweets or pastries of arabic origin; while those of Syracuse or Modica would be stuffed biscuits.

We will talk about theSicilian-oriental mucatoli.

<u>*Dough*</u> *– base on which to apply the filling -*

Grams 800 Flour type zero – grams 120 sugar – grams 200 lard – a tablespoon of honey - warm water just enough to form a soft and alestic dough.
NB – For vegetarians: Lard can be replaced with eggs
Once composed, divide the dough into loaves and let them rest well covered.

<u>*Filling*</u>

Dried Fruit : Grams 500 almonds, - grams 100 kernels of walnuts - 150 grams of dried figs.

Boil, for a short time, the almonds, shell them and grind them together with the walnut kernels.
Boil dried figs until soft. Combine the elements.

Hyblaean Honey: about 250 grams

Spices: 10 grams cinnamon powder
      5 grams clove powder
      candied orange peel q.b.

Liqueurs: Sweet liqueur type 'Strega' or: Sweet Marsala wine.

<u>Ingredients for the Glaze</u>

Knead: 200 gr icing sugar with egg white and lemon juice.

<u>Procedure</u>

Combine dried fruit, ut supra, with Hyblaean honey, spices and liqueurs.
Arrange the elements of the filling, so combined, in the fridge to make it better firm.
Roll out a dough dough with rolling pin and make rectangles 10 cm by 4 cm.
Take the filling from the fridge and with a touch of it form bigoli as thick as a finger.

Arrange a bigolo inside the rectangle of dough, moisten the edges of the rectangle and roll the rectangle to close the filling that in any case part of it must remain visible or clearly visible.

Lightly crush the biscuit and curve it with your hands in the shape of them.

Bake the mucatoli thus obtained for 20 minutes at 180 degrees. Use baking paper.

Once out of the oven, savor the smells and arrange the glaze along the filling: drawing curves.

NB – In the filling of Modica mucatoli is also inserted powder chocolate.

*   *   *

TETU AND TEIO BISCUITS

Give to Caesar what is Caesar's
We will give Palermo what is Palermo.

In order not to be provincial, we pay homage to the Sicilian capital, presenting these typical biscuits – alsocalled: *Catalani* – present in the Palermo pastry shop on the occasion of the feasts of the deceased.

The characteristic name of these biscuits is linked to the dialect phrase:

- *One for you = TETU - One for me = TEIO*

Or: One leads to the other.

The characteristics of these biscuits is that they are soft inside and crunchy outside and also the glazes used: the white one and the cocoa one; they are well crispy. They could well be included in the category of biscuits called: *Bones of the Dead;* of which there are various compositions.

Flours : 500 grams of double zero flour – 150 grams of almond flour
Sugar: 150 grams of granulated sugar
Fats : 150 grams of lard - One egg
Liquids: 150 ml whole milk
Spices : Seeds of a vanilla bean - Pinch of sea salt - Pinch of baking soda
Sodium – three tablespoons of unsweetened cocoa powder
Glaze: 250 grams of icing sugar – two egg whites – three tablespoons of bitter cocoa

Procedure

If you had a kneading machine available it would be better; failing that proceed manually: add the two flours, sugar, baking soda, vanilla seeds and salt. Incorporate the softened lard, the whole egg and gradually the flush milk; until a homogeneous dough is composed.

Divide the dough into two parts and incorporate the 3 tablespoons of bitter cocoa into one of the two loaves.

Obtain, both from the white dough and from the black dough, balls a little larger than a walnut. These balls must be well smooth and shiny; both white and black.

Now we will proceed to place these two-tone balls in a tray equipped with paper and proceed to bake in the oven for twenty minutes at a temperature of 170 degrees.

While the *Tetu and Teio* are in the oven; prepare the glaze: Mix the icing sugar with the two egg whites; until it is smooth and without lumps.

Separate the glaze into two containers; in one of which incorporate the three tablespoons of bitter cocoa.

Once out of the oven, glaze white biscuits with white icing - possibly enriched with a little lemon juice - and chocolate biscuits with black glaze.

Everything is again placed in the oven, for five minutes, in order to dry the glazes; so as to be crunchy on the palate.

*   *   *

We go down from Palermo to Catania where, of course, the confectionery tradition, on the occasion of the celebrations of the dead, is not lacking indeed it is of particular prominence.

One of the traditional biscuits of the Catania pastry shop are: *I 'NZUDDI.*

The term refers to those lying by name: *Vincenzo;* one of these was certainly the composer *Vincenzo Bellini;*to whom the people of Catania, as good fellow citizens, dedicated to him:
the urban villa, a monumental statue, a city museum, the municipal theater and - *the last but not the least* - the pasta alla norma.

At this point even the *'Nzudd*i could be a tribute to the world-famous Maestro Catanese; whose musical notes made the no less famous Gaetano Donizetti gnaw so much and made the Bourbon Prince rejoice at the San Carlo theater in Naples in 1826, who after attending the opera Bianca e *Gernardo or Bianca e Fernando;* he shouted among the riots of the audience: - *Fora u Guaglione* - that is, an invitation to the composer to show himself on stage to receive the tributes of the King and the audience present.

A historical event, linked to the *'Nzuddi,*could be connected with the terrible earthquake of Messina in 1908. On that ominous occasion some Sisters of Catania, called *Vincentian;*went to the City of the Strait to help the wounded and needy.

In order to carry out their charitable works, these Vincentians were guests of the messina monasteries; therefore, a gastronomic-cultural exchange between Catania and Messina may have taken place in the kitchens of the monasteries.

Proof of this is that the *'Nzuddi* are part of the Messina pastry shop and are particularly used for the celebration of their Patroness: The Madonna Della *Lettera.*

Double tribute then one for Catania and one for Messina.

RECIPE BISCUITS 'NZUDDI

Flours: 500 grams of double zero flour
Dried Fruit: 400 grams of almonds, peeled from the skins + toasted almonds
Sugar: 400 grams + 100 grams
Spices: A taking of peels of candied oranges, - Cinnamon: according to taste Grams 5 ammonia for desserts
Liquids: Egg white, whipped until stiff + Water to compose the dough

Procedure

Combine all the ingredients, except the toasted almonds, to compose a homogeneous dough.

From the dough obtained form balls, which must be larger than a walnut.

Arrange these balls in a dashboard, equipped with baking paper and gently crush the balls to give an oval shape.

Decorate by attaching a toasted almond over each ball.

Bake for 20 minutes at a temperature of 175 degrees centigrade.

*   *   *

An example of funerary food, according to Sicilian traditions, would be *U Cunsulu or Cuonsulu;* which would be a dish prepared by the neighbors to give food comfort to the members of a family, in which a dear relative has passed away.

PASTA FOR CUNSOLO

The *Cunsolo* would therefore mean a tribute, a consolation, an offer of food addressed to those who are in a state of pain, of tears; for the mourning of a missing person.

Ingredients for egg noodies
500 grams of durum wheat flour, 5 eggs, salt

Compose the dough for tagliolini, arranging the flour in a fountain, add the eggs and salt.

Knead the ingredients until the mixture is smooth.

From the dough obtained; form, with rolling pin a thin sheet of one millimeter.

Now cut this dough into strips as wide as lasagna, about seven centimeters wide.

Overlap these strips on top of the other and cut them finely. Let the tagliolini rest, in a large tray, to let them dry.

II - Ingredients For Meat Broth

A kilo of beef for boiled meat
Two carrots, one onion, celery stalks, salt and black pepper

Prepare the meat broth, according to the uses, placing the ingredients in a large pot, cover them with cold water and cook over low heat, after boiling, for over two hours.

III - The Meatballs

350 grams of veal for broths, One Egg, Chopped Parsley, Salt and Black Pepper
50 grams of grated caciocavallo ragusano.

Combine the minced meat, with the whole egg, parsley, caciocavallo and spices; knead everything to make a roll of meat.
From this roll you get many balls with a diameter of two centimeters.

Assembly Of Elements

Once we have everything ready, strain the broth, set aside the solid parts, boil the liquids of the broth again; add the meatballs or *meat paddunedda* to the broth, then add the tagliolini. Make sure that the pasta is cooked and does not appear al dente.

Now cover the cooking pot with the appropriate lid and wrap the container in a large white cloth.
Have everything delivered to the family of the deceased, presenting the necessary condolences.
As you can see, for the anniversaries of the dead, home kitchens and pastry shops are quite busy for the preparation of sweets and biscuits; whose characteristics, in general, are compositions of dried fruit with sugars, honey and glazes.

Natural almonds or in the form of pastes or flours are the typical ingredients of these compositions in which no use is made of creams or whipped creams or sparkling decorations.

Our deceased loved ones are remembered with long visits to cemeteries, with the adornments of tombs with flowers and candles, with that religious spirit that is expressed in the suffrage of Holy Mass and in the devotions of prayers addressed to the souls of deceased loved ones.

Certainly foods and sweets contribute to renewing the uses and customs in honor of those who, when they were alive, gave *birth, fed, raised, educated* and above all: they *loved* us.

I MONSÙ E LA CUCINA DEL GATTOPARDO

Se vogliamo che tutto rimanga com'è, bisogna che tutto cambi.
Don Fabrizio, Principe di Salina - detto: Il Gattopardo.

Although the above sentence may seem a paradox, there are absolute truths; because, in the Sicily of that time, despite the values, the battles of the Risorgimento, annexations and connections; the name of the king owner had changed but not the status of things.

In the plot of the novel, the life of the Prince Salina is characterized by a continuous almost perpetual discontent that leads him to observe the ruin of his class; which, however, does nothing to avoid it. Disappointed by the historical and political present of Sicily, he proudly refuses the role of Senator of the new Kingdom of Italy proposed to him by Montezemolo: the Piedmontese official who had specifically come for the parliamentary proposal.

The novel of the Gattopardo was written by Giuseppe Tomasi da Lampedusa between 1954 – 57, a copy of the writing was sent, through the poet Lucio Piccolo who was a cousin of the author, to the Publishing House: Mondadori and Einaudi.
The text was rejected by the aforementioned authors and later by mondadori's literary consultant: Elio Vittorini.

The publication of Tomasi da Lampedusa's work took place a year after the author's death; when a copy of the novel was delivered to Mrs. Elena Croce, daughter of the economist Benedetto, who passed the afore mentioned copy to the Feltrinelli Publishing House; whose director was the writer: Giorgio Bassani.

The latter understood the historical and literary importance of the work and went personally to Palermo to recover the original manuscript; which was found by chance in a drawer of the Author's desk.

In 1959 the Gattopardo received the well-deserved recognition of the *Strega Prize,* becoming, as we know, a: *Best Seller of Italian literature.*

The same happened to a gastronome writer from Forlimpopoli, who lived in Florence, who presented in 1891 an essay entitled: *La Scienza in Cucina e l'Arte di Mangiar Bene.*

The name of the writer-essayist was: *Pellegrino Artusi,* who paid for the publication of the book out of his own pocket, having found no publisher willing to finance it.

Well it was the public to decree the success of the gastronomic work, which reached the heights of popularity so as to still remain in print more than a hundred years after the publication of the first draft.

We can give these examples to all those, myself included, whose research has been rejected by publishers; to then be approved by the popularity and genuine faith of the readers.

We would have to admit that *in our Bel Paese,* like all things, even Publishing, at the present time, is in the deep economic crisis.

Returning to the novel, in the kitchen of the Prince Salina, we find numerous gastronomic references:

DINNER AT VILLA SALINA

This is a normal family dinner in the sense that guests are missing.
The diners were usually more than a dozen: The prince, his wife, children, the preceptor Father Pirrone and the person in charge of the administration of the prince's properties: Don Onofrio.

As Tomasi tells us: Dinner was served with the pomp that was then the style of the Kingdom of the Two Sicilies: the table was covered with an embroidered fine tablecloth that shone under the light of Murano chandeliers; massive silverware and splendid glasses bearing, among the ashlars of Bohemia, the initials - F.D. - in memory of the royal munificence of the Bourbon King - *F.D. - Rex Ferdinand Dedit.*

As for the food, the prince focuses on his favorite dessert: *Jelly Rum:* It was threatening, with smooth and slippery walls impossible to climb; manned by a red and green garrison of pistachios; however, it was transparent and flickering and the spoon sank into it with amazing ease.

After dinner there is a break in the saloon: The traditional coffee, the strong one, to be enjoyed with the almonds of Monreale, procured by Father Pirrone; or the light one of the nuns of the Monastery of the Holy Spirit, accompanied with pink and greenish almond biscuits packaged according to centuries-old recipes.

SOLEMN LUNCH AT DONNAFUGATA

In this case it is a lunch offered by the Prince of Salina to the notables of Donnafugata; in particular in honor of the Mayor of the county: Don Calogero Sedara who was the father of Angelica who would soon join in engagement with Tancredi, the well-liked nephew of the prince; who militates in the ranks of Garibaldi.

On this occasion is served for each diner guest, in a huge silver platter, a towering *Timballo di Maccheroni*.

Tomasi da Lampedusa, endowed with a strong sense of epicureanism, describes the satisfaction of the prince in seeing this timbale tasted; a reaffirmation of food as a pleasure of life:

The burnished gold of the casing, the fragrance of sugar and cinnamon that emanated from it, were only the prelude to the sensation of delight that was released inside when the knife tore through the crust; at first a smoke full of aromas broke out and then you could see the chicken livers, the hard eggs, the filleting of ham, chicken and truffles in the greasy mass of short macaroni.

THE BUFFET AT THE BALL

This is the engagement party between Tancredi and Angelica Sedara. In the famous dance, Tancredi will not be the knight of the betrothed; but the prince personally to let himself be dragged into the swirling waltz.

This character of the prince depicted as skeptical, dissatisfied with his family, pessimistic to the point of invoking death, at this juncture of the dance is lost among the beauties of Angelica and in his heart he feels the feelings and perhaps the frenzy of love beating.

The triumph of the gorge is found in that buffet in the salon of Donnafugata.

Gaston, the prince's monsù, will have worked hard to be able to compose many magnificences; stuff not to sleep on:

Live boiled lobsters – Sea bass immersed in soft sauces – Aurora-colored jellies -
Boneless spouts recline on mounds of amber croutons – Consommè -
Rosy fatty liver pies under gelatin armor.

The triumph of the throat merges with the triumph of pleasure when you discover the table of sweets.

Tomasi da Lampedusa describes these sweets with musical metaphors and a colorful language baroque, where throat and eros still marry:

- *Huge BABÀ saurians like the coat of horses*
- *BEIGNETS DAUPHINE that the almonds mottled with white and pistachio*
- *PROFITTEROLES hills with chocolate*
- *PARFAIT rosei - PARFAIT champagna*
- *PARFAIT bigi*
- *IMMODEST MINNI OF VIRGINS*

The kitchen of the Gattopardo can be well inserted in the broad framework of the *Cucina dei Monzù;* which has a founder: Queen *Maria Carolina of the Royal House of Austria Habsburg Lorraine;* married, in the last decades of 1700, to *Ferdinand of Bourbon* - King of Naples and Palermo - to later become, in 1816, Sovereign of the Kingdom of the Two Sicilies with the name of: Ferdinand *I.*

*   *   *

Allow me, before arriving at *the monzù,*to mention another Queen: *Catherine of the Medici;* which in 1533, at the age of 14, was given in marriage to the King of France: *Henry II of Valois.*
Catherine of the Medici became sadly known, in the historical annals, for having been responsible for the tragic: *Night of St. Bartholomew – August 1572 –* on that night in Paris took place the massacre of French Protestants, called: *Huguenots.*

Historical legends define her as a dominating, irritable and jealous woman.
To these unedifying attributes it was added that Catherine was adept at Machiavellianism; in that she put into practice the norms - *De Il Principe -* the famous political essay that Messer Nicolò Macchiavelli had personally donated to: *Lorenzo II dei Medici, Lord of Florence.*
Still Catherine meant magic and occultism; have been ascertained by historians, the meetings between the Queen of France with the astronomer: *Michel de Nostredame or Nostradamus.*

The legend that most interests us, here, would be that Catherine in moving from Florence to Paris; brought with her a bevy of Italian chefs who had the task of transforming the *primitive* kitchen of the French court into a cuisine: Elegant and Sophisticated.

From this it could be deduced - but do not tell the French - that they were the Italian cooks, of the Florentine Renaissance, to trace the furrows of the *Finesse* or the *Hoo-la-là* in the universally renowned cuisine of the Alps.

The facts mentioned above have not received feedback from scholars of gastronomic literature, who have stated that, at the arrival of the Medici in Paris, the French cuisine was not so primitive; as Catherine would have defined it.

The event was then considered unreliable by historians and included in the category delle: *Legends of Culinary Mythology.*

Of one thing, however, we are certain; that the béchamel sauce was born in Tuscany with the name of: *Salsa Colla* and was introduced in France by Caterina de Medici.
Later in a recipe French book of 1656, the name *Salsa Bechameil appears;* in order to honor a noble courtier: *Louis Bechameil.*

*   *   *

When the King of Naples and Palermo asked the Habsburg court to demand Caroline's hand, the marriage proposal was accepted by Maria Theresa and her son, the heir Joseph, in order to tighten relations with Spain; but Ferdinand was considered, by the Austrian royals, a little coarse, not to say crude, to be able to take care of the future bride who had been raised with all the wealth, doctrines and comforts, worthy of his rank.

Indeed, the chronicles report that, on one occasion, while he was in the Palace of Vienna in conversation with the emperor; Ferdinand emitted a thunderous fart - forgive my scurrility - to which the emperor moved, remaining incredulous but Ferdinand reassured him: *Do not worry, my brother-in-law, it is all health of body.*

However, for reasons of state that can not be postponed; the infant Caroline, willy-nilly, was given in marriage to the Bourbon of Naples and Sicily.

It cannot be said that it was an unhappy marriage; Caroline were granted all the honors of the court and the Sovereign played an active part in the policies and intricate events of the kingdom.
In marriage relations the royal couple produced several infants who were part of the nobility in the European courts; she also had a lover: *John Acton,* his personal secretary; and a mistress: *Emma Hamilton* - in short, she did not have it so badly.

Carolina did not like the Neapolitan cuisine, although she had at her disposal two Viennese cooks, she was horrified to see her husband and the courtisans eating tomato sauce macaroni with their bare hands.

In fact, even in Sicily pasta was eaten with hands, but in our part of the world the fresh Neapolitan sauce was not used; the pasta was seasoned with spices and oil and, even if eaten with the hands and on the streets, the gaze of the Sicilians was turned to the skies.

In our area, the tomato sauce was not used fresh but in the form of an extract; the fact may derive from the Arab civilization that introduced the technique of transforming the fresh sauce into: *Extract or tomato puree* through the drying of the sauce to the beneficial sun.

*   *   *

To repair the inconveniences of the Neapolitan gastronomic customs, Carolina decided to appeal to her young little sister: *Toinette,* who resided at the Palace of Versailles, where labels, parties, dances, theaters and certainly lunches; had reached their apogee on the European courts.

Now that we have talked about Versailles we can not refrain from making a gastronomic visit to the sumptuous lunches of the French court of that time.

The chronicles report that Louis XVI was an excellent fork while Marie Antoinette was, in meals, a little frugal but not picky; the Queen's favorite foods were chicken and milk; as far as alcohol is concerned, it seems that Marie Antoinette was a teetotary.

We have a menu from 1788 about a lunch at the *Petit Trianon* of the Palace of Versailles offered by Marie Antoinette to the *Mesdames Les Tantes* that is, to the ladies aunts, such as the sisters of her husband and the sisters of Louis XV.

The meal consisted of;
- Sequela of Patè
- Herbal ribs.
- Fried turkey à la Ravigote
- Veal sweetbreads en papillotes
- Spit-made milk pig
- Duckling in orange sauce
- Chicken in white sauce
- Veal shank
- Capon with bread crumbs
- Westphalian hams
- Scrambled and Poached Eggs
- Cream puff
- German Pods
- Selection of Cakes

Stuff to do pale even the appetites of the freedman *Trimalcione* and the noble leader *Lucullus;* united in the same table.

As you would say: *Good weather does not last so long.*

From the glitz of *Versailles* to the humid prisons of the *Consiergerie;* Marie Antoinette was sentenced to death by the revolutionaries; the chronicles also report the last meal of the Queen of France and Princess of Austria; it was a chicken broth prepared by the affectionate caregiver: *Rosalie Larmoriere.* Marie Antoinette barely tasted it, so as not to hurt the caregiver.
Rosalie did not find the fortitude to give *The Ultimate Farewell* to the sovereign when she was loaded on a chariot heading towards place de la *Revolution,*now Place de *la Concorde;*where the executioner who had just polished the sharp and heavy blade of the guillotine was waiting for her.

To conclude the stories, which from good become sad, there would be the last word or the famous phrase of those condemned to death:
Marie Antoinette, stumbling on the last step of the gallows, touched the foot of the executioner, *Charles-Henri Sanson;* who, a few years earlier, had guillotined, among many, also *Luigi Capeto;* very embarrassed by what happened; the *Capet Widow,* nickname that was given to her by the giacobini evolutionaries, addressed to the executioner the necessary apologies - Je *suis desolè, Excusez-moi, Monsieur.*

Marie Antoinette's death sentence provoked for her sister Queen Caroline an immense hatred against the French revolutionaries and republicans; which, as we will see later, had considerable repercussions in the Kingdom of Naples and in the repression of the Neapolitan Republic.

* * *

Returning to the speech of before; Marie Antoinette did not disregard Caroline's heartfelt and fraternal appeal: the Queen of France, without delay, immediately arranged a bevy of French cooks who were sent to the court of Naples with the tributes of the Parisian court.

Well these *Messieurs* were called in their functions: *MONZÙ* in Neapolitan dialect and *MONSÙ* in Sicilian *dialect;* they were employed in the service of the Neapolitan court and the wealthy houses of nobles and patricians of the Kingdom; for those gastronomic tasks that were defined: *Offizi della Bocca and Cure del Ventre.*

* * *

Subsequently, even the rich of the kingdom, in order not to fail the nobility that began to give signs of decay, had in their residences the personal cooks; which were called: *Cuochi Paglietta;*because they did not wear the cook's hat the high one in folds, that when the monsù had to pass from one room to another, they were forced to bend down to prevent the hat from colliding with the arch of the door.

The straw hat was also a sign of citizenship, because the Sicilian peasants wore the *Coppola,* while the knights, almost knights and citizens in general, carried the straw hat.

Among these *Cuochi Paglietta,* the chronicles report the name of Alfredo *Senisi,* personal cook of the industrialist *Don Ignazio Florio,* and his wife: *Donna Franca,* nicknamed: *The Queen of Palermo.* Mr. *Senisi* always accompanied Don Ignazio, even on his trips abroad, to take care, in all circumstances, of the person of his employer.

The Florio family of Palermo was called: *I Padroni del Mare or The Lions of Sicily* because of the Florio Fleet composed of steam merchant ships that headed daily from Palermo to Naples and from Naples to the port of Marseille in France in the 19 century.

* * *

To get to the point we made a review of Queens: Catherine of the Medici, Marie Antoinette, Maria Carolina; in these historical plots it can be said that the Italian chefs of Caterina de Medici will have brought benefits to the French cuisine; in turn the French chefs of Marie Antoinette, on the instructions of Maria Carolina, as we will see, will bring a significant culinary contribution not only in the kitchens of the nobles but also in the cooking of the people household.

At that time many typical Neapolitan dishes took the name French: *Gattò – Crocchè – Ragù;* the influence of Frenchism and taste beyond the Alps also appeared clear in the culinary descriptions of the gastronome *Vincenzo Corrado,* who in 1773, published the text of: *Cuoco Galante.*

* * *

Queen Maria Carolina had at her disposal a fork with four ongs made by the blacksmith of one of her *monzù: Gennaro Spadaccino;* and from then on, the royal husband and courtiers were forbidden to eat tomato sauce macaroni with their hands.

Nevertheless, the habit of eating macaroni on the street remained in Naples, using their own hands, even after the invention of the fork.

At the beginning of the 1800s the Tuscan poet Serafino Bonaiuti, visiting Naples, reported: *The lower class, usually eats macaroni with their fingers; when they do not have time to stop by the maccaronaro, they take their red caps, press the upper part and put the macaroni in it; after paying, they walk and eat; when they are finished, they put the cap back on their heads again.*

The Neapolitan habit of eating on the street using the hands did not go unnoticed even by foreign travelers, just to mention one of them; the American writer J. Sanson, in the year 1802, noted, in the diary of his journey from Paris to Naples: *In Naples everything is done on the street or in the same place where the Lazzaroni sleep, the merchants sell, the beggars cry, the animals play, the carriages ran and dinners and lunches were cooked and consumed.*

* * *

Leaving Lazzaroni and macaroni, we can say that the effects of the Monsù cuisine did not stop at the bourbon kitchens but the phenomenon expanded like wildfire; as every noble or patrician house, present in every city, town or district of the Kingdom; came to hire a monsù in his employ.

These *monzù,* in their culinary functions, in addition to the products and techniques of French cuisine; they also used local products, creating a combination and a fusion between cuisine beyond the Alps and popular south mediterranean cuisine.

Returning to the kitchen of the Gattopardo we know that the name of the cook of the prince was: *Gaston,* who had as his assistant a local housewife, called: *Agnes.*

Now if the cuisine of the monsù is to be considered a heritage of southern cuisine, the merit and the awards are due to both characters:

- Gaston for having put in place the refined dishes;
- Agnes for having had the merit of giving, transmitting these dishes and adapting them to a popular cuisine.

The phenomenon of the Cuisine of the Monsù became the heritage of the cultural heritage of a Kingdom; to subsequently integrate well and take root in the indelible culinary traditions that make up the characteristics and wonders of Neapolitan and Sicilian cuisine.

* * *

The term *Timballo,* synonymous with *Sformato,* is also recognized in the diction of *Pasticcio;* in the Hyblaean cuisine are mentioned: *the Pasticcio di Sostanza and the Pasticcio di Noto;*the term that the people of Palermo consider most appropriate would be: *Sfinciune;* among which are: *U Sfiunciuni of San Vito and U Sfiunciuni of Bagheria.*

These compositions are little different from the original timbale of the Gattopardo.

THE TIMBALE OF DONNAFUGATA

We already know from the previous description what we are talking about; for the recipe we rely on good luck and the wishes of Monsù Gaston.
I limit myself to the descriptions of the composition without mentioning weights and measures to avoid delays in the preparations and, in the knowledge that my readers are erudited cooks and cooks; better than myself can be.

Pasta Brisè : Double Zero Flour – Butter - Cold Water

- Butter and water must be of the same size; whose common weight must be about the same weight as flour. It is good to compose the dough with cold water and let it rest for at least an hour.
- If you cook for four people, 300 grams of flour will be enough.

Ingredients:

Meat: Ham, Julienne chicken, livers of Chicken
Vegetables: Finely chopped onion, Petit-Pois in frost
Liquids: Oil for frying, White wine for blending
Spices: Salt and Pepper q.b.

- Fry everything in olive oil and towards the end deglaze with white wine.

Béchamel sauce : Butter, Flour, Restricted broth, Nutmeg, Salt

In cooking techniques to compose any sauce; we will always need three elements: *Fats, Starches and Liquids.* In this case: Fats are butter, starches are flour and liquids are broth. Once composed, sprinkle the béchamel sauce with nutmeg powder and a pinch of fine salt.

Reinforcement Cream: Egg yolks, Flour, Whole milk, Cinnamon powder.

Beat the red of three eggs, two tablespoons of flour, half a liter of whole milk, a teaspoon of ground cinnamon and a sugar intake. Cook these ingredients over low heat, until they are lightly thickened.

First Procedure

Combine and mix the béchamel sauce with the reinforcement cream, in order to obtain a smooth and homogeneous mixture.

Put the two sauces well mixed over low heat and incorporate the chicken sauté and mix everything thoroughly. Turn off the heat when we have composed a fragrant velvety; as you will release the smells of cinnamon and nutmeg.

Boil the pasta: *Maccheroncini,* possibly homemade; drain and season with melted butter.

Arrange the macaroni in a large container. With 500 grams of macaroni you can well serve four people.

Divide the brisè dough into two loaves and obtain two sheets with a rolling pin.

Place the widest dough in a baking dish, previously buttered and sprinkled with breadcrumbs. Make sure to overflow the sides of the brisè dough on the edges of the pan.

The choice of the baking dish is important as it is the shapes of the same; the shapes of the timbale will be obtained.

You could coat this baking dish with buttered baking paper and sprinkled with breadcrumbs; so that it can be easier, once cooked, to free the timbale from the container.

Additional Ingredients – Optional -

Find or prepare: Veal meatballs, Boiled quail eggs, Black or white truffle slices, Fresh cow caciotta in chunks.

Assembly of Ingredients

Take the large container with the macaroni inside and season them with the elements that we have prepared and well amalgamated in the first procedure.

Then add the additional ingredients: fried meatballs, truffle slices and pieces of cheese.

Mix everything carefully.

Now arrange the macaroni so seasoned, inside the dough that is lying in the baking dish; making the dough adhere well with the contents; make sure there are no air pockets.

Arrange on the surface of the macaroni boiled quail eggs.

Close, now, with the other leaf of brisè dough and compose the *riefico* between the two discs of dough in order to seal everything well.

Make a hole in the center of the timbale and wanting with the residues of the dough create leaves or squiggles as decoration.

Grease the surface of the timbale with your hands wet with oil and salt water.

Bake for 30 minutes at 160 degrees; note that the surfaces of the timbale are perfectly golden and are crispy.

Wait a few minutes before proceeding to get the timbale out of the baking dish; using the necessary precautions.

The Timballo is Vostro - *Bon Appetit*

⋆   ⋆   ⋆

PARFAIT CHAMPAGNA

We read among the desserts at *the Buffet del Ballo* these *Parfaits* that, in our area, are known as: *Semifreddi;* very popular in Sicilian cafes.

It is therefore a cold dessert in which the base creams seasoned with liqueurs and flakes of dried fruit, are combined with *sponge cake* or spongy biscuits or other sweets such as meringues.

A first choice concerns the presentation of *the parfait;*if you want to use molds variously decorated; or, failing that, you can use large glasses.

In the case of silicone molds, the biscuits arranged in a crown around the semifreddo; if the composition occurs in the glasses, the cookies are used crumbled and arranged in layers between the creams.

Procedure

Boil 10 cl of Champagne with 150 grams of icing sugar, for two minutes; then add to the mixture a gelatin lamella previously dissolved in cold water.

Clearly instead of champagne you can also use a sparkling wine.

We also need 30 cl. of whipped cream.

The last ingredient would be egg yolks: You have to whip six egg yolks until they reach three times their volume. To facilitate the task it may be useful to place the container on very low heat and proceed to the beating with a metal whisk.

Assembly

Combine the beaten eggs with the whipped cream and sweetened champagne.

At this point the mixture can be used to full the silicone molds that should be placed in the freezer for six hours; and then subsequently put in the fridge to soften them.

At the time of serving, the *parfait* or semifreddo can be decorated with meringue biscuits arranged around the circumferences and if necessary tied with a ribbon.

The designs in the surfaces and the shapes of the *parfait* depend, of course, on the ornaments and the size of the silicone molds at your disposal.

If you use glasses, crumble some Savoyard biscuits and soak them with sweet liqueur.
Put a semifreddo base in the glass, place a layer of biscuits on it; and then: Semifreddo biscuits, semifreddo.
If you do not want to put the glasses in the freezer, you should use more gelatin in the champagne-sugar mixture.

*　*　*

HUGE BABA SAURI LIKE THE MANTLE OF HORSES

The author of the Gattopardo referring to the spongy sweets, dripping with liqueur nectar, connects the color of the Baba to the equine coat; both colors are a reddish-brown and both sizes are huge.

Babà turned out to be a frank or mead sweetened bread in use in Eastern European countries.

In the twelfth century the Danish chronicler *Grammaticus* described a bread related to the festivities of the put into use in the Baltic countries, round in shape and disproportionately high; this bread was called Babà, whose meaning referred to an elderly woman who could symbolize a mythical figure.

In tsarist Russian cuisine, molds suitable for baking, 40 centimeters high and fat shapes such as their dolls called: *Matriosche,* have been found.

In 1979 the gastronome journalist *Savilla Stechishin* reports that, in Ukrainian cuisine, the bread called Baba, was part of a recurring bakery for the Easter celebrations of the Orthodox Church: The name *BABA* referred to the figure of the *Grandmother;*there would also be the term *BABKA* which would be the diminutive of babà, that is: *Granny.*

The same writer reported that baba bread may have originated from a prehistoric matriarchal system, existing in Ukraine; apparently they were pagan priestesses who would celebrate religious rites connected with female fertility that fell in the spring season.

It can therefore be said that '*baba* bread was part of the customs in the bakeries of the Baltic States, Russia and Poland.

In comparison with other types of bakeries that, in those parts, were used on the occasion of holidays; including the *Kulich and Krendel,* the latter composed in the shape of two joined circles, which were seasoned with dried fruit and hazelnuts; the babà was a frank bread in home functions or flavored with mead for festive anniversaries.

The composition, as it presents itself, with spongy dough and condiments, especially soaked in sweet rum syrup; this is due to the cuisine French, when the baba was transferred from east to west; to the lands of Alsace and Lorraine, which seems to have happened from 1700 onwards.

Following the changes made by the French pastry chefs, the Babà becomes a well-known *Confection*.

I think I have already said that in things that last over time there are always legends.

In this case it is said that the promoter of this dessert had been the 'former King of Poland Stanislaus, abdicating the throne in 1736 settled in Paris; as his sister, Maria Leszczynska, was the Ruler for having contracted marriage with Louis XV; the sovereign who went down in history for having had so many lovers; among the most famous: the Marquise *De Pompadour* and Madame *Du Barry*.

While the former King was at the table, his servant overflowed, carelessly, a bottle of sweet wine that went to soak the baba bread that was on the table.
To the deep apologies of the servant; Stanislaus did not worry too much and began to eat soaked bread; fully enjoying it.
Subsequently, the former King had his personal cook called and gave him the task of transforming the baba into a liqueur composition.

How is Baba made?

It is not really a very simple composition, composing it manually is not advisable, due to the incorporation of eggs and melted butter into the dough.
A blender to compose a small babà could be enough; I stick to, however, to provide basic indications.

Combine flour with egg whites, whip the contents and wait for autolysis.
This would be what is called: Pasta di Riporto whose functions are to make the dough softer, more elastic. Method also used for the composition of Pan Brioche and Pane Ciabatta.

Whip: Egg yolks with sugar.

Assemble the yeast, with the carry-over dough and with the whipped egg yolks, to compose a dough.

Once this dough has been composed, and after the BFT - *Bulk Fermentation Time* - the dough must be enlarged with melted butter so that the effects of yeasts are exploited to the maximum to produce those pores and spongy effects, characteristic of the dessert.

The dessert will be soaked in the liqueur fragrances after cooking; the presence of rum in these solutions must be preponderant, to give that vigorous taste of liqueur.

The sweet babà have recently abandoned the huge cylindrical shapes and assumed a circular presentation of smaller dimensions, in the center of which is inserted a ball of whipped cream and the candied cherry.

The Babà has a cousin, in the kitchen French, the so-called: *Savarin;* in honor of the aforementioned Father of Gastronomy: *Brillat-Savarin.*

The dough is similar to that of Babà, - in the Savarin more eggs are used - and it is the invention of the Parisian pastry chefs: Julien Brothers, in 1840.

The forms are different from the baba; the Savarin looks like a pudding with a central void that can be filled with a fruit concoction and the inevitable Chantilly Cream; with regard to the use of rum syrup; it seems that there are secrets that the pastry chefs have not revealed.

*   *   *

IMMODEST MINNI OF VIRGINS

Of these Don Fabrizio was given two and holding them on the plate looked like a profane caricature of St. Agatha exhibiting his severed breasts.
Why did the Holy Office, when it could, not think of prohibiting these sweets?
The breasts of Sant'Agata sold by the Monasteries, devoured by the revelers – Mah.
From Il Gattopardo, Milan 1969

Minni di Vergini are in Palermo some pastries imitating the small and rounded breasts of the girls.
It is known that there is a Monastery, that of Montevergini, where these pastries are made however.
G. Pitrè: Medicina Popolare Siciliana, Florence 1949

The instances which June Di Schino lists of sexually allusive confectionary include several belongings to the category of Vergins's breast cakes such as Minni Chini, *decribed as a kind of breast shape filled with cassata, with sugar icing, topped with a cherry; and the smaller* Minnuzzi di Sant'Agata *from Catania, which were small pasties shaped like an immature girl's breast.*

From: The Food Companion, Oxford University Press 1998 - Author: Prof. Alan Davidson quoting the Dott.sa June Di Schino in the Text: The Waning of Sexually Allusive Monastic Confectionary in Southern Italy, 1995.

How can we deduce *I Minni di Vergini* in the Palermo pastry shop and I *Minni di Sant'Ajata* in the no less illustrious one in the Catanese pastry shop; they have been the subject of panic by illustrious Sicilian writers: Tomasi da Lampedusa and Giuseppe Pitrè; while, in international cuisine, they have had a less taboo recognition in topics concerning sexuality and food:
Gender/Sex and Food.

The *Minna,* dolcetto or cassata in the forms of female breast, is a composition of ancient origins, possibly linked to propitiatory rites of fertility; the female breast also represents the first source of nutrition of the newborn, the first act of maternal love; then there would also be the Christian sources linked to this dessert, such as the Martyrdom of the Virgin Agatha to whom the breasts were torn.

In the ancient recipe of 1725 presented by Sister Virginia Casale reference is made to shortcrust pastry, stuffed with *cucuzzata* and stuffed with ricotta, closed with another sheet; which is given an oval shape similar to a female breast.

Minni Di Vergini - *Recipe*

- *Shortcrust Pastry*: One Kilo of Double Zero Flour, 180 grams of Lard, 500 grams Sugar, Three Egg Yolks, Marsala Wine q.b., Vanilla Sachet Powder and Cinnamon Powder

Filling: A Kilo Cream of Sheep's Ricotta, 150 grams of icing sugar, *150* grams of Pumpkin or candied fruit, A Bar of Dark Chocolate.

- Glaze: 350 grams of icing sugar, an egg white, lemon juice and candied cherries.
- *Tools:* Aluminum or Silicone molds of rounded shape.

Procedure

Let's start with the shortcrust pastry keeping in mind that in manual procedures we must not knead for too long, otherwise the product overheats, causing the fats to melt.

Like other compounds, shortcrust pastry can also go crazy, or crumble; in these cases it would be enough to add a couple of tablespoons of cold water to recover the dough and make it elastic again. If you have time limits the pastry you can buy; even the commercial products, regarding the bakery, are of good workmanship.

Work the flour with the lard, then arrange the mixture in a fountain and add: Sugar, eggs, marsala and spices. Knead everything and let the dough rest properly covered.

Knead the ricotta with sugar, candied fruit and chocolate flakes.

Roll out the pastry with the *lasagnaturi* until you get a thin sheet; from which you can get circles, which must be the same size as the molds you have available.

Then roll out the first circle over the mold, previously buttered and floured, stuff with ricotta cream and cover the filling with another circle of pastry.

Bake at 180 degrees for 20 minutes; pay attention to baking in the oven otherwise the *minne* burst.

While the desserts are in the oven; proceed with the glaze, mixing the egg white and lemon juice. with sugar little by little. The glaze, in these desserts, must be consistent and is applied when the *minne* are baked and cooled.

All that remains is to apply the nipple-like cherry on each treat.

These sweets are also reflected in the kitchens of the Southern Regions of the Peninsula, whose references are deductible: *Tits of the Nuns, Sise of the Nuns.*

There are many names with which it is usual to call this Sicilian dessert present particularly in Puglia and Abruzzo; the most modest prefer the term: *Sighs of the Virgin.*

From the story: Le Paste delle Vergini included in the book: I Segreti del Chiosco by Prof. Maria Oliveri of Palermo. - Ed. The Genius. March 2019 -

The grandmother greeted the nuns who knew her by now and began to choose sweets, with unnerving slowness, for my hungry stomach of a child. -Then for the uncle we take two cannoli, because if you eat one he says that it is little, that he can not even grasp the flavor ... For the mother who is always on a diet we take the ladyfingers, they are light ...

After mentally examining what each family member desired,se began to order: - So, sister.... Give me a big tray, we put six cannoli, four sfince, a little ladyfingers and .... arrived at the word Minne the grandmother start coughiinng.

We had just left the Church, she had confessed, communicated, was in the grace of God ... It could never come out of the mouth of a mother of a family, fearful of the Lord, that coarse word, which would make the girls blush well, from head to toe.

- *Chest – it was said, not minne.*
- *The children clutched their chests*
- *Chest out and belly inside*

The nuns, however, called their pasta: MINNE.
Grandma did not lose heart, after all she had survived two world wars
Then... Uh... the ladyfingers put them? Well... and also give me two...
A small cough, providential, occurred while the grandmother pointed to two minne of glossy icing, took away from the embarrassment.

Every time we went to buy sweets from the nuns of St. Catherine, a stinging cough manifested itself, at any time of the year, to drive away that disrespectful word: - Minne -

One day a new nun arrived, young and full of modern ideas.
Grandma began: - So... there are six of us for lunch, but maybe in the afternoon we are waiting for visits and...
Madam, what do you want? The nun cut short: Tell me how many pastriees you take, so I prepare the tray.

The ways of the religious nun were sharp and quite irritating.
The grandmother, began stuttering to order: Six cannoli, a little Martorana stuffed and four ...
Four sfince? Said the nun.
No – Four....
Four Santa Caterina sandwiches, then?

The grandmother shook her head and in vain pointed to the sweets beyond the grate, the nun pretended not to understand or perhaps she did not understand seriously, because suddenly exclaimed: Ah - the Minne - How many Minne of Virgo, Wants?

The grandmother took the blow, remained in apnea for a few seconds to beckon yes and then abandoned herself in a violent coughing attack.
Her face, covered with a thin layer of powder, was crazy.

From that day we didn't buy the minne anymore

From this story it is easy to understand how fearful sicilian women were in expressing the hidden and private parts of their body.

EFFETTO MONSÙ NELLA CUCINA POPOLARE SICILIANA

In Sicilia non importa fare male o fare bene;
il peccato che noi Siciliani non perdoniamo
è quello di: FARE

Dal romanzo il Gattopardo – Autore: Tomasi da Lampedusa

We should now examine some aspects of monsù cuisine related, no longer to court or palace parties; but in a simple and dignified family canteen, in whose kitchen there is no Monsieur Gaston but the candid Agnes: Bride, mother, housewife and expert Sicilian cook.

There would be the inevitable story of the sparrows belonging to the *Silvidi* family or *Ortolano* birds of the *Emberizidi* family; these birds were caught, in the autumn months with nets, because they travel in flocks, land in the fields to feed themselves and then rise in flight all together but may get entangled in the nets specially prepared by poachers.

The passerines are caught alive, kept in special cages and fed with fig fruits, so that their entrails could be clean and edible; becauase the delicacy of the dish consistes precisely in the fact that the beccafico, once cooked, is eaten whole and in one bite.

This dish was and still is part of the French cuisine and as such was introduced by the monsù in the southern kitchens of the nobles.

The ritual French custom provides that the one who is about to eat the birth, covers his head with a white virginal cloth; as a sign of repentance to accomplish what would be a sin of gluttony towards the ornithological nature.

An admirer of this dish seems to have been the late President of the French Republic: *Francois Mitterand,* who died in 1996; in the last years of his Presidency was suffering from prostate cancer.

As we know in Sicilian cuisine this dish was transformed into: *Sarde alla Beccafico* of which there are several culinary devices concerning the use of cheese, spices and baking methods.

Providing you with the recipe of Sarde alla Beccafico would be like adding nothing to what has already been written and rewritten on this dish.

Sicilian cuisine makes use of this type of compositions of sardines, anchovies, blue fish; resorting to the use of stuffing or fillings that, in the appropriate case, would be a mix of: *Stale bread crumb, grated caciocavallo, chopped garlic, whole egg, capers, passolina grapes, pine nuts, oregano, olive oil, salt and pepper.*

These would be the elements that make up the filling of sardines; which honestly, from a culinary point of view, is not a trivial matter.

Tradition has it that the union of the afore mentioned elements that make up the filling, would provide the sardines with the same flavor of the entrails of the bird that had fed on figs.

A personal opinion, about this dish, would be to proceed to the cooking in the oven of the sardines stuffed with the afore mentioned mix and with the fillets joined one on top of the other; the use of bay leaves and certainly a round of olive oil is also recommended.

Another example of aristocratic food transformed into a popular canteen would be *La Melanzana a Quaglia;* in the sense that instead of the fat quail, which - good for *her* - ran away, there would be a round eggplant; which is cut into four parts, leaving the slices attached to the petiole.
At this point it is required to fry the so decorated eggplant in *deep frying* way; in other words, to immerse the cutted aubergine in boiling oil at about 140 degrees; until completely gilded.
Once the work is done, the eggplant may be served crushed so that the two outer slices represent the wings of the quail and the two central slices would figure the body and tail of the bird.
For seasoning the dish, only a intake of sea salt would suffice.
As for the peck bird, transformed into sardines and the quail in an aubergine; these culinary techniques conceal the most noble culinary creations of the monsù cuisine .

* * *

There would be the *Pasta del Principe*, in which it is spaghetti seasoned with wild fennel. The problem would be to find which prince you are referring to: If it were the Gattopardo or some other Sicilian prince. In this regard, one theory would be that the name of the dish would mean: *Treat yourself like a prince.*

The preparation of this pasta is simple. Boil the spaghetti and store a part one ladle of cooking water. Arrange in the blender the wild fennel with shelled pistachios, flakes of pecorino or caciocavallo cheese and add also to the mixer some olive oil in order to tie the elements.

Obtained the so-called *Pesto,*it would be enough to add the drained spaghetti and, if required, dilute the contents with the ladle of cooking water.
Then season the pasta with a savory: *Muddica Atturrata* or roasted breadcrum

Subsequently, the crumbs, can be put in a pan over low heat and proceed with the seasoning of a little olive oil, accompanied with chopped garlic, oregano, fresh parsley, capers and scent of red chillie pepper or chillie flakes.

It is necessary that these elements are absorbed by the crumbs so that they remain full of flavor; to prevent the botttom of the pan from craping the compounds these elements must be rhythmically mixed, when they are on fire.

Someone recently enriched the prince's pasta by inserting canned tuna or anchovy pulp in the ingredients which is not, on the culinary point of view, a bad idea.

*   *   *

A more substantial dish would be the *Falsomagro or Meatloaf*

Someone has found its origins in Spanish cuisine; but the sources speak of the Angevin derivation in the thirteenth century; therefore, at the time of the Sicilian Vespers; however, even this composition can be considered part of the gastronomic culture of the French monsù introduced in the Kingdoms of Naples.

The name *False* could refer to the stuffing, which in French would be *Farse,* another French term is *Maigre;* it could mean that the filling, in the original version, was rather lean; something that is no longer at least in Sicilian cuisine.

Leveraging our diction could also well mean that the composition would seem a lean food but in reality it is not.

She is a False Skinny: it is an attribute that referred to already adult girls who seemed thin; while in reality when they wear bikinis you could see voluptuous curves, the mountains of Venus and other feminine features, which drove all the boys a bit *crazy.*

Then we leave the beaches and move to the kitchen as the preparations of the falsomagro would require a little attention.

The recipe refers to the composition of the falsomagro according to the canons of hyblaean cuisine; except that it is cooked in white and without sauces, broths or further sautéed.

Ingredients:

- *Meat* : A large slice of Lean Veal
- Minced meat mixed beef and pork
- Salame ragusano *suppissatu*, Slices of Mortadella.
- Spices : Nutmeg, Cinnamon, Cloves, Bay leaf, Black pepper, Salt
- Liquids : Red wine, Milk
- Vegetables : Leek and celery, Finely chopped, including leaves
- Other : Whole beaten egg, Boiled eggs, Caciocavallo flakes, Stale bread crumbs, tomato extract.

Procedure and Assembly

Soak the whole slice of veal in milk for about an hour.

Compose the filling by mixing the minced meats with the spice powders described above, the beaten egg, the caciocavallo flakes, the breadcrumbs, the red wine, salt, black pepper; and if required, part of the milk where the meat was put to macerate can be used.

Now use the slice of macerated veal, place it in a working surface, dry it and, if required, beat it to make it softer.

Once well opened, place the *suppissed* salami cut into cubes on the slice of veal, then the filling, without the bay leaf, as tanned above, place the leek and celery vegetables on top of the filling, enter the slices of mortadella to cover and finally align the boiled eggs cut into three parts eliminating the hemispheres.

Everything should be arranged for a long time and make sure to cover the entire inner surface of the slice; leaving the edges free.

We must now try to close everything, wrapping the sides of the slice of calf to obtain a cylindrical roll. If you want to avoid ligatures: spread the surfaces of the roll obtained with tomato extract or tomaato purree sauce, garnish with a few bay leaves and turn the meatloaf in a previously buttered aluminum foil.

Cooking must take place in the oven, taking care to practice with a fork holes on the aluminum foil to facilitate the exit of the vapors that will form during cooking.

Oven preheated to 220 degrees centigrade cooking control after at least 25 minutes; remove the aluminum foil in the last 5 minutes of cooking.

Once ready and out of the oven, slide any juices and wait another 10 minutes before cutting it and presenting the slices of falsomagro in a special tray garnished with potatoes or butter peas, with what you like.

Certainly the falsomagro would also marry with an excellent sauce, which does not necessarily have to be a tomato sauce, you can use white sauces such as Bernese with tarragon, sauce with reduction of full-bodied red wine with forest blueberries.

It would be better to serve the sauce proposals, knowingly, in special saucers.

This, in my opinion, would be the falsomagro that the expert Donna Agnese would have served at the table on a public holiday, having also invited the demanding and picky mother-in-law.

* * *

We talked in the previous paragraph; on the occasion of the dinner at Villa Salina of the Prince's favorite dessert: *Rum Jelly, manned by a garrison of green pistachios.*

We propose then: Moscato jelly with *Exotic Fruits;*without forgetting the garrison or the garnish of green pistachios of Mount Etna Volcano.

The courtly French cuisine of the '700 certainly abounded in huge compositions with colored jellies with entire depictions with floating fish, swans in a pond, flowering trees, towers of castles and many other sculptures. These gelatinous compositions were presented, in the royal canteens, in a succession of servants in livery who carried, almost barely, capacious silver pottery, above which these statuary works towered.

In the following post-revolutionary century; we have the phenomenon of *Caremism,* a term born from one of the greatest, if not the greatest, parisian chef *Cousinier* so far existed: *Antonio Careme.*

After opening some *Patisserie* shops in Paris, he became increasingly famous and in 1810 prepared Napoleon's wedding lunch with Marie Louise of Austria.

This was followed by the publication of books such as: *Le Patissier Royal Parisienne. Le Patissier Pittoresque.*

After the defeat of Napoleon at Waterloo he was summoned by Tsar Alexander to the court of St. Petersburg; later Careme traveled through Continental Europe, cooking for all the most important ministers, rulers and wealthy of that time.

Of his last book: *L'art de le Cuisine Francaise,* only three volumes were composed, as the author passed away in 1833.

The art of Careme is most remembered in the historical annals of the kitchen for having created more than 400 ornate designs to be performed on pastry of all kinds.

Draw on the plates but avoid The Caremism -: It was the recommendation – loud and clear – that was, expressed and invoked by the distinguished Master *Paul Bocouse,* Spiritual Father of *Nouvelle Cuisine;* which was a reccomandation addressed to his students in the cooking school established in the City of Lyon, French region of the Rhône.
What could be said: time changes, we hope for the better.

*   *   *

Muscat Jelly With Exotic Fruits

One of the elements, in this dish, would be the substance that is improperly called: *Fish Glue:* the term derives from the scales of sturgeon fish caught in the Caspian Sea.

However, the gelatin sheets or powders that are bought in supermarkets or pharmacies are mainly produced using the dense broths of the pork rind, with bones and cartilage also of bovine animals.

A variant to the above jellies, which are predisposed in thin, transparent, odorless and tasteless leaves; would be the vegetarian jellies, among which the most renowned takes its name: *Agar-Agar* composed of seaweed.

Gelatin is an important element not only to compose domestic sweets but above all for its wide use in the packaging of industrial sweets and ice creams; as they have the ability to transform quantities of liquids into an apparently compact form.
The molecules that compose it are endowed with special properties that make these transformations possible.

These molecules are hydrophilic – in the sense that they attract water – and are endowed with a filiform structure.

When liquid is added to the gelatin and the mixture is heated to the fire, the gelatin first swells by absorbing water and subsequently dissolves.

At this point the gelatin molecules move freely in the mixture; when this begins to cool, the molecules lose energy and form a _mesh_ in which the water or liquids used are retained.

ELEMENTS

Fresh Fruit: Papaya, Mango, Pineapple
250 grams of each exotic fruit: cut the pulps of the fruits into cubes, trying to obtain even the natural juices.

Liquids: Half a liter of Moscato white wine or Spumante Amabile

Spices: 30 grams of flaked or crumbled pistachio seeds
Three tablespoons of Granulated Sugar

Other: 15 grams of Gelatin Sheets

TOOLS: Four oval crème caramel molds

Procedure

Put the two sheets of gelatin in cold water.

Arrange the fruit cubes with the juices obtained, together with 3 tablespoons of sugar, in a bowl and cook these contents for 10 minutes over high heat.
When cooked and when the mixture is warm; take the fruit nuts and place them in a colander and place this colander on top of the same bowl; so as not to disperse additional juices that will come down from the cubes.

Pour the muscat wine into a new saucepan, bring the contents to a boil and reduce or evaporate a third of the contents.
Remove this saucepan from the heat and insert the gelatin, wringing it out of the water.
Incorporate the fruit juices into the wine now.

Gently mix the contents of the saucepan with a spatula and when the liquids have warmed and the mixture will become colored and viscous; insert into the mixture the cubes of exotic fruit, which stood in the colander.
Mix everything thoroughly with the spatula and mix the liquids with the fruit.

Now full the molds with the mixture obtained and place them in the refrigerator, for at least three hours; to give time to the gelatin to form compactly. The British would say: To _Set-Up_.

To serve the dessert you may need to quickly immerse each individual mold in hot water; to do better slip the contents into the serving dish.

Decorate the exotic fruit jellies with whipped cream around the bases; placing the pistachio flakes scenically on the surfaces.

*   *   *

It should not be missing among the disquisitions on the effects of the monsù cuisine, towards the Sicilian cuisine: *Le Blanc Manger;* whose composition, in the sweet version, was conceived by Maestro Antonio Careme in the 19th century: You can avoid caremism; but you can not avoid the consequences of caremism.

It would be enough just to say that Biancomangiare is a simple homemade recipe; basically a milk pudding thickened with starches, variously flavored and decorated.

In fact, the history of *blanc manger* is a little more complicated for those who, in the historical annals of cuisine, have sought sources in classic Roman cuisine, or in Middle Eastern, Turkish or Persian cuisine.

It has long been speculated that white-ingew comes from the Middle East due to ancient European imports of rice and almonds from the Arab world.
It should be noted that in Sicily there were no imports of rice and almonds from the Arab world; but cultivation and production of these goods; because the Arab domination has brought, in our island, a cultural integration between East and West.

The English scholar of Arabic culture and cuisine, *Arthur J. Arberry* in 1939, found, as proof of the above, a dish deriving from medieval Arab cuisine, known in persian diction with the term of *Isfidhabaj;* whose meaning would be "White Food" in which it would be a stew of lamb meat in almond milk.

This dish, according to Arberry himself, could be associated with the French and English compositions of the 14-15th century; in which the blanc manger was cooked with chicken breast meat, sugar, rice and almonds.

However, other scholars, including the American historian *Charles Perry* in 1989; have not endorsed this theory, adducing that the aforementioned Arabic or Persian dish was an end in itself, consequently not associated with compositions of European ' white foods'; coming to the conclusion that the European blanc mangers have not suffered any Eastern influence and that the sources were untraceable and obscure.

The only source, at our disposal, about the Biancomangiare can be found in the *Liber de Coquina* by an anonymous author, written at the Angevin court of Naples, at the beginning of the fourteenth century. This *book* was written in vulgar Latin and is one of the most important testimonies on the eating habits of the late Middle Ages; at the Italian and European courts.
According to the dictions of this important work, it appears that the origin of the biancomangiare was French and, in the medieval version, it was prepared with the simmering of: Chicken breasts, rice flour, goat's milk or almond milk, pork lard and sugar.

Remaining among the authors of modern gastronomic literature, in 1993, the lexicologist *John Ayto* of the University of Oxford, found a dish, coming from the classical Roman cuisine, called: *Cibaria Alba* in which it would have been a coarse food; intended more towards slaves than to the citizens or patricians of the empire. This dish was mentioned in the book of 1475 written by Bartolomeo Sacchi, better known by the nickname: *Il Platina;* author of the first printed cookbook: - *De Honesta Voluptate et Valetudine* - who cited as the source of the recipe the Roman writer Marco Gavio APICIO, who lived at the turn of the years before and after Christ, at the time of emperor Tiberius.

By *Voluptate,*Platina means pleasure; which in order not to make it become *libido,*the author adds the attribute of: *Honesta;* while by *Valetude,* we mean the health and energy of the body.
Despite the literal efforts and manual verifications of Prof. Ayto no recipe in this sense was found; following the sheeting carried out on the residual work of Apicius; I say – residual – because part of the original work: De Res coquinaria; it was irretrievably lost.

The research of the University of Oxford also extended towards the writings of *Maestro Martino,*a close friend of Platina and Prince of Cooks in the service of Pope Julius II Della Rovere;
but the hopes of Oxfordian students to find the White Food or Cibaria Alba, in Roman times, were unsuccessful and unfulfilled.

Abandoning now the medieval recipes and the sources of biancomangiare, obscure or obvious, we stick to the sweet and traditional compositions of this amalgamated compound that, in Sicily, is also known as: *Milk Cream.*

The theory would be that the recipe provided by the learned *cousinier Antonio Careme* has found a large following in Sardinian and Aosta Valley cuisine; while in Sicily, and in particular in the Hyblaean territories, there are elements different from those indicated by Careme; such as almonds, honey, pistachios, lemon peel and cinnamon.

Always remaining in our part, the *jancu-manciari* has been associated among the traditional Lenten foods; since the name and the features of the dessert denote purity and candor of the spirit.

We can, from Sicilian culinary techniques, obtain two versions of white creams: A basic method and a version with almond milk.

In the basic recipe, the ingredients would be:
Milk 500 ml, Sugar 100 grams, Starch for cakes 50 grams, bag of Vanillin or vanilla pod, lemon zest.

We must not forget the use of our women to present the white-inging on top of an embroidered fig or mulberry leaf.

Provide you with the methods of preparation or cooking of the aforementioned cream; it would be an offense to your superfine culinary skills.

White-eat with almond milk

The method used by the peasants to obtain the natural almond milk was to crush the almonds until a real cream was obtained. Place the almond cream obtained in a napkin and dip the napkin several times in a cup of cold water; then squeeze the napkin into another container until the almond juice is exhausted.

Ingredients: One liter of cold water, 250 grams of peeled ground almonds, 220 grams of sugar, 110 grams of starch, lemon peel.

Procedure: Put the crushed almonds and leave them to stand for at least 10 minutes in a container of cold water.

Strain the liquid into a gauze and place it in aa cooking pot. A squeeze to what remains in the gauze is advisable. Now that we are there, add the sugar, starch and lemon peel to the liquid obtained and bring the solution to a boil.
Mix the contents with a spatula, to prevent the elements from craping.

As soon as the boiling of the contents begins, turn off the heat.

After about ten minutes, after having given a final turn, you can precede to place the obtained white almond cream in the appropriate mold (s) .
After depositing the mold in the fridge for at least two hours, slide the contents into a serving dish; turning the mold *upside down.*

Sprinkle the surfaces of the pudding with chopped almond and ground cinnamon.

This would be the recipe of Mrs. Teresa da Scicli, kindly offered to me by Anna, my friend from Ragusa.

CAPITOLO SECONDO:
LA NOSTRA STORIA

PARAGRAFO I - LA FINE DI UN REGNO

PARAGRAFO II - L'INFAUSTO INIZIO UNITARIO

PARAGRAFO III - FONTI E CONSIDERAZIONI SULLA CUCINA SICILIANA

LA FINE DEL REGNO

Un classico ancora attuale è il racconto di mille uomini
che sbarcarono a Marsala e sbaragliarono un esercito
di 42 mila soldati; comandati da fior di generali.
Non è incredibile?
Appunto è incredibile.
Io non ci credo -
Carmelo Santillo, Storico, 2017

We have previously talked about the marriage between Ferdinand of Bourbon and Maria Carolina of Habsburg-Lorraine that took place in 1768.

At the time of this marriage Ferdinand was Sovereign of the Kingdom of Naples – *The lands on this side of the lighthouse* – and King of Sicily – The lands beyond the *lighthouse* -.

It is well understood that the Lighthouse in question would be the one on the Strait of Messina, that wonderful marine monument that bears on top the statuette of the Virgin Mother with the cubital inscription: *Vos Et Ipsam Civitatem Benedicimus.*

If this statement was truly understood and applied in the practice of our customs; we would certainly have a better society.

The two realms, despite having a common ruler, were legally separated; in the capital of Palermo, although there was a Parliament, this had no legislative power and the Bourbon monarchy could be considered absolute both in Naples and in Palermo.

Mangiatori di maccheroni (Macaroni eaters)

It seems that the Kingdom of Sicily enjoyed tax breaks compared to that of Naples and the young Sicilians were exempt from military service.

*   *   *

A grain for the Bourbon King were the French revolutionaries; as the Kingdom of Naples had supported the Austrian Empire against the French Revolution.

Napoleon's victories in the Northern Italian campaign against the Habsburg army inflamed and stirred the minds of fervent Italian patriots who saw, in the French revolution, republican yearnings for freedom against the *ancienne regime.*

In the name of the revolution, the *Republic of Genoa, the Cisalpine Republic and the Roman Republic* were founded by fervent pro-Jacobin patriots and with the help of the French army.

In 1798 Napoleon decided to conduct his *armée* in Egypt with the intention of defeating the British Kingdom and the Ottoman Empire with the conquest of the East.

The Kingdom of Naples entered the war against the French, with the support of Nelson's English fleet and with 70 thousand men, under the command of Austrian officers, they entered Rome to establish papal rights and powers against the newly established Roman Republic.

An armed counteroffensive French defeated the Neapolitan army at the Battle of *Civita Castellana,* near the city of Viterbo.
Following this defeat, in December 1798, the Bourbon royals with the treasures of the crown, embarked on the flagship *Vanguard* under the command of Horatio Nelson and with the entourage of ministers, aristocrats and graduates, headed towards the coasts of Sicily, in that phase that is defined by historians as: The escape to *Palermo.*

In the same wake of the *Vanguard,*there was the frigate of the Neapolitan navy called La *Sannita* under the command of Admiral Francesco *Caracciolo;*which served as an escort to the sovereigns.

Following the escape of the Bourbon, shortly thereafter, it was established by the Italian-Jacobin revolutionaries, with the consent and help by theFrench army, the *Neapolitan Republic.*

Those who defended, in vain, Naples against the pro-French revolutionaries, were the *Lazzari or Lazzaroni.*

The term *Lazzarone* comes from St. Lazarus, who was resurrected from the tomb by the work of Jesus Christ following the supplications of the Magdalene: *Lazarus get up and walk,* was the order given by Jesus and the man was seen, wrapped in bandages, staggering out of the pits.

Lazzarone was therefore referring to people dressed at best in white cloths, who laze in the city streets and who were ready for any assignment proposed to them: legal or illegal that could be,

* * *

Thus the city of Palermo, from 1798 to 1801, became the residence of the royals Bourbons and British diplomats in their wake.

Among these English characters we can include:

- *Sir John Acton* born in 1736, after a career in the British Navy, became commander of the fleet of the Grand Duchy of Tuscany. In 1778 Queen Carolina asked Grand Duke Leopold, her brother, to allow Acton to go to Naples to organize the Neapolitan Bourbon Navy. Acton accepted the post of Secretary of State of the Kingdom of Naples. It was certainly not a wrong choice, thanks to Acton's skills, was founded, in 1783, the shipyard of Castellammare di Stabia. John Acton was highly esteemed in the court of Naples and became personal secretary of Queen Carolina with whom it seems that intimate relations also took place. For the record, Acton recognized the talents of Lieutenant Francesco Caracciolo and appointed him to the highest ranks of the Bourbon navy. In turn, Caracciolo fought in 1782 with Nelson, in the naval battle of Genoa to prevent the French fleet from making a landing on the island of Corsica. When the Neapolitan Royals were ready to leave Palermo and head back to Naples to retake the Kingdom of Further Sicily, John Acton asked for leave as Secretary of State and preferred to stay in Palermo where he married a young bride who was the daughter of his brother and with whom he had three children. For the services rendered to the Bourbon Crown, to the Adimral John Acton was conferred the title of *Duke of Modica;* however, his name is not among those who have held offices, albeit honorary, in the County of Modica.

Lord William Hamilton and Lady Emma Hamilton.

William Hamilton was an archaeologist, antiquarian, volcanologist and diplomat, accredited by the British *Foreign Office* to the Bourbon court of Naples, with the task of drafting and informing the British government about political or economic events in the Bourbon kingdom.

Emma Lyon or Hart was a young model with a dark past who had an affair with the English MP Charles Graville, grandson of Sir William Hamilton. Subsequently, Graville became engaged to a wealthy English heiress and the relationship with Emma had become a bit cumbersome; he then decided to send Emma to Naples with his uncle William, promising that he would come and take her back within three months. Emma accepted the proposal and went to Naples to see William Hamilton, awaiting the coming of the Graville. Sir William Hamilton was a widower and the presence of a young woman did not displease him completely and Emma, for her part, realizing that Charles Graville did not show up, nor would he make himself alive; he accepted the hospitality and court of Sir William. To make a long story short, in 1791, William Hamilton, aged 60, married Emma Lyon, aged 26, in England, who became: *Lady Emma Hamilton.*

On their return to Naples, Sir William introduced the young bride to the Bourbon royals and Emma became close friends with Queen Caroline. The Hamilton couple began to give parties in the halls of their Palazzo *Sessa* in Naples in which important guests such as Johan Wolfgang Goethe, sculptors, writers, artists of the time and certainly nobles and courtiers of Europe participated. Emma Hamilton entertained guests by impersonating Greek-Roman mythologies of the classical period or characters such as Medea or Cleopatra, she was very good at singing, dancing and in the poses and attitudes of the body as she had previously been a model of painters and sculptors.

The best tailors of Naples were called to make the tunics, shawls and clothing of Lady Hamilton. Among the welcome guests was Admiral Horatio Nelson, a close friend of Sir William who, after the Naval Battle of the *Nile,*in which he had devastated the fleet French to the Bay of Aboukir, become, as indeed he was, the hero of the seven seas, who would save the Kingdom of Naples and the whole of Europe from the French Jacobins and napoleon's army. Lady Emma Hamilton, who had well learned Italian language, became Nelson's secretary, who even came to live in the same house as Sir William and certainly the mutual admiration between Emma and Horatio also led to love or carnal desire. Her husband Sir William did not oppose his wife's relationship with Nelson; what the Latins called: *Tria Juncto In Uno* or we could use the term French *Menage a Trois;* finally, to put it in the Sicilian way, William Hamilton became: *Curnutu Accurdatu*

For his part, Nelson divorced - or rather repudiated - his wife and dedicated himself to the beautiful Emma.

The British government realized that Nelson and the Hamiltons had become very attached to the Bourbon regime; when the Neapolitan Republic fell, Nelson and Emma Hamilton were protagonists of the return of the Bourbon royals to Naples, decreeing executions and penalties for the leaders of the Republic and of Admiral Caracciolo himself who, having become commander of the Republican Navy of Naples, had managed to block the English Navy at the island of Procida.

By order of Nelson, Francesco Caracciolo was hanged in his own ship and by his own sailors, who certainly reluctantly carried out the given order.

Lord William Hamilton was then replaced by another diplomat and Admiral Nelson was recalled by the Royal Navy.

Once Naples was abandoned the Tria Juncto in Uno did not dissolve but they came to live under the same roof in the London residence: Sir William spent time fishing in the Thames, Nelson most often was at sea and Emma looked after his daughter Horatia, had in 1801.

As we know, in the victorious naval battle of Trasfalgar in 1805 against the French fleet, Nelson was shot dead; William had previously died of natural causes and Emma found herself the widow of her husband and lover.

Apart from an annuity left by her husband William, Nelson's possessions were inherited, by holographic will, from his brother. In his will, Nelson also asked the British Government to grant Emma Hamilton an annuity; unfortunately for Emma, no measures were taken into consideration by the English tax office. At the time Emma Hamilton was 46 years old; as the saying goes: *time erases beauty.*

Subsequently, for having contracted debts, without being able to pay them; she was imprisoned for twelve months; upon release, to escape creditors, she moved to Calais in France with her daughter Horatia; where Emma lived, in misery, the last years of her existence.

*   *   *

So in December 1798 the Bourbon Royals were in Palermo, where Ferdinand and Maria Carolina lived in their residence, called: the *Chinese Palace* in the Favorita Park.

Ferdinand of Bourbon received, a few days after his stay in Palermo, the visit of Cardinal *Fabrizio Ruffo,* a well-known exponent of the Roman Papal Curia; who had gone, on his own initiative, to ask Ferdinand: ships, men and money to regain the lost kingdom of Naples.

The Bourbon king adhered to the request of the cardinal, who was appointed *General Commander of the Army of the Holy Faith.*

Landing in Calabria, his native land as belonging to the family of the Princes of Bagnara, Cardinal Ruffo addressed an appeal to the Calabrian population to which about 15 thousand peasants responded who, shortly thereafter, formed an army of 25 thousand men, heading towards Naples to free the city from the Republicans and the French.

This army was also joined by brigands of the place, clearly in view of loot.

Among these was *Michelangelo Pezza,* who was ordained Captain and Column Commander of the Army of faith; Pezza was better known by the nickname of: *Fra Diavolo.*

Michelangelo Pezza belonged to a very religious family and his mother dressed him in the habit of a friar and his companions called him ' Friar Michael '; when he went to school the boy proved listless and did not want to learn the Catechism, so the priest instructor told him: *You, you are not 'Fra Michele - sei 'Fra Diavolo;* from this event was born the nickname that instilled terror in enemies.

With Napoleon stranded in Egypt, the grip of the French army in Naples began to fade and the Republican patriots were left without the protection of French cannons.

Cardinal Ruffo entered Naples on June 13, 1799, with the Lazzaroni celebrating and following the surrender of the supporters of the Republic; although officially the Kingdom of Naples will return to the Bourbon dynasty following the *Peace of Florence* in February 1801.

It seems that there had been agreements in the negotiations between Cardinal Ruffo and the members of the Neapolitan Republic. Following the surrender of the latter, the Ruffo would have granted the Neapolitan revolutionaries a safe conduct to be transferred to France or in any case not to be prosecutable.

Despite these agreements and without respecting the offers made by Ruffo, a military junta was formed, in fact under the orders of Admiral Nelson, subservient to Emma Hamilton who transmitted to Nelson the wishes of justice and revenge of Queen Maria Carolina.
In the trials against the Republicans: 124 of them were executed in Piazza Mercato in Naples, by hanging and beheading; 222 people were sentenced to life imprisonment.

The historian and philosopher *Benedetto Croce,* reports, in his writings, the ferocious repression against the members of the Neapolitan Republic, expressing a negative and unedifying judgment of the Bourbon Royals:

- *King Ferdinand has done too much honor by calling him: Tyrant.*
  He thought of hunting, females and good food; as long as they let him do such things, he was ready to order war, to flee, to promise, to perjure, to forgive, to kill; often laughing at the bizarre spectacle.

Queen Maria Carolina of Habsburg was defined :

A woman who, beyond the improprieties and turpidity of private life, has been seized by a series of lies and violation of solemn commitments made on honor and faith.
A turbid spirit, he had neither mental highness, nor precautions and prudence; she continually did his own and everyone's damage.

Dismissed from command, Cardinal Ruffo, although he had been the architect of the provisional restoration of the Bourbon Rulers in Naples, returned to the commitments of the Roman curia.
To Admiral Nelson was conferred by King Ferdinand, for services rendered to the Bourbon crown, the property of the *Ducea or the Feud of Bronte, on the hills of the volcano Mount Etna* of which we will be interested in the pages to come.

* * *

Following the peace of Florence in 1801 the Bourbon rulers returned to Naples, but the story of the escapes does not end: Napoleon manages to escape by sea from Egypt and return to France.

Out of fear of Napoleon and Caroline's desire for revenge against the French, the Bourbons asked the Russians and the British for help.
In fact, in 1805 20 thousand soldiers of foreign troops landed in the port of Naples who joined the 40 thousand Neapolitan Bourbon soldiers.

Almost nothing was done about this agreement because Napoleon, in the battle of Austerlitz –*The Battle of the Three Emperors* – defeated, within two hours, Russian and Habsburg armies.

The Bourbon hastened to negotiate peace, but Napoleon did not even received the Neapolitan ambassadors; expressing itself categorically: *The Bourbon Dynasty has ceased to reign.*

In January 1806 Giuseppe Bonaparte, Napoleon's brother, set out for Naples.
and the French regained possession of Naples in the following month, amid popular indifference in the city.
For Ferdinand there was no other choice but to make a second escape to Palermo.

In September 1808 Joseph left the throne of Naples to assume the title of King of Spain; in his place Napoleon conferred the Kingdom of Naples to his brother-in-law: *Gen. Joachim Murat,* husband of *Carolina Bonaparte.*

*   *   *

With a new French King there was a second gastronomic fusion between French cuisine and Neapolitan cuisine.
The table of King Murat and his wife Carolina was managed by French chefs but was rich in fish and delicacies of the Campania coast: *Mullet of Morza, Capitoni, Sturgeons, Seafood, Clams and Mussels of Fusaro;* including all the deliveries of Capodimonte dairy products : *Butirro di Sorrento, Stracchino di Carditello, Mozzarelle, Ricotte;* along with cured meats of various kinds, hams, sausages and bacon.

Queen Bonaparte at the table was much more reserved, according to the nurse of her princely children, the English lady *Catherine Davies;* Carolina got up at eight in the morning, had breakfast with fresh milk, checked that the milk was fresh even for the breakfast of the princes, visited the bathroom and returned to bed to get up at one o'clock in the afternoon; then have a second breakfast with tea, coffee, chocolate and cocoa; accompanied by toast and crepes prepared by the Neapolitan cook; while muffins were prepared by Davies herself.

The two reigning spouses seem to have not understood each other, so Carolina had no particular political powers; she took care of the decorations of the royal palace of Naples, was interested in the archaeological excavations of Pompeii; in the economic field she made the silk and cotton factories more modern and established a new factory for the processing of coral sea, whose trade in Naples became famous.

When things went wrong for Napoleon, in his first exile on the Island of Elba, Murat had tried to contact the Austrian government in an attempt to preserve the throne of Naples but the Austrian minister *Prince Von Metternich,* at the Congress of Vienna, recognized the sovereignty of the Kingdoms of Naples and Sicily to the Bourbon dinasty.

Unable to return to France, Murat landed with a few men in Calabria trying to raise the people against the Bourbons; it was instead the people who revolted against Him; he was captured by the Bourbon soldiers in Pizzo Calabro and, after a short trial, he was sentenced to be shot: In October 1815 he presented himself to the firing squad in a sparkling uniform of general of the Hussars and recommended to the soldiers: *Aim at the heart and spare my face.*

Prince Metternich himself declared Caroline Bonaparte a prisoner of state; but he was lenient towards her, the English ship *Tremendous* was made available to lead Caroline and her four children: Achilles, Letizia, Lucian and Louise; to France.

Carolina had time to prepare her things and was embarked with her children and with a cow – called Carolina – to provide fresh milk for her and the former princes during the journey. In reality the English ship landed in Trieste and Carolina spent her time wandering around Europe under the title of: *Countess Lipona* whose term would be the anagram of her lost Kingdom.

As for the *Carolina Cow,* she became famous in the television carousels, in the years of the Italian economic miracle, which praised the consumerism of Invernizzi cheeses; together with the other characters they remained dear to the Italian television audience: *Silvester, Calimero, Topo Gigio, Jo Condor, Speedy Gonzales, The Flintstones, Popeye . . .*

*   *   *

This time the stay in Sicily of the royal family lasted for about ten years; during this period, the first proposals for reforms appeared by the Sicilian Parliament against Bourbon absolutism.

Help with these claims was provided by the British; in particular Admiral *Lord Bentick,* who acted as an intermediary for the establishment of a liberal constitution in Sicily.

This constitution was promulgated in 1812 with the signature of the Vicar Prince Francis on behalf of his father Ferdinand; who stated that he could not preside over the ceremony due to health reasons. The constitutional references were of English style and provided for the establishment of the bicameral system: The one hereditary and the one elective, the legislative power belonged to the Parliament to which the King could affix the Royal Sanction.

Among the substantial changes was contemplated the abolition of feudalism and a new administrative structure of the island.

At that time, Sicily, since the Arab conquest, was divided into three valleys and three points:

- **Mazara Valley**: *Which was configured in Western Sicily*
- **Val Demone:** *North-Eastern Sicily with the cities of Palermo, Messina, Catania*
- **Val di Noto:** *South Eastern Sicily*
- *Capo Passero: In the Province of Syracuse*
- *Capo Lilibeo: In the Province of Trapani*
- *Capo Peloro: In the Province of Messina*

These three points are symbolically depicted by the legs of the trinacria of the Sicilian flag; sites of extraordinary scenic beauty full of history and legends.

With the Constitution of 1812, in order for Sicily to be better administered, the three aforementioned valleys were abolished and 23 districts were created; among which the districts of Noto was the 20th and the next was the district of Modica.

The abolition of feudalism in Sicily became effective with the decree of confirmation and implementation of December 1816.

* * *

The glorious County of Modica, *Regnum in Regno,* born in 1296 with the investiture of Manfredi I Chiaramonte, came legally to an end .

Since the Feudo Modicano was the subject of multiple claims; The title in 1816, was recognized, to the house: *Fitz-James Stuart.*
This family, even today, is recognized in Spain with the title, purely formal, of *Count of Modica.*

The origin of the County of Modica was born from the Sicilian Vespers.

To Peter III of Aragon, after the expulsion of the Angevins in Sicily, in 1282 we owe the institutions of the County of Ragusa with Gulfi and the County of Modica with Scicli; with the investiture respectively of *Pietro Prefoglio and Federico Mosca,* who will be reunited in 1296 and form that stable territorial, political and economic identity; which will take the name of: County of **Modica.**

A very important historical event in the County took place between 1550 and 1564 following a subdivision of 30 thousand hectares of land divided into 1700 lots; which were conferred in special emphyteusis to private individuals; this subdivision of such a vast area represented an exclusive and positive episode because it broke the latifundium in South-Eastern Sicily and a new class of small and medium owners was created.

In total, in the County of Modica, from 1557 to 1713 a total of 134 thousand hectares of land were granted in emphyteusis, corresponding to 40 thousand plot.
The events were caused by the economic need of the family of the Counts *Cabrera y Moncada* and their personal absence from the rural life of the County.

Unfortunately, similar events will not occur in other parts of the island, where the crisis of the old feudalism, established by the Norman domination, will have as a consequent only the multiplication of the feudal Barons, formenting the latifundium.

*   *   *

Returning to the Sicilian Constitution of 1812 it was clear that the Bourbon did not want to make any social or constitutional changes either in Palermo or in Naples; nor did it show that it pursued such purposes.

Meanwhile, Murat's fortunes plummeted with Napoleon's defeat at Waterloo.
In 1815 the sovereign Ferdinand returned to the realm of Naples and its peninsular possessions.

The following year 1816, following the Treaty of Constance, sovereign Ferdinand of Bourbon issued a *Basic Law* with which he established the unification of the two realms into a single entity.

This entity took the name of **Kingdom Of The Two Sicilies:** Sicily Further was the Kingdom of Naples and *Sicily Citeriore that of Palermo;* whose Absolute Sovereign was *Ferdinand I of Bourbon;* that is, the same Ruler; who from Ferdinand III of Naples and Ferdinand II of Sicily, became *S.M. King Ferdinand First of the Two Sicilies.*

The city of Naples was named the capital of the Kingdom of the Two Sicilies; as an obvious consequence there was the suppression of the Sicilian Constitution of 1812 and the eviction of the Sicilian Parliament of Palermo.

With the acts of 1816; the Bourbon King, while keeping the Sicilian Constitution in words, destroyed it in fact; this constitution died a violent death, leaving behind legal and economic laws that were never implemented and with it the expectations of the Sicilian people towards a constitutional government were extinguished.

The discontent of the Sicilians manifested itself with the independence revolts of 1820 and 1848.

With the law of 1816 a new administrative subdivision was made; in Sicily seven Provinces were established, which in 1927, in the fascist era, became Nine; the City of Ragusa was added, which was preferred to Modica because of the interest of the Minister *Filippo Pennavaria;*the City of Castrogiovanni or Enna which was preferred to that of Caltagirone, which was the birthplace of the clerical anti-fascist *Don Luigi Sturzo* who, after the fascist era, found the *Italian People's Party;* from which was born, subsequently, the political party of: *Christian Democracy.*

Sicily slows down ties with the Bourbon dynasty due to the formation of this new kingdom; as in 1816 it came to cease, after 700 years, the Kingdom of Sicily and the Sicilians would aspire to greater political autonomy without feeling subjects or accepting the role of being a colony of the Kingdom of Naples

In 1830 the new Bourbon King Ferdinand II – granchild of Ferdinand I - rather than meet the needs of the Sicilians; he accentuated the processes of centralization of his Kingdom, convinced more than ever; that it was the only way to govern.

The new King used to say to the Sicilian representatives: *The Kingdom rests on my shoulders.*

In the revolutionary uprisings of 1848 the Sicilians demanded the restoration of the Constitution of 1812 which had not been legally abolished.

The General Parliament of Sicily was established, with a revolutionary government presided over by: *Ruggero Settimo;*which required the independence of the island at least in the form of separation of the two crowns.

The insurrection of Palermo led Ferdinand II to a prompt and hasty conclusion:

- On January 29, 1848, the King issued a Sovereign Act in which a new Constitution was granted in his kingdom with a bicameral parliamentary system and freedom of the press.

Paradoxically, Ferdinand II of Bourbon became the first constitutional ruler of Italy.

This Constitution of the Kingdom of the Two Sicilies was promulgated almost immediately; which had similarities with that French of 1830, granted by the King of France Louis Philippe; instead of the Sicilian one of 1812, which was of English style.

This new system kept the central authority intact, except for some reservations according to the needs of the Sicilian population.

The equality of citizens was enshrined and individual freedom was guaranteed.

The legislative initiative was the responsibility of the ministers who presented it to the Chambers.

In a separate Chapter the legal personality of the sovereign and his powers over the armed forces, judicial rights, closure of the Chambers, sanctioning and execution of laws were exposed.

This Constitution was short-lived as it was overtaken by events: after a few days from the promulgation in Naples; the kingdom French of Louis Philippe collapsed and with it the constitution that he had bestowed on the French people.

Although the Chamber of Deputies in Naples was convened after a few days it was dissolved and was never reconvened.

In other words, the Sovereign Act of Ferdinand II was never enforced; he remained in retirement until the fall of the Bourbon dynasty.

Nor did things get the better of sicily; in the Spring of 1849, the established Parliament of Palermo, just 16 months after its birth, attacked from the outside and weak on the inside, will be forced to close its doors.

Subsequently, the Bourbon decided to use force to repress Sicilian separatism, so towards the end of 1849, the situation was restored with weapons; the chronicles report the bombing of Messina; from which Ferdinand took the nickname of *King Bomba*.

Ferdinand II appointed *Gen. Filangeri,* the one who had cannoned the city of Messina, Governor of Sicily; then imposing on the island a debt of 20 million ducats.

From these events, the Sicilians realized that: the resurgenation of the ancient kingdom of Sicily was and could only be a mere illusion; reason why you had to take another road.

Pure utopia, mere illusion: If ever we had a Kingdom of our own; with Frederick II – *Stupor Mundi* – emperor in Palermo, with the Poets and singers of the Sicilian School, with the philosophers of the Ionian School, with Archimedes in Syracuse, with Ceres the goddess of the harvest and with Eros, Bacchus; with the Cyclops of Etna and with all that is real or unreal should be forfeited in a kingdom that was: *The cradle of Mediterranean civilization.*

*   *   *

What did the economic situation look like in the Kingdom of the Two Sicilies?

Opinions are conflicting as one of the historical tasks of the future Savoy governors was, precisely, to denigrate: *the ancien Bourbon regime.*

Agriculture, which occupied the la most of the Sicilian population; poured into its simplest and most primitive form: *graniculture and pastoralism.*

The extinction of feudalism in fact did not bring any social benefit for those employed in the agricultural field; as feudalism was simply replaced with the latifundium: the agricultural contracts, which the large owners or large tenants imposed on the peasants, remained unchanged; that is, in the Medieval state. Therefore, no radical change had taken place, designed to give a new character to the economic and social situations of the island.
The arrogance and preponderance of the noble owners, for them exercised by the campieri, towards those who manually worked the land remained a socially disconcerting fact.

Yet these landowners were the ones who supported Garibaldi's expedition; because as the aforementioned Prince Salina well said – in the novel of the Gattopardo: *everything must change so that everything remains as it is .*

The fear of the big owners were the new social reforms demanded by the Sicilian separatists; what was historically called and invoked, as the future: *Socialism*.

The sectors in which few Sicilian companies excelled were the shipbuilding and shipowning industry.

In 1847 the *company FLORIO* was founded; one of the most prestigious names of the island that won the contract for weekly postal services between Naples and Palermo; it was created: the first steam shipping company in the world.

Maritime merchant activities favored the development of the insurance sector in the city of Messina, several insurance companies were established for the presence of many English merchant ships.

In the first decade of 1800, in the city of Catania, Paolo Geraci opened a factory to carry out all the phases for the processing of silk; about the same period several companies dedicated themselves to the tanning of leathers and cotton processing; a spinning mill with steam engines was opened in Trapani by F.lli Adamo.

Of particular importance is the marble industry, the development in the chemical department and the paper mills of Comiso and Castelbuono.

In Campania was born the largest industrial metalworking complex and the largest naval-mechanical industry; among which we can mention:

- The first steam warship
- The first propeller-propelled ship
- The first railway in Italy: Naples-Portici
- The first railway tunnel, equipped with lighthouses, near Nocera

An important industry of that time were the zolfatare mines in Agrigento; in 1816 the British government had been granted by Ferdinand I the monopoly for the exploitation of Sicilian sulfur.
His successor Ferdinand II decided to entrust this monopoly to a French company which granted a payment of more than twice that made by the British.

The British, to enforce the pacts of the monopoly, sent a fleet to the Gulf of Naples; Ferdinand, in turn, put his fleet and army in a state of war.
The matter was then resolved peacefully by the intervention of the King of France Louis Philippe; despite Ferdinand had to compensate the interested parties.

Among the company's activities we must mention the foreign investments of the *Woodhouses family,* who created several factories and cellars in the Lilibitane areas: the *Sweet Marsala Wine* established itself commercially in European markets; even in the Royal *Navy,* during the Napoleonic naval wars, sweet Marsala was offered to sailors instead of Jamaican Rum.

There would be to complete the economic picture the exports of Sicilian products such as sea salt, wheat and citrus *fruits - Le Lumie di Sicilia -*

What was the financial situation like in the Kingdom of the Two Sicilies?

Taking up the Piedmontese rhetoric of passing off the Southern Kingdom, oppressed by the Bourbons, as a poor and backward land; of which the Alpine North would have committed, with disinterest and magnanimity of soul, to the economic development of these backward lands.

Well it has recently been recognized that the Kingdom of the Two Sicilies was, in fact, the richest and most financially advanced state, compared to the other states of the peninsula.

One of the indicators of this wealth comes to us from the indices of the financial system of the *Banco Delle Due Sicilie;* which according to the balance sheets and accounting books, boasted in 1861, the year of the Unification of Italy, a capital of 440 million lire in gold coins.

From 1861 onwards there was a huge and rather strange transfer of capital from the South to the North; subsequently the Banco di Sicilia and the Banco di Napoli were established.

Nowadays these southern banking institutions do not really exist: Banco di Sicilia is owned by Unicredit which is a Milanese banking institution; Banco di Napoli is part of Intesa San Paolo, which would be the richest credit institution in Italy, based in Turin.

In the 1990s the Cassa Centrale di Risparmio per le Provincie Siciliane also closed its doors.

In conclusion, it can be said that, towards sunset, the Bourbon Kingdom had managed to make all the other European kingdoms, England in particular, enemies; but the real enemy was not so much foreigners as, in fact, was the Piedmontese Prime Minister *Camillo Benso di Cavour,* who tried to put the Bourbons in a bad light towards the other powers.

* * *

There would have been the last Sovereign Act that of Francis II issued on June 26, 1860; when by now the Bourbons were with water at their throats.

This statute read:

- *As for Sicily, we will grant similar representative institutions that can meet the needs of the island.*

An act that came too late to the ears of the Sicilians and was completely disregarded.

Francis II of Bourbon became King of the Two Sicilies in 1858 at the age of 23, politically unprepared to take office; as the death of Ferdinand II occurred almost unexpectedly; also following an attack by a Bourbon soldier named: *Milan;*who wounded the King with a bayonet shot.

Francis' mother was *Maria Cristina of Savoy* who passed away a week after giving birth to Francis himself.

Maria Cristina would have been a prodigious Queen if she had remained alive; deeply religious enough to have been beatified by the Catholic Church in 2014; she did not venture into the political affairs of the Kingdom, but rather devoted himself to good works and actions of goodness to the poor and needy. In the four years in the title of Queen Consort; no death sentence was carried out in the Kingdom, she made sure that her husband pardoned all the condemned and at the same time led Ferdinand to prayer, so that the Lord could show the King the ways to better manage his Kingdom.

Francis had married Maria Sophia of Bavaria, Elizabeth's sister better known as *Sissi,*consort of the Emperor of Austria and Hungary: *Fancesco Giuseppe.*

For the sake of history we must report that, in his long reign, one of the last official acts of the Habsburg Emperor was to sign, to his great regret, the declaration of war in 1915.

Franz Joseph, during his reign became a witness to too many bereavements that concerned his family: His son Rodolfo died by suicide in Mayerling together with *Baroness Vetzera* his lover; his brother Maximilian shot in Mexico, Sissi stabbed in Genoa by a psychopathic anarchist who is not the case to pronounce his name; his nephew Franz Ferdinand and his wife Sofia, designated as successors of the empire, they were killed in the Sarajevo attack; and, as the last gift of fate, his Empire will be involved in a world war that will mark the end of the Habsburg dynasty.

Francis II was a person of good nature, very attached to the Catholic religion, the chronicles call him bigoted and even superstitious; he was convinced that the deceased Mother preserved his person and the Kingdom by divine will.

As we have said, the relations of the Bourbon kingdom with the other European states were very bad, particularly, since 1856 diplomatic relations with England had been interrupted; Emperor French Napoleon III had militarily engaged with Victor Emmanuel II in the Second Italian War of Independence against the Habsburgs.

His father Ferdinand II, on his deathbed, addressing him and Maria Sophia, gave him only one piece of advice: - *Do not trust the Piedmontese relatives* - honestly he was not all wrong.

Francis concentrated on domestic politics to try to meet the needs of his people and improve their living conditions.

To this end, he granted more autonomy to the municipalities, halved taxes on the ground, reduced customs taxes and emptied prisons by granting amnities.

After the second war of Italian independence against the Austrian Empire, Vittorio Emanuele II gained Lombardy from the Austrians but had to cede to Napoleon III, as compensation, the counties of Nice and Savoy.

This gouverment act aroused the faith of Garibaldi, who was a native of Nice, who ideally approached the programs of Masonic, Republican and perhaps even anarchist: Giuseppe Mazzini.

Mazzini, in his comfortable residence on Laystall Street in London, plotted revolutionary acts against all the kingdoms of Europe: the Bourbon, the Habsburg, the Piedmontese, the French and the papal.

Without ever intervening personally; that is – Without *putting a finger in the hot water* - Mazzini concocted conspiracies, plots and terrorist acts of all kinds and against all the kingdoms of the European continent.

Mazzini's proselytes in Sicily; among them the politician Francesco Crispi, of Albanian origins, the patriot Rosolino Pilo; they invoked the help of Garibaldi to carry out an expedition to Sicily against the Bourbons.

Mazzini did not disregard the cry of pain, Garibaldi could not wait to unsheath his sword; it was only necessary to find a sponsor, that is, a valid financier.

The Savoy Prime Minister, Count of Cavour, did not have so many economic possibilities at his disposal, the finances of the Piedmontese State were under pressure from the Rothschild Bank.

The Royal English Navy, on behalf of Freemasonry, then thought of financing the Garibaldi expedition.

How did Garibaldi use the money he received from the British?

In this context we must admit that *Our Liberator* acted very diligently because, instead of paying compensation to those who followed him in the expedition; he invested the money buying the enemy: in the sense that he paid the Bourbon generals to beat the retreat in the battlefields, the troops of the enemy *Garibaldi* had become, in reality, for some boubon generals the friend *Garibaldi*.

In the light of these events, in the battle of Calatafimi, Gen. Landi withdrew 3,000 Bourbon soldiers against 1,000 Garibaldi soldiers and 500 Sicilian picciotti; in the Calabrian area of Soveria Mannelli 10,000 Bourbon soldiers surrendered without firing a shot in the air – *Perhaps they were afraid of injuring some traveling pigeon* – and finally; in the decisive battle of the Volturno another 10,000 Bourbon troops withdrew without engaging in fighting.

The Neapolitan Navy, does not take part in any of the fighting, surrendered peacefully to the Piedmontese one; far inferior in means and armaments; certainly blocked by the *British Royal Navy* which in fact reigned throughout the Mediterranean.

After all these disconcerting victories, Garibaldi proclaimed himself *Dictator of the Two Sicilies;* Victor Emmanuel II, in turn, seized the opportunity of the moment and with his armed troops, headed for the South; the meeting of Teano with the Garibaldi troops was immediately sanctioned with the historic phrase of Garibaldi to the Piedmontese king: *I obey.*

VIVA L'ITALIA – Someone then said that italians had to be made too.

Francis II and Maria Sophia took refuge on the rock of Gaeta and never set foot again in Naples or Palermo; with the few troops remaining faithful, they resisted for three months the attacks and cannonades of the Piedmontese troops of Gen. Cialdini or who for Him; in the end all that remained was to declare the surrender to the Piedmontese and go into exile at the papal court.

In that of Gaeta the last King and the last Queen of the Kingdom of the Two Sicilies; they showed courage and ardor in the now useless defense of the lost Kingdom; in particular Francis wanted to save his wife, but Sophia refused and remained in the stronghold to incite the soldiers and treat the wounded; one of the reasons for the surrender of Gaeta were also caused by the epidemic outbreak of typhus.

Defeated the Bourbons; all that remains is to incorporate, as promised, the Neapolitan officers in the Piedmontese troops or one could say now Italian; few adhere; a Bourbon officer invited to change uniform said: *In life you swear only once and I have sworn allegiance to the Bourbon.*

Francis II never abdicated his reign and when government officials asked him to sign the act of abdication so that the real estate of Naples, which had previously been confiscated, was returned to him, Francis replied to them: *I am sorry, but my honor is not for sale.*

Before dying, Francis II addressed his former subjects:

I am Neapolitan, born among you.
Your customs are my customs;
your language is my language;
your ambitions are my ambitions.

I am a Prince of Yours who sacrificed all his desire
to preserve peace, concord,
prosperity among his subjects.

*   *   *

In 2011 they celebrated the 150th anniversary of the Unification of Italy and on the internet a user asked a question: *What can we prepare in the kitchen to celebrate this important event?*
What would be the dish or course that unites us: Brothers of Italy?

The request of this user was not satisfied because, We Italians united, we do not have a dish that unites us; we are as different in the kitchen as we are in customs, traditions, language and perhaps even in aspects of life.

*   *   *

To the liberator and conqueror Garibaldi we have named the squares, avenues and city streets, monuments, statues, villas, palaces; but there would be no gastronomic recognition of him, from us; for example: a soup, a pizza, an ice cream or an omelette, dedicated to the *Hero of the Two Worlds*.

To fill the gaps of this serious lack of ours, the British thought about it: what would we have been if we had missed the British?

The recipe that we will read will be in English, so we will learn when fate gives us a new liberator, to dedicate at least one currant cookie to it.

These biscuits were invented in 1866 by a Pastry Chef from Newcastle: *Johnathan Carr; nowadays* they are packaged by the American Multinational Company: *Kellogs Corporation.*

For the record Garibaldi visited the English town of Newcastle Upon Tyne, in 1859; the reason for this visit has not been revealed, perhaps Garibaldi just wanted to take an ecological walk to visit the walls of *the Vallum Hadriani* built by the Roman Emperor in the year 122 d.C.

DELIA SMITH: GARIBALDI BISCUITS

Ingredients:

110g self-rising flour – pinch of salt – 25g spreadable butter – 25g golden caster sugar – 2 tbsp milk – 50g currants – a little, light beaten, egg white – a little granulated sugar.

Method:

Put the flour, salt and butter into a mixing bowl and rub to the fine crumb stage.

- Then add the sugar and after that enough milk to mix to a firm dough that will leave the bowl clean.
- After that transfer it to a lightly floured surface and roll it out to a rectangle 20cm by 30 cm.

- Now sprinkle the currants over half tthe surface and then fold the other half on top and roll everything again so you end up with a rectangle 20cm by 30cm.
- Then trim it neatly using a sharp long-bladed knife, so you end up with a shape about 18cm by 28cm.
- Cut this into 24 fingers approximately 3cm by7cm.
- Now place the biscuits on the baking sheet, brush with a little egg white and sprinkle with granulated sugar.
- Bake near the centre of the oven for 12-15 minutes at 200C, then cool on a wire tray and store in an air light tin.

The author of this recipe is the English gastronomer Mrs. Delia Smith who has published several cooking essays; in particular, the cookbook: *How to Cook or About Cooking,* published in 1999, reached 11 million copies.

So I chose Mrs. Delia as a leading Goddess so that this research of mine can receive, I do not say 11 million copies but at least 11 readers if then, these readers, become a dozen: <u>I have achieved my goal.</u>

* * *

A common economic good could be wheat whose grains, once cooked, are used for confectionery compositions such as *the Neapolitan Pastiera and the Sicilian Cuccia.*

The custom of consuming boiled wheat is linked, according to tradition, to the memory of a miracle performed by Saint Lucia, which is celebrated on December 13 and is the protector of sight and eyes. To the prayers of the faithful: *Saint Lucia pani vurrja, pani nu nn'haiu;*in the year of grace 1646 in the sky of Palermo, the Saint made a dove appear announcing to the people of Palermo the arrival of a ship loaded with wheat, which was enough to feed the entire city.

Saint Lucia is also the Patron Saint of Syracuse and the citizens of Syracuse claim to the people of Palermo the primacy of the invention of the *Cuccia;*placing the episode of the wheat famine in the year 1763.

Boiled wheat can certainly be considered a primitive food of the ancient Greeks, which was also used for propitiatory purposes, to ensure prosperity and fertility.

KENNEL or CUCCIA OF SAINT LUCIA

First you need to make the wheat grains edible.
Soak 500 grams of wheat for three days, changing the water every day.
Drain the wheat and put it in a pan, cover it with water and a pinch of salt; cook for up to eight hours over very low heat and let it rest in the same cooking water for up to 12 hours.

Ingredients

500 grams of edible wheat, 1.5 kg of fresh sheep's milk ricotta, 450 grams of granulated sugar, 300 grams of candied pumpkin, 150 grams of dark chocolate chips, chopped pistachio and cinnamon powder.

Procedure

Prepare the cream: knead the ricotta, previously sifted, with sugar; add the candied pumpkin cut into small pieces and the dark chocolate chips.
Drain the wheat well and incorporate it into the cream, stirring the mixture.
Serve the Cuccia in a bowl or glass glasses, sprinkling the surfaces with chopped pistachios or ground cinnamon.

*   *   *

There would also be the Neapolitan Easter dessert, called *PASTIERA,* in which wheat grains made edible are used.

It seems that Queen Maria Theresa never smiled, she was a statutory example of feminine seriousness. Once Ferdinand II invited her to eat a slice of pastiera; after tasting the dessert, the Queen expressed herself with a captivating smile of thanks to her husband; the rather smug King said that, in order to receive the next benign smile from his wife; we had to wait until next Easter, when she would eat another slice of the same dessert.

NEAPOLITAN PASTIERA

It is in fact a sweet tart inevitable in the Neapolitan Easter canteens.
The pastry used as the basis of the tart is the shortcrust pastry and as far as edible wheat is concerned, you can use packages already industrially prepared; failing this you can proceed to make the wheat edible, using the same techniques as the Sicilian kennel.

Ingredients

400 grams of shortcrust pastry, 250 grams of fresh sheep's milk ricotta, 250 grams of granulated sugar, 250 grams of pre-cooked wheat per pastiere, 50 grams of candied orange peel,
Three eggs, bag of vanillin, milk q.b., aromatic drops of orange.

Procedure

Place the shortcrust pastry on a baking sheet previously greased and floured; make it adhere well in the corners.
Mix together the ricotta with 150 gr. sugar, the day before composing the cake tatter, and flavor the mixture with aromatic drops of orange or other aromatic syrups.

Whip the red of the eggs with the remaining sugar, insert the sachet of vanillin and the candied orange peel; add the pre-cooked wheat to the mixture and incorporate the previously processed ricotta.
Check the dough that must be amalgamated neither too liquid nor solid, pour milk if it is solid.

Spread the cream obtained inside the coated baking sheet and with segments of puff pastry scenically arrange seven strips in the surfaces, crossing them with the other.

Bake in a preheated oven 180 degrees for 30 minutes.
Remove the pastiera from the pan when it has completely cooled.

The pastiera could be sprinkled with icing sugar at the time of serving at the table.

Certainly the Neapolitan Ladies could offer, regarding the Pastiera, further advice and more voluptuous tricks from those indicated by me in this composition.

*   *   *

We have indicated the nicknames of Ferdinand II: *King Bomba* was given to him by the Sicilians because of the bombing of *Gen. Filingieri* perpetrated in the city of the Strait in 1849; his first wife Cristina of Savoy, following a joke by the King to move the chair where he was sitting, told him verbatim: *I thought I had married the King of Naples and instead I married a lazarone;*finally it was given as a nickname, by the people: *King Lasagna;*by Via that Ferdinand was of corpulent ton.

There are two methods to compose lasagna sheets: one farmer and one Franciscan.
The peasant one is a simple union between flour, salt and hot water.
The Franciscan method: 600 grams double zero flour, 6 eggs, a glass of water, a pinch of salt.

As soon as we talk about lasagna comes to mind the seasoning of the sauce: *The Neapolitan Ragù* turns out to be richer than the Bolognese one as others to the stew of pork and beef, meatballs, boiled eggs, savory slices of provola and pieces of Naples salami are added which contains more fat than the Milanese one.

We will try to compose a lasagna with peasant dough using a corpulent Black Cabbage, sausages and ricotta. This composition will be well approached to a nineteenth-century home cooking in a canteen of the Kingdom of the Two Sicilies.

LASAGNA OF THE TWO SICILIES

Dough: 250 grams of durum wheat flour – Re-milled Semolina -100 grams of hot water.

Make the fountain with flour and pour boiling water, little by little, knead with a fork. When all the water is absorbed and as soon as the mixture becomes easy to handle, knead everything vigorously.
Let the dough rest for 20 minutes properly covered.
Roll out the dough with *lasagnaturi* or rolling pin and form a sheet as wide as possible and as thick as a couple of millimeters.
Let it dry, if necessary, and then cut it, with a cogwheel, into strips two centimeters wide or three centimeters for a baked lasagna.

Ingredients: Black cabbage of about a kilo, pork sausages, two each, fresh ricotta, butter or lard, olive oil, salt, red pepper flakes, white wine.

Procedure

Decorticate the stalks of the cabbage and boil the leaves in boiling salted water for 10 minutes after the resumption of boiling. Collect the boiled leaves and arrange them in a colander, with a scissors cut said leaves into four or five parts.
Boil the sheets of lasagna in the same water where the cabbage was boiled which should be a beautiful green color.

In a pan arrange the pork sausages and with butter or lard fry them with whole garlic undressed over low heat. When it is believed that the sausages are well advanced; raise the heat and deglaze with white wine. Once the wine has evaporated, add the cut cabbage leaves with a ladle of cooking water, continue cooking for another five minutes.

During these five minutes, recover the sausages and crumble them quickly, put the sausage and lasagna back into the pan; use chili pepper and a round of olive oil.

Arrange the contents of the pan in the serving dishes and season each dish with a generous tablespoon of ricotta *scaniata* with melted butter and white pepper.

To be honest, this lasagna is my culinary idea: we hope it works.

* * *

There would be some Catania biscuits called: *THE COPPER OF NAPLES;* designed precisely by Sicilian pastry chefs on the occasion of the establishment of the Kingdom of the Two Sicilies.

We see that then not all the Sicilians rebelled against the union of the kingdoms; at least the pastry chefs tried to get economic benefits.

For the record: the copper coins in circulation in the kingdom were called: *Tornesi;* in fact, there were coins of the denomination of 2 – 5 – 10 tornesi; then there were the *Tarì or Carlini* coins that were minted in silver; last gold coins, called: *Ducati.*

Ingredients

Double zero flour 250 grams, 110 grams of sugar, 75 grams of butter, 160 ml of milk,
50 grams of bitter cocoa, 5 grams of ammonia for desserts, 1 tablespoon of honey, a teaspoon of cloves powder, a teaspoon of ground cinnamon grated orange peel.

For Gaskets

100 grams of orange jam, 150 grams of dark chocolate, 25 grams of butter,
chopped pistachio from Bronte.

Procedure

Combine flour, sugar and bitter cocoa; mix the ingredients and add: honey, butter in chunks, orange peel, clove powders and cinnamon powders; ammonia for sweets.

Pour the milk and compose a dough which must be soft and a little sticky.

Now compose the balls as big as a walnut and arrange them, well apart, on a baking sheet equipped with baking paper.

Bake the biscuits in a preheated oven for about twenty minutes.

Remove from the oven the biscuits and let them cool.

Form the glaze; melting, in a water bath or in the micro-waves, 150 grams of dark chocolate with butter; make them well join or mix.

Brush the surfaces of the baked biscuits with orange jam.

Glaze the *Copper of Naples* by immersing the top of the biscuits directly in the melted chocolate.

All that remains is to sprinkle the surfaces with the chopped pistachio of Bronte and let the applied glazes dry well.

L' INFAUSTO INIZIO UNITARIO

Pur troppo s'è fatta l'Italia,
ma non si fanno gli Italiani.
Massimo Taporelli, Marchese D'Azeglio
1798-1866

After the annexation to the Kingdom of Italy; the Sicilians were worse off, the Savoy Prime Minister Camillo Benso di Cavour did not grant any form of self-government; imposed new and heavier taxes and compulsory conscription was established, which could last, for young conscripts, up to eight years of active or reserve service.

The new Piedmontese government officials were completely insensitive to Sicily; of which they ignored the customs and traditions not to mention the idiomatic expressions of the Sicilian people, which they did not understand.

To better facilitate the Garibaldi expedition, the republican Francesco Crispi, realised and made publically some proclamations to the sicilian people with the purpose to agitate the peasants against the Bourbon istitutions.
Crispi's proclamations, clandestine and devious, were also misinterpreted by the people and the uprising were extended even against honest state officials and the local bourgeoisie; cause of which many people were innocently slaughtered .

Garibaldi, in turn, with his decrees addressed to the Sicilian people, gave the possibility of giving birth to a new society, free from miseries and injustices and gave a glimpse of the long-awaited division of land to the peasants.

These hasty and untruthful statements ignited the souls of peasants, artisans and the minute people, causing a bloody revolt in the countryside, giving rise to fires of houses and personal vendettas.

*   *   *

One of these events took place on the slopes of Etna and precisely in the municipality of Bronte, where in 1799 the Feud or Ducea Nelson was established as a personal gift from Ferdinand Bourbon to the family of the English admiral; for the services rendered by the same to the Bourbon kingdom during the Napoleonic wars.

The peasant revolution of Bronte and the neighboring Etna tawns caused several mortalities among guards, civilian population and bourgeoisie.

The English owners of the afore mentioned Ducea Nelson then turned to Garibaldi to try to quell these peasant revolts against their properties.

The liberator could not escape these requests also because the British were the financiers of his expedition; immediately instructions will be given to Gen. Nino Bixio to go to Bronte to do justice.

From the descriptions of the events narrated by Prof. Benedetto Radice, in his writing: *Memorie Storiche di Bronte;* who at the time of the riot was only six years old, when He and his family miraculously escaped the massacre of that horrendous night.

From the deposition of the facts it can be well understood how adverse were the souls of the parties in question: the peasant class towards those who were called: *Cappelli or Harts* .

Allow me to expose the events as reported by Radice.:

The plebs of Bronte, however, did not see only in Garibaldi the liberator of the Bourbon tyranny; but the liberation of the harsh tyranny, called: **Misery.**
It was also in the consciousness of the people that the revolution would seize, for the benefit of the community, the goods of Nelson's Ducea.
What could not be achieved in ordinary times or by law; it is customary to try to achieve by violence in revolutions.
What was not possible in '48 is tried again in '60.
Some agitators had returned to Bronte, from prisons rather criminals, known for killings and thefts.
They went through the streets with caps and tricolor bows, proud of the recovered freedom; stirring up, for the countryside and for the houses, the people to the riot, demanding the lack of division of the lands, misunderstanding and interpreting, according to their evil soul, the words of the dictator against the Bourbons: that it was a duty to hunt down the realists to make themselves meritorious to the Fatherland.
A citizen considered crazy, Nunzio Ciraldo Frajunco, surrounded by the head of tricolor pieces, was announcing through the city streets: Cappelli, look at you, the hour of judgment is approaching. People Do not Miss the Appeal.
So that trouble they gave themselves with wild joy to put to fire houses of the believed Bourbons, assaulting and looting; between the ringing sound of trumpets and drums; to the cry: **Viva Garibaldi, Viva l'Italia.**
The most angry invaded by the demon of destruction and the greed of the booty, ramshackle the windows, began to throw out mattresses. chairs, coffee tables, cabinets; and set them on fire.
It is a macabre dance, made more grim by the sinister flashes of the fires: a spectacle worthy of the soul of Nero or the brush of the Goya.

Tired they break into the cellar, opened by the owners to avoid the sack of their homes; they eat, drink, refresh the burnt throats and drunk with wine and fury, at the command of improvised generals, like torrents of lava from the torn sides of a volcano; they run here and there towards new looting and new fires. The theater, the archive of the Municipality, the casino of civilians were burned.

On the dawn, at the sight of the burning village, pitiful crowds of women, praying in the streets, run to the Church of the Annunciation and with a loud voice and tears, prostrate knees, asked the Virgin to calm the wrath of the furious.

Following the chronicles of several massacres perpetrated on that night of horror and the pleas of the unfortunate who were captured and subjected to the most unfair tortures; whose corpses were then burned in the embers lit by the fires.

The Governor of Catania, on the lively requests of those who had managed to escape from Bronte and at the request of the English Consulate; sent to Bronte a garrison of eighty soldiers, to restore the disturbed order.

These troops, under the orders of *Col. Poulet,* headed towards Bronte, in whose vicinity they came into contact with a religious procession of people and clergy praising white flags; who begged the commander not to open fire towards the village but to enter it peacefully.

Those who had fomented and carried out the riots of Bronte and the peasants who had participated in it; once the fumes of wine and fury have been simmered and the spirits have cooled; also thinking of their own danger and already seeing in front of the penalty that awaited them; they esteemed well to be safe, giving themselves to the countryside or finding refuge in the slopes of Etna.

The fire of sedition was already beginning to extinguish by itself, as naturally that of a volcano is extinguishing, after its period of destructive activity.

Other peasant riots had occurred in the slopes of Etna; Gen. Bixio was in Giardini-Naxos when he received the order of Garibaldi to move his troops to Bronte, Randazzo, Linguaglossa, Paternò and other districts.

After forced march Bixio and his troops arrived at Bronte on the sixth of August.

Having Bixio gathered the delegates of the Town Hall, he ordered them with threats to confess the names of the main culprits of the riot; later he gave orders to Col. Poulet to occupy all outlets of the country and to arrest the main culprits; about a hundred brontesi.

The lawyer Nicolò Lombardo, who represented the rights of the peasants in the possible division of the state lands and the Ducea of Nelson, was approached by some friends and personally by Col. Poulet; informing him that his name had been spoken as the leader of the riot and they warned him to get to safety.

The lawyer Lombardo, however, trusting in his feelings, in the awareness of not having advised evil; having indeed worked to calm the spirits, for having helped Poulet to enter Bronte; he felt that he should not fear the wrat of Bixio; who, having presented himself spontaneously, burst forth: **Ah, You are the President of the Rogue.**

Lombardo was immediately arrested and imprisoned by Bixio.

Particolare del pannello dipinto da Onofrio e Minico Ducato di Bagheria (1955)

Subsequently, the Bixio invented a decree in which he ordered a curfew on Bronte, the delivery by the population of all firearms and cutting weapons; dissolved the Municipality and the municipal authorities; imposed on the citizen a heavy war tax, ordered the state of siege and appointed himself the absolute arbiter and highest authority of Bronte; in the name of the dictator: Garibaldi .

This war tax had to be paid by the citizens of Bronte and daily people knocked on the houses to collect the money to be paid into the coffers of the Bixio; even the families who had had the house looted, the furniture burned, the husband killed; they had to pay the taxes imposed by the patriot Bixio.

On the morning of August 7, the Mixed War Commission arrived in Bronte to instruct the trial of the accused of the riot; composed of: the President, three judges on the sidelines, a tax lawyer, a secretary and a registrar. The stormy agitation in the days of terror had been followed by a frightening calm, a harbinger of disaster. Mutual suspicions agitated the souls of relatives, friends and even more of enemies, offering themselves, for private hates, the easy opportunity to accuse.
Many were charged with a crime; just for having been there .
The War Commission met on August 9, at 12 o'clock, when the accused were notified to present their exoneration within the unadromatic one-hour deadline.

Lombardo protested his innocence, he accused the accusers as liars; he said that he had worked to the triumph of the revolution and to quell the turmoil; who had promptly informed the competent authorities of public order in Bronte and invoked the sending of troops by the Governor of Catania and he pointed to witnesses in his defense.

None of the witnesses indicated by Lombardo were summoned by the Court.

At 8 pm of the same day, the War Commission represented the sentence that condemned five of the guilty people to be excecuted: Nicolò Lombardo, Ciraldo-Frajunco, Spitalieri, Samperi, Longhitano.

By a strange combination, apart from Lombardo, all the other condemned were by their own name: *Nunzio.*

The other accused were sent to Messina, for a further trial.

The relatives of the Lombardo, presented themselves to Bixio to implore to be able to give the last hug to the relative condemned to death; He proudly rejected them; furthermore a boy, in charge of bringing boiled eggs to the condemned, was sent back by Bixio with harsh words: **They do not need eggs, tomorrow they will have two balls on their heads.**

The historian Radice gives us some details of the shootings.

On the morning of August 10, at eight o'clock, the condemned were sent to torture; arrived at the Piazza di S. Vito; they were seated in a row.

Lombardo said to a woman who was crying and shouting her name: **I am innocent like Christ.**

Read by an officer the sentence was ordered fire: all five fell against each other.

A condemned man, holding in his hand the image of the Virgin, like a talisman on his chest, kneeling turned to Bixio: **Our Lady gave me grace, now you do it to me.**

He was the crazy man: the soldiers had not had the courage to hit a crippled person, whose fault had been to make only noise, beating a tin drum.

Grace was not granted: A Garibaldian officer, on the beckon of Bixio, chilled him with a blow to the back of the head.

Carmine Radice, before concluding the chronicle of these events, comes to a consideration towards the Gen.Bixio: *The Garibaldian revolution was propitious to him to save him perhaps from an ignoble life, and made him a bronze type hero; the Ajax of our age.*

Questioned, years later, about the facts or misdeeds of Bronte, Bixio, who had become a Parliamentarian, to his exoneration, said: *I could not do anything for those poor wretches received a regular trial.*

The fact that He calls the *condemned 'Poor Wretches'* means that He knew that those people were innocents.

How can the patriot Bixio, now parlamentarian can define a trial in which a popular jury has not been constituted, in which a panel has not been appointed to defend the accused, in which eyewitnesses of the facts have not been heard by the Court; inspite themselves had requested to the Court to be heard.

The sentence was issued in the name of Victor Emmanuel II King of Italy; if the facts were prior to the unification of the Kingdom of Italy; the legitimate King would have been Francis II of Bourbon.

If, even before the sentence had been issued, the Bixio had already informed the liberator Garibaldi of the death sentence of the defendants.
Basically Gen. Bixio, was in a hurry, could not stay in Bronte and do justice or flush out, in the slopes and countryside of Etna, to find the real culprits of the riot.

Garibaldi was in Milazzo and was about to cross the Strait and He had to be at his side to earn a place in history; so that the destinies of the Fatherland would be fulfilled, which were those of overthrowing with weapons, deceptions and money received from the British; a legitimate King and attribute the Kingdom of the Two Sicilies to the Savoy usurper.

*　*　*

On March 17, 1861, following Garibaldi's victory and the fall of the Bourbon kingdom, *Vittorio Emanuele II of Savoy-Carignano* passes of role; from: *King of Sardinia to King of Italy.*

However, in order to obtain a *National Unification,*according to the geographical configuration of our Peninsula, the following parts were missing: *The Venetian Region. The Trentino Region, the Papalino Kingdom with the coveted Roman City.*

From Livy – Urbe Condita: Abi nuntia Romanis, caelestes ita velle ut mea Roma caput orbis terrarum sit. Go and announce to the Romans the will of the Heavenly Gods is that my Rome becomes the Capital of the World.

*　*　*

In early 1866 Prussia left the German Confederation and declared itself an independent state ruled by Chancellor *Otto Von Bismark;* subsequently a treaty of alliance was signed in Berlin between the new Prussian State and the new Kingdom of Italy; with the good wishes of french Emperor Napoleon III's .

In that treaty it was agreed that: if Prussia had attacked Austria, so would Italy, in order to obtain, from the latter, the regions of Veneto and Trentino.

The Austrian Empire, having become aware of the aforementioned Italo-Prussian agreement and the support conferred on it by France; proposed to Italy the peaceful concession of Veneto behind a substantial outlay of money; if Italy had withdrawn from the alliance with Prussia.
In June of the same year Prussia invaded Saxony: war had broken out within the German Confederation; Italy entered the war on the side of Prussia.

Thus began the first military commitment of the Kingdom of Italy which, in the history of the Italian Risorgimento, is recognized, as: *Third War of Independence.*

The command of the armed forces normally belongs to the Savoy Sovereign and the army was divided into two army corps: One under the command of *Gen. Alfonso Lamarmora* who holds the positions of Prime Minister and Chief of Staff; the other to *Gen. Enrico Cialdini* appointed Duke of Gaeta; title obtained for having conquered the Bourbon stronghold.

Cialdini, as a historical figure of Risorgimento hero, has recently been the subject of revision for massacres perpetrated against helpless citizens, in the province of Benevento, in the City of Palermo and almost everywhere in the regions of the former Bourbon Kingdom.

The statues and city streets named or raised in memory of this person, have been removed in several cities of Italy; and some Italian parliamentarians such as *Giuliano Amato and Graziano Delrio,* on behalf of the Italian Government, have felt the duty to publicly present the government apologies to the Municipal Administrations of those places that have been theaters of useless shootings and reprisals of Savoy troops against the population.

The strength or ability of a Superior Officer, who is at the head of armed troops, should not be assessed on the basis of the degree of ferocity against peasants, armed with pitchforks and unjustly stirred up; but they should be evaluated in a field of glory when facing the armed enemy, and the tactics put in place should be aimed not only at defeating the enemy; also to preserve human lives on which its conduct depends.

These considerations were not put into action in the battle of Custoza by the two commanders as Cialdini refused to take orders from Lamarmora and, during the war, he would have acted on his own.

The mood of the two commanders should have been taken into account by the King; who should have acted in order of putting some peace among his generals: Lamarmora and Cialdini to overcome personal envy of degrees; at least when you are in a state of war and in front of the enemy; during military actions.

The Italian forces fielded consisted of 20 divisions with a total of 260 thousand men.
Lamarmora's troops settled on the western banks of the Mincio River; those of Cialdini settled on the banks of the river Po'.
On the other hand, the Austrian troops under the command of *Duke Alberto Teschen,* brother of the former Queen Maria Theresa, second wife of Ferdinand II of Bourbon Two Sicilies; they were strong of 190 thousand men; of which 75 thousand were fielded in the battle of Custoza.

The fate and events of this battle were also followed by British and French foreign officers and the international press of the time gave extensive communication of the military and political events of that time.

On June 23, Lamarmora began hostilities by crossing the Mincio to attack the enemy behind the Adige; in reality the Austrians were not behind the Adige; but on Lake Garda: *He should have also be aware, before the attack, where the enemy was.*

As soon as the Lamarmora troops moved from the Mincio, they were attacked by austrian forces from Verona; the battle of Custoza took place mainly between Mantua and Peschiera del Garda.

During the course of military operations it turned out that General Lamarmora was not aware about the enemy's deployments, he began to lose his head as he could not realize the enemy forces in the field and the plans of attack; urgent dispatches followed to Gen. Cialdini to support his troops; but Cialdini did not take orders from Lamarmora; he would have moved his troops from the Po, when and if he feels like.

Despite the numerical superiority of the Italian army and the value of the soldiers and officers for having conquered important bridgeheads, the troops received withdrawal instructions which were followed by the order of *prompt retreat;* the Italian troops went back and the defeat turned, as usually happens in these cases, *into a route;*allowing the Austrians to take the city of Custoza and block the Italian attack in the Veneto.

For the record, Gen. Cialdini decided to cross the river Po six days after the defeat of the Lamarmora at Custoza.
The two Savoy Princes also participated in the battle of Custoza: Umberto and Amedeo, the first will become the future King of Italy and Amedeo, who was wounded in the clash, will become, even if for a short time, King of Spain.

The Italian attack on the Austrian Veneto ended with the defeat of Custoza; on the other side, that is, from the Prussian one, came news of the victory in the Battle of Sodowa, in the Bohemian Region of Czechoslovakia.

Austria still renews the peaceful proposal to grant independence to Prussia and Veneto to Italy.

Chancellor Bismark, who, as a statesman, was not a fool but was the Father of German unification, adheres to peace; also because he came to fear that the Austrian troops of Duke Albert could be used against them.

The King of Italy wanted to show that he knew how to win and the exponents of a War Council met in Ferrara, in whose conference were present: King Vittorio Emanuele II, Gen. Lamarmora, Gen. Cialdini, and the ministers: Visconti Venosta and Pettinengo.

At this conference it was decided to continue the war against Austria:

- Gen. Cialdini were entrusted with 14 divisions that were to proceed towards the Isonzo river and, subsequently, towards Vienna and conquer it.

- Gen. Lamarmora would maintain the block of the Quadrilateral.
- Admiral *Persano* or Carlo *De Persano* would attack the Austrian fleet, in the next eight days, with the order to destroy it.
- Garibaldi, with his troops *I Cacciatori delle Alpi,* would conquer Trentino and head towards Croatia and Hungary.

As a friend of mine used to *say: To Speak in the square we are all good.*

If Cialdini had been *Napoleon I;* Lamarmora, *Julius Caesar;* if Persano, *Oratio Nelson;* and Garibaldi had been, nothing less than: *Alexander the Great or Genghis Khan;* perhaps – *I said: Perhaps* – such a plan could have been put into action.

On June 20, Admiral Persano had received an order from the Minister of the Navy to transfer the Italian fleet from Taranto to Ancona, in the Adriatic Sea; meanwhile the Austrian Fleet was stationed in the port of Pula in Dalmatia.

On July 14, Admiral Persano received the peremptory order to act without delay, otherwise he would have been, ipso facto, dismissed from naval posts.

The Italian Navy then decided to shell the fortified island of Lissa; this operation would have forced the Austrian fleet to expose itself in battle on the open sea.

The bombing of Lissa begins unsuccessfully; but, the next day, shows up at sea, unexpectedly for the Persano, the Austrian fleet, under the command of *Gen. Tegetthoff,*which penetrated into the Italian lines; ramming and sinking the battleship *Re d'Italia,* was subsequently lowered to the bottom the battleship *Palestro* and an unknown number of warships that found themselves unmanned with cannons because the mouths of fire had been transferred to the sunken battleships.

The Austrian attack took place at 11 a.m. and at noon; Admiral Tegetthoff disengage from the fight and leads, somewhat satisfied, his fleet out of range.
Persano tries to chase him but the Austrian ships are faster as they are equipped with more efficient engines.

When Persano came ashore, he declared himself victorious because, according to him, he had put the enemy on the run; in reality it was the Italian fleet that had lost two battleships not the enemy.

The only consolation would have been Garibaldi's victory in Trentino, in the *Battle of Bezzeca.*
In fact, in this battle, it was a clash between the Trentinos who were in favor of becoming Italians and Trentinos who wanted to remain Austrian; after several clashes in the heights of the place; the Trentino consorts of Austria withdrew because they had run out of ammunitions.

Once defeated by land and sea, it remained for the Sovereign Vittorio Emanuele to accept the non-vexatious proposals of Austria: The Venetian region and part of Trentino with Trieste, were ceded by Austria to the France of Napoleon the Third; who, within a short time, delivered them to Italy.

Garibaldi's troops were recalled from Trentino with the order to cease hostilities towards the Austrians; to the telegram of Gen. Lamarmora, that imparted the order; followed a second: *I obey;* by Garibaldi.

*   *   *

The conqueror Garibaldi, after the unification, had a problem: how to get rid of those forty thousandsSicilians who had followed him with weapons and with their lives, in his victorious expedition against the Bourbons.

Confessing to a friend of hers, Garibaldi had the opportunity to write: *If I were to return to Sicily, they would stone me.*

All the promises of freedom, well-being, assignments of cultivated and uncultivated lands; remained *Only Words.* The hopes of a population, dedicated to simple agriculture, were faintly extinguished; whose young sons were removed, from their arms and their lands, to be coecatively framed in the Piedmontese army to perform a long military service.

Garibaldi entrusted, to his Sicilian-Albanian friend Francesco Crispi, who by now from Mazzinian, revolutionary and republican had turned into a parliamentary monarchist, minister and prime minister of the Kingdom, and then also became a colonizer of Libya - *what would not be done for his career* - the unfortunate task of getting rid of all these people or mobs, who were on his stomach or from his stomach down.

Crispi entered a proclamation in which he did not spare the praise of the Sicilian people for having sacrificed themself to the Garibaldian cause and having been associated with the fate of the new homeland that welcomed the Sicilian children with open arms; then he completed the proclamation, with the textual words: *Now that all is finished, return to your huts.*

In this last line of the government proclamation, the harsh reality of the new Sicilian political situation transpired; He could have said to the people: Go back to *your homes,* or to your *families* or go *back to your work commitments.*
He said, *Go back to your huts;* that is: Go back to your *miserable huts* because there is nothing to share or to divide: *The Party is over and our friends leave.*

I don't know if you've ever read the book: *The Cabin of Uncle Tom;* in this novel we talk about the miseries, labors and harassment to which negro slaves were subjected on cotton plantations in American segregationist states.

This would have been the moral of Garibaldi's fable; transform Sicily as the State of Mississippi of the 1800s; in which the peasant and non-peasant population would have been composed of many slaves, such as Uncle Tom.

*   *   *

Incipit of the novel: *Biography of the Changed Son*, written by Andrea Camilleri; on the life of one of his distant and fellow countrymen; the writer, poet and playwright from Agrigento; *Luigi Pirandello*, Nobel Prize for Literature in 1936:

A tinted morning of September 1866, the nobles, the wealthy, the borgisi, the wholesale and retail traders, the lords of both coppola and hat, the garrisons and their commanders, the office employees, non-commissioned officers and government officials; that after the unit had invaded Sicily like grasshoppers, were suddenly and badly waked by a frightening of voices, shots, noises of wagons, nitrites of horses, running steps, cries for help.
Three or four thousand peasants of the countryside near Palermo, armed and commanded for the most part by former foremen of the Garibaldian enterprise, were assaulting the city.
Palermo capitulated, almost without resistance; to the peasants had been added the populace, unleashing a revolt that at first seemed even indomitable.

From these descriptions it is well understood that in Palermo and in the interland; a riot had broken out that will pass under the name of a card game: *The Seven and a Half*; as it lasted seven days and a few hours.

Certainly the History of the Risorgimento of Italy, like the events of Bronte, will not mention these events.

Against the new political regime that in Sicily had proved to be centralizing and despotic; they moved:

- Former and disatisfied follower of Garibaldi,
- expropriated ecclesiastics,
- republicans,
- socialists, independentists,
- peasants and artisans.

It was therefore not a political uprising but a revolution of the proletarian people, of the city people, of the Sicilian nobility and of the clergy.
To the latter were expropriated lands and monasteries and also the Patron Saints.

Sicily and the South of Italy have always been a God-fearing people, devoted to religious traditions and to the Catholic and apostolic faith; in the city of Palermo will be prohibited, by the rulers and municipal officials, the religious celebrations that the citizens of Palermo pay in honor of the *Patron Saint Rosalia,* which fall on September 4 of each year of grace.

This explains that, all that was unacceptable for the Sicilians, were the impositions of these northern foreigners, against a Sicilian culture of their own, against their own faith and the faith of our ancestors; they considered the South Italians as a subject population not yet reached their degree of civilization; that is, we were, in the eyes of these hard-working officials: *barbarians* .

Well to us Sicilians you can appeal as you like: *Villans, zappaterra, terroni, mafiosi, bastards* - because, thirteen dominations, will have produced legitimate and illegitimate descendants - you can also call us *Sons of Bitch;* we will not be offended; we only want to bring to the knowledge of those who call us: **Barbarians;** that civilization has spread from the **Mediterranean** to the **Alps** and not vice versa.

In Sicily we have a proverb that has been interpreted and translated into almost all languages:

- *Cu cancia a veccia 'ca nova; sapi chiru cà perdi ma nun sapi chiru cà trova.*
- Who changes the old with the new; he knows what he loses but he doesn't know what he finds

With the proclamation of the Kingdom of Italy; it was realized that: the New was worse than the Old.

*   *   *

Let me report a summary of an analysis entitled **"Terroni"** composed by the Apulian journalist and writer: Pino *Aprile.*
The author, in his analysis, reports the massacres carried out, in the 1860s, by the Piedmontese generals, comparable to the Nazi genocides; such as the looting of southern cities, similar to that of the *Sack of Rome in 1527,* the establishment of *concentration camps, mass shootings in mass graves, imprisonment without charge, deportations and torture of all kinds;* towards not only those who were part of the *Brigandage;* even towards the defenseless population.
The analysis continues with the claims that the South was robbed of its belongings and all its wealth was transferred to the North; such as bank capital, works of art, public and private goods.

The results of the Savoy conquest, within a few years, reduced the South of Italy to a country of absolute poverty: The assets expropriated from the Bourbon House, which at present would amount to billions of euros, were invested in the North to cover the debt exposures of the House of Savoy towards the Jewish bank of the Rothschilds and to give impetus and favor the progress of industrial infrastructures in the Northern Regions.

Pino Aprile's considerations have not been shared by modern historians, who have asserted that these are anti-Risorgimento hoaxes; however, 160 years after these events concerning the annexation of the

South to the Italian North, there are conflicting opinions and our Risorgimento should be historically revised in the light of new documents.

∗   ∗   ∗

In the city of Palermo in September 1866, about 35 thousand insurgents gathered in the squares and city streets; red flags were hoisted and the principles of *Republic and Freedom* were praised by those presents.

Although there was no promoter who had put himself at the head of this uprising; a Revolutionary Committee composed of nobles and clergymen was established.

To be honest, a brigandage operation was recorded in the Municipality of Misilmeri, near Palermo, in which local peasants, led by criminals and bandits; massacred 16 carabinieri, despite the fact that they had surrendered.

The number of fallen by the government was 161 people; but no one was interested in calculating the number of dead killed among the insurgents; which were several thousand.

Palermo and Castemmare del Golfo were savagely borbanded by the Italian Navy for four days, without any restraint; subsequently came ashore, in the port of Palermo, gen. *Raffaele Cadorna,*a man of heavy hand, with a total of 40 thousand men including: Bersaglieri, grenadiers and infantrymen.

Armed forces from Naples and Florence carried out, in their advance towards the city, random killings and brutality of all kinds; who discredited the royal army; as it was necessary to take into account that: the insurgents were not only brigands or bandits, but citizens exasperated by the suppressions, by the arrests without just cause, by the unjustified assignment of the forced domicile, by heavy taxes imposed, by the long period of compulsory military service, by unemployment, by miseries, by the non-allocation of land, by political corruptions and by the suppression of religious corporations.

A first attempt for pacification was put in place by the Revolutionary Committee which, through the French Consul of Palermo, sent to the governors of the city, the intentions to end the uprising.
The authorities in charge, who had their backs covered by as many as 40 thousand soldiers, refused the compromises of the Sicilian Committee for reconciliation.

Once the occupation of the city by the troops of Cadorna took place, it was proclaimed by the latter: The state of siege, the prohibition to leave the city, the disarmament of rifles and cutting weapons; subsequently, three military war tribunals were established; which will issue, in record time, very heavy and severe sentences.

Mass arrests were carried out that will reach the number of 3,600 people, making it the prisons unusable, it is no coincidence that cholera broke out, which in the winter months, will reap, only in Palermo, eight thousand victims. Came to light, in the following years, based on the stories referred by some Savoy officers who participated in the suppression of the uprising; the implementation of various mass executions; the detainees were thrown into wells by the dozens to be better machine-gunned.

The insurrection is quelled with unprecedented force; the streets and squares of the beautiful Palermo, became deserted by fear, hunger, misery and cholera.

With the suppression of religious communities and charitable works, the distribution of aid to the population was also prohibited, relief for cholera patients and the donation of food to the hungry were denied.

1866 can historically be considered the darkest period that had ever existed for the capital of Sicily, which was the seat of the Sicilian Poetic School, the seat of the splendors of the Swabian dynasty and Arab culture.

Once the riot was quelled, the military actions did not cease; there was the hunt for the reluctant to the levy service; the gendarmes went to the homes of those who missed the recruitment appeals and if they did not find the person, they would arrest the parents or family members and if they did not find the family members they would arrest friends and neighbors; once a midwife was also arrested for having given birth to the reluctant.

Then a young man in his twenties was found on the streets, who was immediately arrested by the gendarmes as a reluctant and taken to the military barracks to be interrogated or rather to be tortured; the military doctor with a burning ember, produced in the body of the unfortunate man wide signs of burns; before he realized that the guy was a deaf-mute.

This doctor, whose name should not be mentioned, at the end of his mission, was conferred, for services rendered to the Crown, the Savoy honors of the Knightly Order of St. Lazarus: *Poor Lazarus, if he had been able to resurrect for the second time, he could have personally conferred on this luminary of science the due honors of stupidity.*

We can conclude the sad reportage with the verses of Vincenzo Di Giovanni from Palermo, who by profession was not a poet or writer, but a street food seller.

- *Lu vittimu ma lu persimu di vista*
- *Lu setti and mienzu, lasted veru picca.*

* * *

Certainly there were other opportunities for Gen. Raffaele Cadorna to lay bare the abilities of executioner of the Kingdom; when in 1869 he had full powers to repress the revolts that broke out throughout Italy following the introduction of a new tax on the wheat.

The Generals Cialdini, Bixio and Cadorna, were close friends among them, they knew well how to tame the peasant revolts; but in the battlefields against the Austrian enemy, they proved incapable of techniques, logistics and military strategies; they could have been at most: *Iron Sergeants.*

The Gentleman King was a true gentleman towards these executioners, all three were appointed Senators or Deputies of the Kingdom, sitting in the scanni of the Roman palaces, in the now liberated capital.

The more peasants, the more workers killed or shot, the more the possibility grew to become, in the new kingdom of Italy: a court dignitary or advisor to the King, senator of the Kingdom, Father of the Fatherland; on whose chests shone medals and cockades of all sorts.

*   *   *

Cadorna's son, Luigi, in the First World War was appointed Chief of Staff of the Army; for two years in which he held command, in time of war; he did nothing but launch bloody frontal attacks on the Isonzo River and the Carso mounts, against equipped Germanic defensive lines.

To the point that even the enemy had compassion on our infantry: *Enough, Italian Soldier, we do not kill like this* – it was shouted from the enemy trenches.

In our city of Ragusa there is a city street entitled: *Boys of '99; we refer to the fellow citizens who had the misfortune of having turned 16,* at the time of the First World War: they were sent, like beasts to the slaughter, on the heights of the Carso; without even a necessary basic training; to be killed in the charges ordered by Cadorna and if someone had second thoughts, there would have been the task of the Regi Carabinieri, to shot at their own camerades .

Gen. Luigi Cadorna was made aware, by the French and British Allied Military Ambassadors, that there would be, in October 1917, a massive enemy attack against Italy, by the German troops, now victorious in the russian front.

Cadorna and Badoglio his assistant, reassured the Allied envoys that their troops would resist any enemy attack.
Shortly thereafter followed the defeat of Caporetto, October 24, 1917 that is: the worst military defeat ever suffered by the Italian army and the consequent retreat of our army on the Piave.
The data of this defeat: 40 thousand dead, 300 thousand prisoners, 350 thousand soldiers in disarray.

Some innocent soldiers who, because of the enemy fire, swerved, no longer knowing where their units were or what would happen to their commanders; well, they were captured by the Regi Carabinieri, accused of desertion in front of the enemy, gathered together with other comrades, brought before a military court and with sentences quikly issued ; immediately were executed.

On October 28, with contempt, Cadorna issued the following proclamation:

The lack of resistance of the units of the Second Army – referred to Gen.Cappello – *cowardly retreated without a fight or ignominiously surrendered to the enemy, allowed the Austro-German forces to break our left wing.*

Cadorna's accusations against the commanders and men of the Second Army have historically been denied.

If we had been in a more conscious nation; it was not the soldiers who needed to be shot; but the generals.

The French and British allies regretted to the Italian King the Cadorna actions and asked for the removal; otherwise they would not have sent their troops in support of the Italian Army; from these events was finally dismissed the Cadorna and was appointed Chief of Staff Gen. *Armando Diaz*: The fate of the war had a decisive turn towards the coveted victory.

Then there was the Cadorna of the third generation who took the name of his grandfather: Gen. Raffaele Cadorna.

During the Fascist wars, he did not participate in the African War because he was against the African War, he did not participate in the invasion of Albania, because he was against the invasion of Albania, so he was against military operations in Greece, Yugoslavia and the Russian Campaign.

Practically if a General is against wars why be a soldier; he could have done a different job.

Hops – I almost forgot: the title of most renowned Senator of the Savoy Kingdom, belongs to General Bava-Beccaris; when *in 1898, elected Royal Extraordinary Commissioner,* he quelled the riots of the workers in Milan with cannon bullets; leaving on the pavements of the city eighty dead corpses and a few hundred people seriously injured becauase they had stolen some bread loaves from a nearby shop. Later he became personal advisor to Victor Emmanuel III; one of the most appropriate advice – *so to say* – was to entrust the Italian Government to Mr. Benito Mussolini following the Fascist March on Rome, in the year of grace 1922.

*　*　*

THE MILITARY RANCIO

The rancio would be a gathering of people, soldiers in particular, who consume the same food, at the same time and in the same place.

I don't know if you did the military service; my military service dates back to 1967 and when the rancio was consumed; if a superior officer asked: *How is the rancio?* The soldier's answer had to be: *Excellent and abundant for the troops.*

A negative response *to the excellent and abundant;* it would have involved a 10-day delivery of Simple Punishment Chamber or Penalty.

In the third century b.c. we know that the Roman soldiers were equipped with portable mills, of which it was fashionable to prepare a cake ante litteram; call: *Buccellatum;* which would be the promoter of the sweet *Buccellato, which we will see shortly.*
In addition, among the legionaries of the Roman Empire was widely used the *Buccellatum* as was eaten like popcorn; to be, in moments of rest or for dinners, ground and boiled with water or milk.

Julius Caesar, in *De Bello Gallico,*tells us that, among the equipment, the Roman soldiers were equipped with utensils for cooking food; the char was transported in special wagons; that they were often attacked by the Gauls: both to appropriate the foodstuffs and to leave the Romans without food; when the enemy is weak and undernourished, it would be easier to overwhelm him.

In the Middle Ages the barbarians, not the Sicilians but warrior peoples of Eastern Europe, supplied themselves with food and supplies, carrying out raids and looting of what the cities or the countryside offered by violence.

In the modern era, Napoleon used to say that the army marched more with the stomach than with the legs; for which he considered the provisions for the supplies of his troops to be of extreme importance.

Always according to Napoleon: If the soldiers had lacked food, they would have gone to rob the civilian population which was often followed, by the robbed, resentments and revenge; to which the army had to respond; starting a pernicious spiral of violence.
It must be admitted that the French Emperor, called by the Duke Wellington: *The Great Thief of Europe of all time;*in military matters he knew more than others: *Stealing is possible; but not to the poor.*

In the Piedmontese army, as the Kingdom of Savoy was indebted to the banks, the military rancio was distributed in the name of the economy: Black bread, rice, legumes and as regards beef, these were distributed once or most twice a week.
It should be noted that these were not tender meats, but animals used for field work, for milk or for reproduction; only when they reached late age were they slaughtered or decayed naturally
In the post-unification period, pasta and tomato sauce condiments were also introduced as meal for troops.

In the First World War meals for Italian soldiers were improved because the meat could be frozen or bagged and a considerable contribution was given following the preservation of canned meat.

Another breakthrough to provide foods for troops was the mobility of kitchens; field and personal containers such as gavettes.

The meals for the soldiers who fought in the Carso and in the Alpine heights, were transported on the back of mules, using insulated potholes weighing 55 kilos, which were able to preserve the heat of soups, broths or meat stews.

It must be admitted that for the bagged meats there were cases of *Botulinum;* it would be a toxin that develops if the meat is poorly packaged or in preserved foods when the contents deteriorate or if the glass containers are not sterilized.
Botulism is therefore a food poisoning caused by botulinum toxin; provoking gastro-intestinal disorders, nervous disorders and respiratory paralysis; complications that often lead to death.

In general, the military foods for the Italian soldiers and that of the French and English allies; they were far better, more abundant and healthier than those distributed among the soldiers of the Central Powers: to go hungry is to lose the war, which punctually happened, for Austria and Germany in 1918.

In Italy in 1943, during WWII, the alimentation of the Italian soldier was scarce, soldiers had arrived at the last hole in the belt, which was called: *Buco Mussolini.*

In Second World War the rancio consisted of a cup of black coffee with rusks, a gavetta of pasta or rice in broth, with a piece of boiled meat weighing about 300 grams; the weight of the beef was inclusive of the bone.
If the rancio did not arrive, the soldiers could rely on emergency rations: Corn cakes and canned meat.

For the Italian population, during the Fascist war, the general diet was truly in a disarming state; with the municipal card annonaria you could have:

- *200 grams of black bread, composed with floured legumes*
- *One candle a month*
- *Two deciliters of oil per quarter*
- *Little black pasta* – Black does not mean cuttlefish ink.

Living in these terms would have been impossible, and to think that the Duce wanted to win the war.

The only way to survive, at that time, was to resort to the *Black Exchange;*some families in order to survive were forced to foreclose or sell gold, furniture and the most disparate things; sometimes even houses and farms.

The richest and most appropriate rancio was the *Kappa Ration,*used by American soldiers in the wars of liberation of continental Europe occupied by Germanic troops.

The inventor of these rations was the American nutritionist *Angel Keys,* whose -K- was taken as the initial of these rations.

And it consisted of the following products:

- *Wheat cakes*
- *Dried pork or veal*
- *Chocolate bars*
- *Dried fruit*
- *Freeze-dried lemon*
- *Pills for sterilizing water*

The American soldiers, to thank the favors of the Italian population, offered to the festive crowds that celebrated their entry as the end of the war and the end of the famines: Coffee, chocolate and cigarettes.

Imagine the joy of a family who had been eating black bread for three years, having a chocolate bar in their teeth and the grandfather who could not afford to buy the strong chopper for his pipe; have a pack of *Pall Mall cigarettes;* that the Neapolitans called: the *Palli a Manu.*

* * *

BUCCELLATO/*i*, or *UCCIDDATU* in Sicilian dialect.

This dessert can be prepared in a single block of circular shape: The Buccellato; or if properly cut, it can be presented as in many pastries or stuffed biscuits that would take the name of Buccellati.

Ucciddatu: It would then be the Sicilian dialect term that is often magnified on the occasion of Christmas celebrations and subsequent new year's eve and epiphany holidays.

Dough for Buccellato

One and a half pounds of flour, 500 grams of sugar, 3 sachets of baking powder, a tablespoon of ammonia for cakes, eight eggs, 500 grams of lard or melted butter.

Given the presence of fats, it would be better to use kneading machines; if it is not possible, arrange the flour in a fountain, and put in the center the ingredients one at a time, eggs and lard; then try to incorporate everything and compose a dough that will be sticky and soft.
Arrange the dough in the fridge to make it better to absorb the fats.
Next, divide the dough into two parts, roll out each part with a rollling pin and obtain two squares: 35-40 cm per side; on the side near you the filling is arranged and then roll the filling evenly inside the dough.
If you want to compose the pastries, cut the rolls, before being baked, in logs a couple of fingers thick.

Ingredients for the Filling

These ingredients can be different from kitchen to kitchen; points of discrepancy may have in the use or not of chocolate and in the cooking of dried fruit in wine or water.

Since we like to drink we use wine and do without chocolate but not without spices of cloves and cinnamon.

The filling for buccellato would be: *200 grams of toasted and chopped almonds, 200 grams of chopped walnut kernels, 1 Kg. of dried figs, 400 grams of sultana, powders of cloves and cinnamon, candied oranges, grated orange peel, 6 tablespoons of Hyblaean honey, two tablespoons of sugar and two glasses of red wine.*

First, arrange the dried figs in hot water to soften, drain and cut them finely.

Boil in a pan the wine with honey, cinnamon spices and cloves and sugar, reduce the mixture over low heat and incorporate liquids: raisins, figs, almonds and chopped walnuts; mix everything gently for about 10 minutes.

This would be the filling to compose the buccellato; if you want to use chocolate, it would be enough to arrange it in small pieces over the filling without the need to melt it.

The buccellati biscuits will go into the oven for 10 minutes at a temperature of 180 degrees; if instead you want to present the roll of the buccellato, circular in shape, you should cook it for another five minutes.

The cooking time would also depend on the composition of the pastry, so it would be good to carry out, after ten minutes, the progress of cooking.

Once baked and when the cake is cold you can glaze with whipped egg white and icing sugar, once glazed the surfaces of the buccellato should be decorated with chocolate vermicelli or candied fruit.

*   *   *

A tribute now to the Calabrian peasant cuisine; it is said that Sicilians and Calabrians are cousins of ladle.

Once, on a walk in the parts of the Sila, I stopped in a place called: *Botte Donato,* where I ate a plate of spaghetti in white seasoned with two teaspoons of a composition with spicy herbs: I do not remember the name given to the dish but it was something divine, my taste buds masturbated to the maximum until I caused a convulsive hiccup that I had to quell with excellent white wine and an extra glass of full-bodied red: *Cirò Marina.*

SHEPHERD PASTA

400 Grams of Handmade Macaroni Pasta
250 Grams of fresh sheep's ricotta
100 grams of fresh sausage, the Ragusana one with fennel and black pepper seeds is fine.
200 Grams of tomato puree
Tropea onion, fresh basil, oregano, salt
Holy Oil – It is called Holy because it should be used with Sacredness, for the reason that the olive oil is spiced with red chillie.
Smoked ricotta, for grating

Needless to tell you how to prepare it, the only problem would be to incorporate the fresh sheep's ricotta with the tomato sauce; to avoid the lumps of ricotta just mix them with a little pasta cooking water.

*   *   *

Then you can not disregard, based on the aforementioned readings, the *Pistachio of Bronte*.

CASARECCIE WITH BRONTEE PISTACHIO PESTO AND NEBRODI PORK BELLY

Carbohydrates 400 grams Pasta Casarecce or other egg pasta.
Dried Fruit 200 grams of shelled pistachios from Bronte
Two tablespoons of walnut grains
Meat Eight slices of Black Pork Belly
Spices Two cloves of garlic,
Red chili pepper ad libitum
Salt and Pepper q.b.
Fat 5 Tablespoons Extra Virgin Olive Oil
Cheese 75 grams Peppered Etna cheese

Lend pistachio, garlic teeth and grated Etna pepper; using the mortar or a blender, while the blender is in motion pour, flush, the extra virgin olive oil; in order to obtain a soft cream.
Brown the slices of bacon and make them crispy, then cut the browned slices into strips.

Boil the pasta; storing a ladle of cooking water.

Place the pistachio cream in a pan over medium-low heat and combine the homemade and mix the ingredients, using the ladle of hot water if necessary.
Now incorporate the bacon strips into the dough.

Serve the dough and garnish with chilli, and sprinkle the surfaces with walnut grains

If you wanted to make this dish creamy you could use cooking cream in pistachio cream, and use less olive oil in the composition of pesto; in this case the pistachio pesto before being combined with the casarecce; it would need to be cooked for a few more minutes.

* * *

There could still be, before concluding this paragraph, paying tribute to german Chancellor Ottone Bismark, one of the most important European statesmen of his century.

A recipe, now ancient, would be the Bismark steak, when a grilled steak was combined with a fried egg on horseback, if the fried eggs had been two then we would have had: *Bismark steak with Two Horses.*

This dish is still in use in European catering, perhaps with a base of polenta enriched with herbs.

For a homely composition, the steak could be replaced by a Hamburger; as for the egg instead of the fried one you could use one or two poached eggs.

Before placing the poached egg on the hamburger it may be congenial to use glue-type Ketchup, to make the egg better adhere.

Then with everything you could also stuff a nice round sandwich or a brioche, skewer the brioscia with a long toothpick and suspend from the toothpick of the cucumber slices with gardener vegetables.

It could also work for a frugal meal, during an office break.

FONTI E CONSIDERAZIONI SULLA CUCINA SICILIANA

*La cottura del cibo rappresenta il passaggio dalla **Natura** alla **Cultura**.*
*L'alimentazione diventa **Cucina** e la cucina diventa **Gastronomia**.*
Michael POLLAN,
Natural History of trasformation, 2013

A first reference, on ancient cuisine, can be found in the Homeric poems of the eighth century b.c: bread, meat roasted on a spit, wine, fruit of various kinds, cheeses and honey.

These foods appear frequently in the pages of the Iliad and the Odyssey, although specific references to the quality of food, about their origin and any exchanges of goods would be missing.

In the fifth century b.c The acropolis of Athens became quite populated and culinary practices were well developed; the chronicles, of that time, report among other things: *The Excellent Bread of Athens, The Sea Breass of Ephesus and the Swordfish of Byzantium.*

The causes of this copiousness of foods may have been derived from trade with Minor Asia in particular in the Lydia region, where fruit trees and vegetable crops of various kinds were widely cultivated, due to the presence of spring waters.

They were also appreciated by the Athenians of that time, the foods and cooking practices from the settlements of Magna Graecia in the Siciliote and south-peninsular colonies.

With the conquests of Alexander the Great was then established the *Hellenistic Culture* and the cuisines of the Mediterranean area, came to be influenced by the oriental-Persian culinary cultures.

The colonies of Magna Graecia reached advanced gastronomic techniques; practicing sea fishing; bakery, which involves the cultivation and harvesting of wheat; dairy farming, which involves cattle and sheep rearing; olive tree crops, which involve the presence of oil; the crops of the vineyards for winemaking.

Particular importance reached, in the colonies of Magna Graecia, the *Syracusan Cuisine;* very popular in the city of Athens and Corinth, for the research on fish foods practiced by expert Sicilian chefs and for the presence of what can be considered the first father of gastronomy: *Archestrato da Gela;* who, in the kitchen was a pure, devoted to the simplicity of food and addressed words of remonstrance against the Syracusan cooks who impinged the fish with cheeses and sorrel brines.

In addition to maritime fishing, freshwater fishing was practiced, in particular eels were caught in the Strait of Messina and Archestrato in his writings of *Gastronomy* reports:

Every eel I praise, but certainly it is by far the best, the one that is fished in front of Reggio, in that arm of the sea.

There you inhabitant of Messina have a great advantage over all other mortals; since you can put in your mouth food so delicious.

In addition to the eels of the Strait, Sicilian fish was highly appreciated in the convivial banquets of the Greeks; are reported by the chronicles: *The imperial prawn of Catania, the shells of Tindari, the sardelle of Lipari, The Sturgeon of Syracuse and certainly the slices of Tuna and Swordfish .*

* * *

One of the most magnificent Greek philosophers present in Syracuse was *Plato* who, while appreciating the local cuisine, complained to his fellow philosophers in the Motherland, about the opulence of the Syracusan siciliotes, who lazed for a long time at the canteens to eat twice a day; while it would have been enough only once: *The philosopher was for frugal lunches and often ate only bread and olives.*

The celebrations are then reported by *Plutarch and Heraclides,* in the Syracusan acropolis, in honor of Goddess *Demeter,* protector of crops and wheat; from this it can be verified how important this grain had been, considered a gift of the Gods and the importance of baking.

Another element, which made the ancient Syracusan cuisine famous, was honey and its use for sweets and medicinal ointments.

* * *

During the Roman period, fishing activities were not only carried out in fishing but techniques for the conservation of fish were implemented.

The Roman sources of *Eliano and Ateneo* provide us with information on the existence of tuna traps in Pachino, Tindari, Cefalù, San Vito Lo Capo, Salunto; particularly interesting were the techniques for the preservation of tuna; that is, the types of salting based on the cuts of the parts of the fish.

From the treatise *Naturalis Historia of Pliny the Elder,*you can receive more than 300 recipes of different types of fish, caught in the Mediterranean, including: Invertebrates, crustaceans, molluscs, tuna, mackerel, red mullet, bream etc.

To be able to understand the cooking techniques put in place at that time, we must get to know two gastronomic writers of ancient Rome.

- *Marco Gavio Apicio from 25 b.C. to 37 a.C. Under the reign of Emperor Tiberius.*

- Apicius is credited with having written the work: *De Re Coquinaria* composed of ten books in which the *Classical Roman Cuisine* was described in its entirety. Now it seems that the original work of Apicius contained only two books: one dedicated to sauces and the other of a general nature. The rest of the books seem to have been supplemented by two other writers, who gave themselves the name of Apicius, to complete the gastronomic work in the year 400 a.C.; after Apicius, the original one, had disappeared, apparently by suicide, for about 4 centuries. From the book of sauces of Apicius there are two important sauces of that time: *The Garum or Liquamen*: Obtained from the fermentation of small fish and the *Defutrum*: That it was the boiling of grape musts, obtaining a sweet compound, used as a condiment.

- *Ateneo Da Naucrati, Greek-Egyptian writer, who lived in Rome in the year 200 a.C.* The only work of the Athenaeum, which has come down to us, would be: The *Dipnosofisti or Dotti a Banchetto*; written in 15 books, of which only a summary was found and currently archived at the Marciano library in Venice. It would be a *Symposium* in which philosophers, doctors and grammarians – 22 people in all - entertain themselves in dialogues concerning human knowledge; with particular regard to food, wine and entertainment. Ateneo brings us important information on the gastronomic culture of the ancient world.

On the basis of these precious treatises it is clear, in the classic Roman cuisine, that the *blue fish,* including entrails, it was the basis of the sauce: *Garum* to which Condimenta was added, like aromatic herbs and sea salt in relation to half the weight of the fish.

The liquid that derived from these fermentations was collected in tanks, to be subsequently stored in sealed amphorae and was used in culinary techniques as a condiment or to compose other sauces.

The *Liquamen* was the flower of the garum; that is, the filtered garum.

These techniques and the writings of Apicius and Athenaeus have allowed us to know different fish recipes of classical Roman cuisine:

- *Sardina fish wrapped in fig leaves with oregano, angelica silvestris, ferula aso-foetida, with the presence of cheese and vinegar; for cooking under the ashes.*
  - Ateneo recipe.

- *Sole fish, boiled with cheese and silfio – Angelica Ferula – called to the Sicilian Fashion.*
  - Ateneo Recipe

- *Moray fish, roasted with pepper, ligustic leaves, saffron, onion, Damascus plums, wine and honeyed wine, vinegar, defrutum, oil and garum.*
  Recipe of Apicius

- *Sea bass of Miletus, roasted and softened by brine*
  - Ateneo Recipe

- *Urchins, with garum, oil, sweet wine, pepper powder*
  Recipe of Apicius

- *Sepia, stuffed with ligustic pepper, celery seeds, carvi, honey, garum, wine.*
  Recipe of Apicius

- *Squid, made in small pieces, sprinkled with fat and stuffed with aromatic herbs, before being roasted.*
  -Ateneo Recipe

Stuff to drive crazy the best modern chefs, you can certainly say that the ancient Romans did not lack the inventiveness of the table; although certainly not everyone could afford certain refinements of food.

It must be said that, in ancient Rome, the sale of food on the street was very much in use also for the reason that it was difficult for the plebs to cook at home, being the accommodations not safe and there was no system of kitchens in which the fires could be regulated; the cooking of food often caused dangerous fires; of which malicious faults were attributed to Nero or Commodus or to the Christians; in fact the fault would be attributed to the unsafe home structures of those times.

From the name Apicius then, it seems that the culinary term may arise: *Alla Scapece,*widely used in Neapolitan cuisine for zucchini or fish; everything derives from the Latin term: *Ex Apicius.*
The Romans used a lot of Sicilian wheat, proclaiming the island: *The Granary of Italy;* in connection also with the production of pasta; always at that time, there was a revealing spread of Sicilian sweets; due to the gastronomic use of almonds and certainly of Hyblaean honey.

* * *

Hyblaean honey was mentioned in the Shakespearean tragedy of Julius Caesar, put in place in 1579; following the English translations of *Plutarch's Parallel*Lives. The most famous part of the work is, without a doubt, the speach of Mark Antony on the dead body of Caesar, the one that begins with the invitation of the speaker to the people to listen to him: *Roman nobles, friends, fellow citizens, lend me ear: Lend me your ears.*
However, our honey was mentioned in the historical *tragedy;* when the four generals: Brutus and Cassius on one side and Octavian and Antony on the other, before fighting at Philippi, held a conference in a tent; it was anything but a friendly conference: *Words before the blows.*
In this meeting Cassius, addressing his adversary Anthony, expressed himself thus: *Your words have stolen honey from the Hyblaean bees.*
Certainly Cassius was referring precisely to the speach of Anthony; which had been so penetrating and persuasive as to raise the wrath of the people and force the conspirators to flee from Rome.
Antonio's answer was: *My words will have stolen the honey from the Hyblaean bees but not the sting.*

This brief presentation of the Hyblaean bees and their honey, are important to make us understand how famous was the product of our land since ancient times.

Bees, as in Great Britain, should be considered by the Italian Ministry of Agriculture a protected species; precisely for that great work they produce for the production of honey and for the pollination of flowers.

* * *

At the fall of the Roman Empire in 476 a.C. the barbarians arrived in Sicily, first Odoacer and then Theodoric, who had Odoacer killed.

Since we have already seen enough killings, we pass in the year 535 a.C. when Sicily was annexed to the Byzantine Empire following the conquests of Gen. Belisario .

* * *

Constantine, the first Roman emperor to embrace the Christian faith, fixed, around 300 a.C., his residence in the Greek colony of Byzantium, near the Black Sea, which was named in his honor: *Constantinople.* The acropolis will become, subsequently, the capital of the Byzantine or Eastern Roman Empire, until the fifteenth century, that is, for over a thousand and one hundred years.
In fact, Constantine could not have chosen, for his empire, a better place; both for the natural beauty, and to favor the land and sea trade of the long-lived Byzantine Empire.

The cuisine of this Roman-Byzantine Empire is historically interesting and surely there will have been correlations with Sicilian cuisine; because, *ab ovo,* it was characterized by the fusion of Greek gastronomy with the Roman one; to build, with the passing of the centuries, the basis of: Ottoman *Cuisine;* with ramifications on *Greek, Balkan and Levantine cuisine.*

The local economy of the Greeks of ancient Byzantium came to prosper for the trade of tuna and other black sea fish products; over the years, important gastronomic discoveries were made in those waters: first *the Bottarga;* subsequently, in the twelfth century, the first experiments of *Caviar* were performed from sturgeon eggs.

In the field of meat, special dishes were composed with game of gazelles, poultry meat for broths and were presented compositions of dried beef, such as: *Pastrami,* still in use in Turkish and Eastern European cuisine.
Byzantine cuisine became famous not only for the discovery of new foods; but for new culinary techniques; one of these were fig leaves used as wraps to turn food and preserve them from contamination or burns during cooking; techniques that gave rise to a series of foods such as *Dolmades or Dolma;* dishes that still and more than ever find wide use in modern kitchens.

Byzantine cuisine came to be well equipped with spices of various kinds; rosemary was used to flavor roast lamb; as well as found wide use the spices of saffron and nutmeg.

The eastern spice routes followed the routes from the Far East to the port of Alexandria in Egypt and, in the passages of caravans or by sea, were purchased, by Byzantine traders, loads of spices to be displayed for sale in the annual markets of Constantinople and Thessalonica.

In the major cities of the empire; particular attention was paid to bakeries, dairy products such as Feta cheese *and Tome*;different fruit jams were composed and put into use such as quince jams, oranges and pears, sweet preparations, combining dried fruit with honey or sugars, such as: *Baklava.*

Spicy wines, muscat and vermouth were used in the drinks; with the use of essences such as: anise, roses and sweet fennel seeds were then flavored soft drinks.

To get an idea of the compositions of Byzantine cuisine, you can admire the following dishes with their sauces:

- *Roasted pork with wine and honey*
- *Fish Breed with cumin*
- *Wild duck with red wine, mustard, cumin*

This would have been the menu of Byzantine cuisine that Liutprand, bishop of Cremona on a diplomatic mission to Constantinople on behalf of King Berengar II of Ivrea in 949, would have chosen.

We can conclude this intervention on Byzantine cuisine by mentioning an oat biscuit and the development of this biscuit among the different European cuisines; this would demonstrate the importance of a historical cuisine and the ramifications that it can have even in terrestrial distances.

The biscuit in question would be, in the original diction, *Paximadion,* and then become:

- *Paximadia, In Greek*
- *Bashmat, In Arabic*
- *Beksemad, In Turkish*
- *Peksimet, In Serbo-Croatian language*
- *Pesmet, In Romanian*
- *Pasimata, In Veneto-Italian dialect*

Another example of Byzantine culture is found in the architectural field: *Byzantine architecture* paved the way for Western *Romanesque and Gothic* architecture; as well as in the East he had a profound influence on Islamic *Architecture.*

In Sicily, as Byzantine architectural works, there would be to mention the *Mosaics,* that is, the decorations of floors, walls or ceilings of the churches; of which some examples can be found in various Sicilian churches.

The Arabs were called in the West *Saracens, that is, inhabitants of the Sahara,* it took almost 50 years to conquer Sicily from the Byzantines, the first Arab landing dates back to the year 827 carried out in that of Mazara Del Vallo.

During the 200 years of their domination on the island, they favored the culture, arts, poetry, mathematics and the Sicilian economy.

The Arab domination, according to the historian Michele Amari, strongly influenced Sicilian agriculture as in addition to wheat other cereal crops were practiced; increased and improved the cultivation of vineyards and olive groves; in particular, new plantations were planted such as: Oranges, lemons, sugar cane and papyrus.

The city of Palermo, which at the beginning of the first millennium had 350 thousand inhabitants, became the seat of the emirate and was distinguished by luxury and wealth so as to be considered the most important and rich economic center of the Mediterranean; in whose waters, trade was favored by the presence of an intense maritime network.

The conquerors did not persecute the Christian faith in Sicily; however, those who did not embrace the Islamic religion were forced to pay more government taxes.

Certainly the Arab culture was also expressed in the field of arts and architecture, even today we can admire in Palermo the treasures of Arab-Norman architecture in places of worship that from mosques became Catholic churches: *The Palatine Chapel* with Norman doors, Arab arches and Byzantine domes; *The Church of San Cataldo, Church of San Giovanni degli Eremiti* with red domes of clear Arab workmanship.

A particular Arabic feature were the decorations of the domes and niches; made from stucco, ceramics or bricks that are called: *Muqarnas.*

It is said that: *Arab cuisine made Sicilian cuisine exploded* in concentrations of flavors of sweeties like: cassata, cannoli, sfinci, royal pasta, sesame nougat,zuccata, marzipan; and again, the first experiments of Sicilian ice cream were carried out which was expressed in dozens of flavors not only in cones or cups; but also in semifreddo, in granitas, scursunera or jasmine ice cream.

Since the introduction of rice crops have been formed in Sicilian cuisines: timbales, arancine and sweet rice; nor can the copious presence of spices and herbs with which couscous are seasoned be omitted; an authentic explosion of culture that has generated gastronomic styles and combined, enriched tastes of the Sicilian culinary style.

One of these gastronomic discoveries, in the ninth century by the Arabs, were the techniques used for the drying of pasta and the popular use of long pasta, seasoned with cheese and spices, eaten by Sicilians with their hands on the streets or open places, possibly with their eyes turned to the skies.

The Arabs have planted the roots of what can be called the gastronomic heritage of the island, it was not a passing fashion but the set of foods and techniques practiced a millennium ago, nowadays, are part of our heritage, culinary traditions and those identities that perhaps will never be extinguished in the souls and traditions of the Sicilians.

With the arrival of the peoples of the north, that is, the Normans, apart from the use of game, no particular innovations or changes were made to an already rich cuisine; they were clever enough not to abolish or destroy the advanced social and economic structures of Arab-Muslim Sicily.

*   *   *

In the year 1071 following the siege of Palermo by sea and by land by norman warriors under the orders of Roger of Hauteville, who had previously seized Calabria; the Arab-Saracens handed over the capital of Palermo to Roger; with the understanding, in the pacts of surrender, to be considered free citizens, not to be politically persecuted and to freely practice Islamic worship.

In 1091 following the fall of the city of Noto, where the last Emir of Sicily *Ibn-El-Werd* had taken refuge with his family and with the conquest, by the Normans, of the island of Malta; the Arab-Saracen domination in Sicily came to an end and the Norman domination began; later in Christmas 1130, Roger II of Altavilla was named: *Rex Siciliae.*

The Normans started the so-called process of *Latinization,* certainly imposed by the Papacy; that is, the transformation of the Byzantine Orthodox churches and mosques into monuments of Catholic worship; this new structure involved a series of not indifferent architectural works and the introduction of new styles, which certainly benefited from the architectural beauties of the island.
However, this process of Latinization did not take place in a coercive manner as some mosques remained unedified and open to Islamic worship; as well as some churches that continued to profess the Orthodox-Byzantine faith; as for example: *The Church of Piana degli Albanesi* in the province of Palermo; where my two grandchildren from Palermo were baptized: *Manfredi and Sveva.*

The culinary influence of the Normans, who were mostly peoples of Germanic origin belonging to the Scandinavian area; introduced in Sicilian cuisine, as previously stated, new techniques for a better cooking of furry game; introducing spit-cooking on lit coals.

They were then presented in sicilian kitchens some fish from the Atlantic Ocean and the North Sea, such as: *Herring, Cod and Stockfish;* the latter in Sicily was called *Piscistoccu,* famous in Messina cuisine; the salting techniques of these products were introduced to be preserved over time.
These new foods were kindly welcomed and received even in the popular canteens for their particular taste and for the not high purchase price.

Sicilian cuisine can be considered as a *Absorbent Paper* for having drawn from the various dominations and those that will follow one another; so many culinary benefits; among which we can also include the use of new tools, introduced by the Normans, such as knives for cutting meat, skewers and the use at the table of two-pointed fork.

From the royal Norman family descended *Constance of Altavilla* who was the parent of an infant of the Swabian House: Frederick II – King of Germany and Sicily and Lord of almost all of *Italy, excluding the Papal Kingdom.*
To Frederick II of Swabia and his Empire; we owe the integrations of the three civilizations: the *Norman, the Arab and the Greek-Latin* that were, at that time, present in Sicily.

In the constitution issued by Frederick II in the Kingdom of Sicily, which dates back to the year 1231, we read:
We grant the same guarantees to the Jews and Saracens because we do not want innocent subjects to be persecuted just because they are Jews and Muslims.

In the years to come, Sicily came to take advantage of a magical period of absolute internal peace among its inhabitants, and the intentions of Frederick and his magnificent Court, were turned to the culture extended in all fields of knowledge; not surprisingly, to Frederick King of Sicily; was conferred by posterity, the attribute of: **Stupor Mundi**.

Despite being King of Germany, his favorite kingdoms were Sicily and the Italian South Peninsular , Apulia in particular; one of the titles attributed to Frederick II was: *Rex Apuliae,* this term referred to the whole southern kingdom.

- He founded the University of Naples
- He was the promoter of the Sicilian Poetic School
- He favored the developments and research of the Salerno Medical School in which nutrition was an integral part, according to the teachings of the Greek philosopher Hippocrates and the Roman physician Galiano or Galieno.
- He made the City of Palermo the intellectual cradle of Italy and perhaps of Europe
- His court was magnificent and opulent composed of scientists, poets, intellectuals of all nationalities.

From recent studies carried out by *Anna Martellotti,*professor at the University of Perugia; could be attributed to Frederick II the set of recipes and related culinary techniques included in the cooking manuscripts, recognized as: *Liber De Coquina and Anonimo Meridionale.*

These important manuscripts were traced back to anonymous gastronomic writers in the fifteenth century; from the careful studies and research carried out by Mrs. Martellotti and other scholars who have endorsed her research; it would appear that the manuscripts in question date back to the times datable to the early twelfth century and therefore written at the time of the Swabians in Sicily.

From these conclusions, the manuscripts in question were codified as:
Treaties or Cookbooks Federiciani .

In her disquisitions Mrs. Martellotti states that: If Sicilian poetry becomes Tuscany, and then becomes Italian; the cuisine described in Frederick's treatises becomes a vehicle of national scientific culture.

The cookbooks in question range over different topics related to food and culinary practices; they would therefore include and deal with different gastronomic topics:

- *De Genere Herborum:* The cuisine of vegetables
- *De Super-Fluilatibus animalium:* Concerns milk, dairy products and eggs
- *De Piscibus:* Related to fish products
- *De Cibis Compositis et Multis:* Gastronomic preparations with different ingredients
- *De Animalibus:* Recipes related to game meat and farmed aninals
- *De Arte Venandi Avibus:* This manuscript, containing illustrations of the time, was written personally by Frederick II, as an expert hunter and falconer; about the hunting art of hunting birds, using suitably trained falcons.

In the gastronomic philosophy of the Frederick Treaties, not only Sicilian recipes are used; due to the continuous travels of Federico during the military campaigns in many parts of Italy we have come to recipes included in the cuisines of different regions; such as: *Crespelle de Quaresima,* would be the sweets that are now called *Cenci or Chiacchere; Lassanis,* which would correspond to our boiled and seasoned lasagna; *Defoliated cake,* would be nowadays the *Tigelle or Crescentine Modenesi.*

In the court kitchen of Frederick II we therefore find an abundance of spices such as saffron, fruits such as pomegranates, spit-roasted meats according to Norman techniques, the best fish of the Mediterranean with the scapece technique, pigeons caught by falcons and certainly a selection of Arab sweets such as cassata, sweets and marzipan biscuits and candied sugared almonds.

To complicate so much magnificence and to be able to encircle the imperial crown of King of Germany and Sicily and other realms, Frederick had to assume towards *Pope Gregory IX,*the commitment to lead the crusades in the Holy Land.
A feat of which the new Emperor was not, in reality, so inclined to accomplish and tried to postpone the expedition to the *Holy Land* as much as possible by citing personal health reasons and political issues to the Pope .

Forced by papal pressure, Frederick headed the *Sixth Crusade* in the Holy Land in 1228, heading for Palestine.

What the previous crusades had failed to accomplish with armed clashes against the Arabs, with weapons, killings and the expenditure of human lives; Frederick managed to obtain with the peace treaties with the Arab emirs and the agreements with the Sultan *Al-Kamil*; obtaining free access to Christians to the city of Jerusalem and religious visits to the Holy Sepulchre; he also obtained the title of King of Jerusalem following his marriage to the heir to the throne *Iolanda of Brenne*.

This was Emperor Frederick II of Swabia, of the Germanic house of *Hohenstaufen*,

Rex Siciliae – Rex Apuliae
Stupor Mundi

The Pope of Rome was not satisfied with agreements, he wanted blood to flow; he therefore did not recognize the agreements stipulated between the Emperor and the Sultan and, at the Council of Lyons in 1248, excommunicated Frederick for the third time, and his descendants, to be deposed and relieved of the titles acquired.

This papal act provoked in Europe and in Italy in particular, a deep division between the feudal lords or the lordships of the Italian cities, establishing the opposing factions of the Guelphs and Gibellini; the consequences of these factions were fatal for all European populations, for the rest of the medieval period, provoking wars and mourning, usurpations and depositions, conspiracies and injustices.

For the record, a seventh crusade was subsequently prepared by the Popes of Rome in which Frederick did not participate because of the excommunication; the papal office was entrusted to the King of France *Louis IX, called the Saint*; the expedition ended with serious defeats for the crusaders also due to the raging cholera epidemic.

Louis the Saint himself was affected by the disease – *cholera does not even respect the Saints* – captured and taken prisoner, was treated by Arab doctors and subsequently a heavy ransom was requested for his release, which was not paid by the Pope but by the French crown.

The Crusader wars did not bring any benefit, neither economic nor religious and are still a cause of disagreement as Muslims accuse Christians of having invaded their lands.

* * *

The Pope French whose surname he had: *Pantaleon – it seems that of a Venetian carnival mask – nomen imposuit* Urban *IV;*he appointed in 1263: Charles of *Anjou, King of Sicily.*
As if Sicily were a property of the Pope for which he designated the rulers.

A French army descended from the Alps towards the south peninsular occupying Naples and later Sicily; after the battle of Benevento in which the only male descendant of the house of Hohenstaufen, *Manfred of Swabia,* was defeated and killed on the battlefield.

Charles of Anjou was definitely not Frederick II and the Sicilian people burdened by heavy taxes and the bullying of the French soldiers; he revolted against the occupiers in the famous uprisings of *the Sicilian Vespers:* the revolt of Palermo and the other Sicilian cities forced the Angevin troops to abandon the island.

Giovanni Da Procida, one of the leaders of the Vespers uprising, on behalf of the Sicilian people, conferred the crown of Sicily on Peter III of Aragon as the husband of Constance of Swabia, daughter of the late Manfredi.

Certainly the Angevins tried to retake the island; but they were not so lucky; the Aragonese Kings, after 90 years of struggles, took the crown of: *Rulers of Trinacria;* the new seat of this kingdom, which in fact was of Spanish origin, was established by the permanence of the Aragonese royals in the city of Catania, at the *Ursino Castle.*

In general, the Aragonese presence in the thirteenth century and the Spanish trade with the East became very profitable for Sicilian cuisine, as more spicy dishes were put in place, very useful for compositions of vegetarian dishes.

Continuing the stories and the succession of the various Aragonese rulers in Sicily would not make sense for our research; the consequences, however, of what happened in 1492, with the discovery of the New World, was something that changed not only Sicily but the face of planet Earth.

* * *

For <u>Columbian Exchange</u> we mean the exchanges, peaceful or forced, between Europeans with the new world; which concern economic goods belonging to the animal, vegetable, mineral kingdoms: in the animal kingdom we also mean people and diseases, by vegetables we mean the exchange of fruit plants, olive groves, vineyards and citrus groves; in the mineral field we refer more to precious metals such as gold, silver, gems, in this field more than an exchange we can speak of embezzlement or robbery by the old world.

Chocolate, Tomatoes, Potatoes, Peppers, Cassava Flour, Peanuts, some categories of Beans, Avocado Fruits, Guava, Papaya, Pineapple and Turkey Meats, Tobacco and Chili; they were some of the new foods that raged on the European continent.

Conversely, the Old World exchanged with the New: *Wheat, olives, grapes, citrus fruits and a series of animals: horses, sheep and felines;* cats were also shipped to the Americas.

From the Asian continent reached the new world: *Sugar Cane, Bananas, and Vegetable Strains.*

These exchanges revolutionized the global systems of cultivation in agriculture, the economic systems of nations; food styles and cooking systems, social lifestyles and health; as well as bringing cultural and biological consequences on the earth's population.

One of the modern historians, the American *Alfred Crosby, Yale University,* in his treatise: *The Columbian Exchange: Biological and Coltural Consequences, 1972* - he found, on the basis of the statistics obtained, that the growth of the population in the globe, in the post-Columbian period, was increased very rapidly because of these exchanges.

There would therefore have been a connection between Columbus discoveries and the increase in population for the use of a new diet suitable for human proliferation.

We have statistics of those born in the post-Columbian period; but we have not calculated the data of deaths due to these exchanges with the new world; perhaps it would be better to say: the yankerie perpetrated in the new world by the *European Conquistadors,* responsible for the demographic collapse in the Americas during the sixteenth century.
More than exchanges, the conquistatores were interested in seizing gold, silver and everything available to them in the territories occupied by the indigenous tribes: *Incas* – Peoples of the Andes – *Aztecs* – Mexico – *Maya* –Mesoamerican – *Tiahuanaco* – Bolivia, Peru, Chile.

Apart from massacres and killings of indigenous people who were partially naked, unarmed or badly armed; against professional soldiers or mercenaries, there would have been the ailments and infections of cruel morbids transmitted by Europeans to the natives; who, having had no previous contact with other peoples: *Their organism was devoid of immune defenses.*

Just to name a few of these contagious and epidemic diseases: *Bubonic plague. Chickenpox, Leprosy, Malaria, Typhoid, Yellow Fever;* the victims of these illness have never been counted and I think it would have been a difficult undertaking, of which it is better to remain silent and not to talk about it.

We could at most deal with mysteries or inexplicable events of phenomena that appeared to the Reigning King *Montezuma of the Aztec tribe;* in the years preceding the landings of the Spanish troops under the command of the conquistadors: *Hernan Cortes and Francisco Pizzarro:*

- *A comet appeared in the sky in broad daylight and at night turned into a pillar of fire*
- *Three important Aztec temples were destroyed: one due to a strong fire, one struck by lightning in a clear sky and another submerged by water.*
- *Strange beings with many heads on one body were noticed in the inhabited centers.*
- *Strange chants were heard of women, not present, singing funeral rites.*
- *A strange bird landed on The hands of Montezuma; through the eyes of the bird, as if they were a mirror, the King saw strange appearances of men landing on the shores of his Kingdom.*

Finding plausible explanations in these events is impossible; however, it can be deduced very clearly that these were not good omens for the kingdom of Montezuma and its inhabitants.

*   *   *

An important event that concerned Sicily was the *Battle of Lepanto:* A naval clash that took place in June 1571 in Greek waters; between the fleets of the Ottoman Empire and those of the *Holy League;*in turn constituted by the Spanish Empire - including Sicily and the Kingdom of Naples - the Papal States, the Republic of Venice, the Republic of Genoa, the Grand Duchy of Tuscany and all other minor kingdoms recognized in Italy at that time; included: Savoy, Lucca, Urbino, Ferrara, Mantua and the Knights of Malta.

Pope Pius V, spiritual leader of this league, appointed *Don Giovanni of Austria,* natural son of Emperor Charles V *of Habsburg,* commander-in-chief of the Christian fleet; *Don Giovanni* represented *the Spanish Empire* and the kingdoms, at that time, connected to it such as those of*Naples, Sicily and Sardinia.*

The aims and context of the naval clash were related to the control of the Mediterranean; as the Ottomans and the peoples of North Africa carried out, with their substantial naval force, acts of piracy both in the open sea and in the Sicilian and peninsular coasts; the Ottomans had occupied the island of Cyprus, which was a Spanish domain, and the Aegean islands, occupied by the Maritime Republic of Venice, were under constant Ottoman threat.

The Battle of Lepanto was an important victory against the Ottoman Empire; although it certainly did not mark its end; an imperial spokesman the *Vizir Mehmed Sokollu* stated that: *In the battle of Lepanto they had lost only their beard but not their arms;*we must remember that in1683 the Ottomans were about to conquer Vienna and with it also the western European part.

The fleet of the Holy League was composed of the Spanish flagship fleet in the center and on the two sides or horns, the Venetian and Genoese fleets were arranged.

The victory was won by the Spanish, Sardinian, Sicilian and Neapolitan central fleet against the Ottoman one; while the two fleets arranged on the flanks had difficulties: the Venetian one that had engaged fire against the Moroccan and Tunisian ships, was then helped by the Spanish fleet not to succumb; very ambiguous were revealed, during the clash, the moves of the Genoese ships, under the command of *Giandandrea Doria;* so much so as to insinuate the possibility that the Genoese commander had stipulated, before the clash, a secret pact with the Ottomans.

*   *   *

We have previously mentioned the figure of Emperor Charles V who, in the mid-1500s, had managed to reunite the Habsburg crown with the Spanish one; becoming de facto and by right sovereign of a great empire: *Spain* – with the title of Charles I – *Netherlands, South-Italy* – including the Kingdoms of Naples and Palermo – The Austrian *Territories, Northern Italy and the American Colonies* under Spanish rule.

To this empire, Charles V would have liked to add the English Crown; as Mary Tudor, daughter of Henry VIII with his first Spanish wife Catherine of Aragon, became Queen of England and Ireland following the untimely death of her half-brother: the reigning Edward VI.

Mary was Catholic like her mother and not Anglican like her heresiarch father; The marriage of Tudor to Infant Philip was then arranged; so that he could marry a Queen; Charles V, appointed Philip King of Sicily in the year 1556; with the name of Philip II.

The marriage was celebrated in London and was expected that Mary could immediately generate an infant who could unite the crowns of Spain and England; something that unfortunately for the royal spouses did not happen.

Philip could not stay in London to be an affectionate hubby; for its European and colonial commitments and domains; he therefore decided to sail for Europe and abandon the sterile Mary Tudor, who went down in history, perhaps unduly, as *Bloody Mary or Mary the Bloodthirsty*; his reign lasted only eight years and, at his undemented death, the English throne was occupied by her half-sister: *Elisabeth I*.

If the couple Philip and Mary had had a descendant this would have been the richest and most powerful ruler in the world; as he would inherit:
The Kingdom of England, the Kingdom of Ireland, the Kingdom of Spain, the Netherlands, Austria, Northern Italy, the Italian South-Peninsular Kingdom, the Kingdom of Sicily and would become Lord of all the *American colonies of Castile and England.*

It is said, however, that history is not made with ifs or with mah.

*   *   *

After the naval victory against the Ottoman Empire, the Mediterranean area of Sicily and the peninsular maritime coasts of southern Italy, came to be relieved from suffering coastal attacks by Saracens and Turks; what was supposed to be a period of peace and serenity for Sicily; it proved to be a period of economic recession; because, once the Mediterranean was no longer a threat from the Turks, the island and the south-peninsular area were forgotten by the great powers that were, moreover, committed to occupying the territories of the new continent, rather than taking an interest in the peoples of the Mediterranean.

The Spanish domination in Sicily and the heavy political and economic crisis that began to dawn in the Spanish motherland; the lack of protectionism of goods, the agriculture of landowners; they were of no benefit to trade, economy, culture and social justice related to the needs of the island.

In other words: since the state of affairs in the *Dominant Part* did notwork; consequently they could not function in the *Dominated Parts.*

＊　＊　＊

One of the negative events for Spain can be found in the very useless *Thirty Years' War, between 1618 and 1648,* which raged throughout Central Europe among the Protestant states that formed the *Evangelical League* against the Catholic States; in the bosom of the *Holy Roman Empire;*which with the passing of the centuries: it was no longer *Sacred,* it was certainly not *Roman* and it was not even *an Empire.*

In support of the Evangelical League were the Dutch rebels who were under Spanish rule, the Scandinavian countries, Sweden in particular and France, which although not Protestant, felt threatened by the Austrian and Spanish Habsburg power.
Spain then went to war with Austria against France and the countries adhering to the Evangelical League to defend Catholicism in the bosom of the Holy Roman Empire.

His Catholic Majesty Philip III of Spain needed money to keep his armies of mercenaries, people with few scruples, deployed in half of Europe.

The Spanish crown asked the Viceroy of Sicily *Di Castro;* the maximum effort in raising funds for a million scudi: a huge sum for that time; to which the Viceroy did not know where to beat his head or to which Saint to turn.

Proceed to the sale of government buildings, state land and feudal rights; it proceeded, for a fee, to attribute noble titles and alienations of patronage rights over religious institutions.

Regarding the attribution of noble titles, the title of ' *Don* 'which would be the lowest step of the feudal pyramid, was awarded for 40 ounces.

In 1620 the Viceroy issued a notice to regulate the title of *'Don',* as many people had begun to use it for free - called the *Don-a-forza* - without having proceeded with the government purchase.

According to the Royal Decree these Don-a-force were fined 200 ounces.

You could also buy the *Jus del Mero and Misto Imperio;* that is to say the right to be a judge and to administer justice; this right allowed the various Barons of Sicily to practice justice at will against vassals and peasants to whom torture and the death penalty were also associated, in the exercise of this justice.
The convict could appeal to the sentences of the master-judge by addressing directly to the Spanish Crown; which for a farmer would have been a rather difficult if not impossible practice.

Thus continuing the state of affairs; the chronicles report that, at the beginning of the 1700s, the Sicilian aristocracy was formed by:

- 142 Principles
- 788 Marquesses
- 1500 Barons and Dukes

It is estimated that 4/5 of the island was under feudal control.

Despite the power attributed to them by the Spanish Crown in the seventeenth century; many Sicilian aristocrats lived on debts contracted with various creditors, as there was the fashion of living in the city, in sumptuous palaces, with an excessive social life; many noble families, even if heavily indebted, casually continued to live in luxuries; disdaining any active economic role.

This noble caste was made up of absentee landowners who preferred to mortgage their property rather than devote themselves to land reforms such as crop innovation or irrigation of fields or improving the lives of poor peasants.
Many of them entrusted their lands to the gabellotti who, in turn, had the sole interest in squeezing the peasants and possibly defrauding the landowners.

Apart from the costs of maintaining the splendor of their palaces, the baron always needs a greater number of servants, eight-horse carriages, effeminate and tight clothes and costumes with silver or gold squiggles.

Many were also, at that time, the rich or extra-rich barons; their wealth that came from the income of the countryside; but did not return to the countryside to repair roads, falling tenant buildings, bridges, dams, canals; the income of the countryside went to the cities for the construction or maintenance of the palaces.

* * *

The Messina hinterland of Val Demone produced few cereals in itself; so the economy of the Peloritan city was oriented towards maritime trade; thanks to its port consisting of a large inlet with a natural arm, in the shape of a sickle, which delimits a port area of about 820 thousand square meters.

The port of Messina was a safe haven for vessels and boats of all kinds and, over the centuries, became a commercial emporium not only with other Mediterranean ports, also for trade with the East; that is, the best means of communication between the West and the East, in the Mediterranean area.

With the production and trade of silk, the cultivation of cane sugar, the activities of private shipyards that carried out construction and repair of vessels and boats, the activities of insurance companies that covered entire loads of traveling goods, the flourishing typographic activity that also produced the modern mold of nautical maps suitable for navigation, trade in fish products and food products such as olive oil and wine; they made the port of Messina an essential base for maritime trade and made the city commercially more alive, richer and proud of its specificity.

Starting from the sixteenth century it became particularly important and profitable in the Val Demone the production and trade of silk, obtained from silkworms, according to the techniques of Chinese silkworm breeding and in relation to these trades the port of Messina became an important market for all the silk produced in Sicily and in the areas of southern Calabria.

The eggs of the bug were kept warm, wrapped in patches that women placed in their prosperous breasts. As soon as the bacherozzi were placed in trellises of intertwined reeds and fed with chopped mulberry leaves, of which the worms were very greedy.
When the amounts of ingested leaves exceeded the very flow rate of the insect's body; a cocoon of raw silk was eliminated from the bug through the slits of their mouth. This cocoon consisted of a single silk thread that could reach the length of 900 meters.

Subsequently, this raw silk, obtained from the worms, was sold by the farmers to the spinning mills that carried out the appropriate processing phases.

In the Spanish domination of that time, the city of Messina was ruled by the viceroy and an Ostrogoth who represented the Spanish crown; then there was the local power, represented by the city senate which was composed of the nobles of the city and the feudal lords of Messina or the surrounding parts.

In 1591, following a donation of 583 thousand scudi to Philip II, King of Spain and Sicily, the city of Messina obtained a tax privilege of government exemption regarding the trade and maritime shipments of silk; which allowed the Messina silk traders to establish a monopoly on the silk produced in the triangle: Termini-Messina-Syracuse.
In other words, as a result of this privilege, all the silk that was produced in Syracuse and Catania, could only be sold by the Messina merchants and could be exported exclusively from the port of Messina.

The activities of the silk sector were regulated by an institution called: *Consulate of the Art of Silk;* in the Peloritan city there was also a prestigious manufacturing activity as it was established, with the consent of the Spanish crown, the *Frankish Silk Fair* which attracted the presence of a considerable number of foreign merchants.

These political-economic privileges enjoyed by the City of Messina were the cause of contrasts with the other Sicilian cities, especially with Palermo: in 1610 the nobles of Palermo managed to have some of the privileges previously granted to the Messinesi businessmen revoked by the Crown of Spain.

The Spanish Crown gave *a blow to the circle and one to the barrel;*in the sense that it once favored Palermo over Messina or Messina over Palermo.

The relations maintained between the Senate of Messina, which represented the local power, with the various Spanish Ostrogoths, in the first half of the '600, began to deteriorate due to the violations of the tax exemptions previously granted.

While in the first half of the 1600s silk had become the most important export product in Sicily; on the second part of the century, signs of collapse in the sector come to light due to economic, political and cultural crises for the most part generated in Spain and by the competition of the silk trade that the city of Messina has to face with the cities of Palermo, Catania and Syracuse.

In the end, the Senate of Messina had to accept the new impositions by the dominant Spain and, as if that were not enough, it was precisely the Senate that imposed new and additional taxes on silk, as the sum of 583 thousand scudi, previously donated to the King of Spain, had been loaned by Genoese bankers at a high interest rate; who demanded payments for the extinction of the debt.

The practice of imposing new and burdensome taxes on silk by government and local institutions set in motion a stasis in the related trade by weakening the economy and finances of the city; as if that were not enough, a vicious circle was created that led to an increase in the costs of essential goods, such as the receipt of wheat and other cereals suitable for the consumption of the city population and the Val Demone, the latter acquired these products from the most profitable Val di Noto and Val di Mazara.

The tax burden of Spain, in the second half of the 1600s, became irrepressible for all the dominated parts: in 1647 the revolt of Masaniello broke out in Naples, now reduced to hunger, and the famine of 1671/72 was very serious and reaped victims throughout Sicily.

In Messina the situation became particularly critical: the poor flocked to the city from the surrounding lands and villages and to the shortage of wheat and food was added an epidemic that easily attacked poor people, because to feed themselves the were compelled to eat sordid foods.

Two factions were formed in the Peloritan city:

- That of the *MERLI* to which most of the artisans, petty bourgeoisie and ordinary people belonged; this class despite being pro-Spanish was against the power of the Ostrogoths, their motto was: Viva o Re e *fora u malu-guviernu.*
- That of the *MALVIZZI* to which belonged the class of the nobility, the great merchants and ecclesiastics, supporters of the local Senate, which had become anti-Spanish with the aim of making Messina a free city or a maritime republic as Genoa and Venice were.

Spain for its part tries to calm the minds of the people of Messina by providing wheat to alleviate the dramatic situation.

A historical event occurred in 1673, following the war between France and Spain within the Dutch situation in which there were Spanish possessions from the time of Charles V of Habsburg.

Holland was attacked by the French of Louis XIV and the English of Charles II to conquer the Spanish dominations from the Netherlands.

In the summer of that year the fleet French was in Sicilian waters.

The Malvizzi faction, which had formed a new Senate of Messina, began to weave contacts with the French emissaries, asking directly to Louis XIV - *the Sun King* - the French intervention to free the city from the Spanish power.

In 1674 a convoy of French ships arrived in Messina and 7 months later the city Senate, broke loyalty to the Spanish crown and swore allegiance to the Sun King; the French commander the *Duke of Vivienne* assumed the functions of viceroy; on that occasion the Spaniards surrendered and abandoning Messina took refuge in their fortress of Milazzo.

Sicily is at war between the cities that remain loyal to Spain and those who are on the side of the french occupation .

The French fleet conquered the port of Augusta in 1675 and the village of Melilli after a bloody siege.

Taormina, that was faithful to Spain, was occupied by French troops; Acireale heroically defended itself by land and sea from the French siege.

Between August and October 1677 the attempts by the French to take the Spanish strongholds of Licata, Milazzo, Syracuse and Catania ended without occupation.

In March 1678, the Sun King, given the impossibility of conquering the fortress of Milazzo, gave the order to prepare the evacuation of the French troops from Sicily, without giving any notice to the Messina senate that had also supported with weapons the French troops in the various sieges against the Spanish fortresses; shortly thereafter the *Peace of Nijmegen* was signed, which put an end to the hostilities between France and Spain.

The anti-Spanish revolt in the city of Messina, which occurred between July 1674 and April 1678, came to an end; the French troops withdrew from Messina, the Senate of Messina was suspended and the senatorial building was razed to the ground by Spanish troops.

The promoters of the Messina revolt were persecuted and their assets confiscated by the Spanish crown. For many members of the Malvizzi faction there was no other solution than to flee and find asylum in France.

The sources of this Messina revolution and full story against the Spanish domination in Sicily in the 17th century, are available in the writings of *Prof. Salvatore Bottari book: Post Res Perditas.*

In this book were also reported the events of the exodus of about four thousand Messina citizen, of which many of them no longer touched the Patrio Suolo, strongly described by *Tiziano De Nardo* who provides a description of the events, which agrees with the manuscript sources of the time when this exodus from the Port of Augusta to French port of Marseille took place.

To torchs those who longed to flee, arrived on the piers, dragging with their arms or carrying with wagons everything they hoped to save: Men, women, children, from the families of the highest lineage, to the most humble people; all equalled in the same catastrophe and in the stressful fate.

Hundreds of lifeboats shuttled between the ships and the docks, from which they detached loads until they *submerged, as in a hellish bolgia, between screams, cries and curses.*
The dawn turned out to be tragic: on the piers turbulence of imploring and cursing madly, they still contended for the last chances of salvation.
On the overloaded ships, the order was given to suspend boarding.
The French sailors brutally, fiercely repelled with oar blows those who still, on the benches and even swimming tried to hug each other at the edges of the boats.
Then an immense cry was raised from the crowd, on one side and on the other; a thousand and a thousand arms were raised to heaven and all the voices, all the feelings were in that cry.
The farewell, the weeping, the love of the earth and the relatives, the hatred, the fury and the curse:
A great, powerful and superb city was dying.

* * *

For historical duty, in 1701, caused the death of Charles II; the Habsburg dynasty came to an end in Sicily.

A few years later, following the War of the *Spanish Succession,* the throne of Sicily was conferred, with the placid good of the English, to Vittorio Amedeo II of *Savoy,* who after eight years, for intricate political issues, exchanged it, albeit reluctantly, with the isle of Sardinia.

Sicily became Austrian from 1720 to 1734; and then return to Spain through the cadet branch of the Spanish crown of the Bourbons who conquered the Kingdom of Naples in 1734 and the following year the Kingdom of Sicily: The Bourbon Kingdom of the Two Sicilies was born which lasted until 1860.

* * *

At the dawn of the nineteenth century the system began to regenerate, industrial innovations began to use machinery; the development of craftsmanship in our country became a great source of economic support; the new means of transport set in motion an adequate distribution of goods and the development of the railway network made Italy more united

In the gastronomic field, the integration and insertion of new foods with old ones made significant changes towards a food system certainly more appropriate for a modern society in the process of economic and cultural expansion.

The Americas freed themselves from European domination and forced slavery.

Despite the European uprisings of 1848 failed and the old rulers returned to their thrones; these revolutions made a profound change for consumers, especially the bourgeois classes and the proletarian classes.

With industrial development, the factory proletariat assumed a greater consistency by maturing a new working class united and associated to improve social conditions.

Charles Marx's manifesto laid the foundations for a new conception of Socialist *doctrines;* giving birth, in Europe: *The Workers' Movements.*

Let's see some developments, in general, over the centuries of the modern age:

- *In the years of 600, 700*

In 600 there followed famines and pestilences that were the cause of malnutrition and infections in the various European populations.

Italian gastronomic literature is silent, at a time when French cuisine triumphs in Europe.

The consumption of slaughtered meat will decrease, due to the excessive cost and the consumption of fresh fish was hindered by transport problems.

Instead, the consumption of preserved fish will increase, such as: *Smoked herring and the use of salted, smoked and dried fish.*

The 700 turned out to be an important century for agriculture with new plantations of *Rice, Buckwheat, Corn and Potatoes.*

Nervine Drinks made their entrance: *Coffee, Tea, Chocolate and Refined Sugar.*

The kitchen stove was invented, equipped with several burners, allowing with the gradation of the fires, a step forward for the cooking of meals and a better culinary preparation.

- *In the 800s*

They improved good table manners also for the use of the fork and other cutlery. Marketing and improvement of preservation techniques, such as: *Canning, freezing, freeze-drying.*

Development of means of transport, possibility of consumption of food produced in very distant places, with overcoming seasonality; predominant role on the use of vegetables in home canteens.

The use of chocolate on a large scale:

- The chocolate bar was invented in America in 1831

- Milk chocolate in 1875 in Switzerland
- In 1879 *Rudolph Lindt* invented chocolate that melts in the mouth

Beer Industrial Revolution:

- The new industrial alcoholic beverage, widely used and consumed, caused by the inventions of steam engines, with the use of thermometers for temperatures, devices for roasting and cooling malt, the study of the fermentation processes of sugar into alcohol and new techniques for bottling, as well as pasteurization and sterilization processes to slow down or eliminate microbial or bacteriological growth in liquids.

Liebig Meat Extracts

- In 1847 *Justus Von Liebig,* German chemist and inventor – Father of Gastronomy – developed a concentrate of beef extracts. The use of these extracts to compose broths for soups or for liquid dishes became an important invention as with a minimum expense and a minimum weight it was possible to feed a mass of people. Although the solid part of the meat was missing, certainly the broths constituted an important source of food; so much so that it was thought to use these extracts to defeat hunger on the African continent. Since it was necessary, for the industrial production of this product, an exasant quantity of lean beef and the cost of the raw material was high in the European markets; it was decided by the Liebig Company - which became a multinational - to carry out productions in South America and precisely in the State of Uruguay, where the cost of meat and labor were far lower than in Europe: it was necessary to find 30 kilos of beef to be able to produce only one kilo of extract. During 1864 about 30 thousand kilos of meat extract were produced in Uruguay and transferred to Europe.

Certainly all these gastronomic inventions were not applied in the same places and at the same times; they have, however, led mankind towards new systems of production and towards an effective diet destined not only to the survival of the population but also to the pleasures of life: Beer, Chocolate, Coffee and towards meditation with a cup of Tea.

*   *   *

Returning to the kitchens of our Sicily, the most specific and effective sources for our research can be found in the writings or gastronomic manuscripts, which our ancestors, in the literary field, have handed down to us or what our mothers have orally learned from the wisdom of their ancestors and transmitted to a future generation; in the hope that this new generation can preserve this cultural baggage and fully appreciate it, because: *Not only of Mac Donald lives the man.*

We have seen previously, based on the research of Mrs. Anna Martellotti, of the University of Perugia, the insertions of anonymous manuscripts: *Liber De Coquina and Anonimo Meridionale,* making them backdate between the twelfth and thirteenth centuries, to confer them in the *Treaties or Cookbooks Federiciani;* to these important sources of gastronomy, we can add the treatises between the fourteenth and fifteenth centuries, previously mentioned: The printed book of Bartolomeo Sacchi nicknamed: *Il Platina – De Honesta Voluptate et Valetudine –* and the manuscript of the excellent papal cook Martino *da Como,* contemporary and friend of Platina; dated back to the year 1460 with the title of: *Libro De Arte Coquinaria.*

We can still add to our sources another anonymous manuscript, dated at that time:
Book Modo Singulare De Cocina, in which culinary practices concerning Neapolitan, Roman and Emilian cuisine are developed.

What I personally believe can be a historical source of extreme importance for the knowledge of the basics of Sicilian cuisine; it would be the manuscript of *San Martino delle Scale,* - Benedictine Abbey located in the Municipality of Monreale, near the capital city of Palermo.
This recipe book in use in the seventeenth century, was written anonymously inside the famous Monastery, in clear seventeenth-century writing, contains a total of 102 recipes of which 82 deal with Sicilian gastronomy.

Recently *Stefano Rapisarda,*professor of philology at the University of Catania, has conducted a widespread study about the contents of this recipe book, inserting them in a gastronomic research entitled: *A Sicilian Baroque Cookbook.*

Before moving on to the review of the Book of San Martino, I think it is necessary to mention the chefs and writers who, in the modern age, with their works have made an invaluable contribution to national gastronomy, constituting precious sources:

- Bartolomeo Scappi: renowned Renaissance cook at the papal court of Pius IV, considered the Father of modern Italian cuisine. His *Gastronomic Work in 1570* contains more than a thousand recipes.
- Giovanni Del Turco: *Epistulary and Various Secrets –* Treatises on Tuscan and Florentine cuisine in seventeenth-century.
- Carlo Nascia: *Quattro Banchetti per Quattro Stagioni, 1684 –* Palermitan cook, at the Farnese Family
- Vincenzo Corrado: *Il Cuoco Galante, 1789 - Il Credenziere del Buon Gusto 1778 Del Cibo Pitagorico, 1781 –* The recipes of Corrado, who was a religious monk, felt very much the influence of French cuisine adapting it to Neapolitan and Roman dishes.
- Francesco Leonardi: *L'Apicio Moderno, 1790 -* He was a cook at the court of St. Petersburg in the service of Caterina The Great. Inventor of: *Fresh Tomato or Neapolitan Sauce..*

- Vincenzo Agnoletti: *Manuale del Cuoco e del Pasticciere, 1832* – Cook at the House of Duchess Maria Luigia of Parma and Piacenza.
- Ippolito Cavalcanti: *Theoretical-Practical Cuisine,* in Neapolitan language *1837* – Neapolitan Cook and Scholar. Among the gastronomic researches of Cavalcanti, we must mention: *Parmigiana di Melenzane, Panzerotto or Fried Pizza, Vermicelli with Clams, Fried Cod, Pasta and Beans, Maritata Soup, Pasta Cheese and Ova.*
- Pellegrino Artusi: *La Scienza in Cucina e l'Arte di Mangiar Bene, 1890* – A great gastronomic work.

*　*　*

In examining the Manuscript *Book of San Martino Delle Scale* Prof. Rapisarda notes different aspects and culinary customs:

- Goat's and cattle milk, eggs and dairy cheeses, such as: *Ricotta, Tuma, Caciocavallo,* are indicated with particular highlights; there are also references to Almond *milk* to replace milk of animal origin during the Lenten periods. The compositions of custards like *Biancomangiare or Mangiare Reale* are also presented; in the latter we have sweetened goat's milk with the addition of cinnamon and pine nuts and dates, which were diped for a long time, in rose water .
- Among the described meats stands out the use of game both; goat meat for stews, pork meat, including: *Friging sugne or lard, Sausages and Hams.*
  Among the fats such as butter and oil are also considered fats derived from the cooking of restricted broths of poultry, used in doughs for pies. Example how to make *Goat Pruning:* it would be a stew where meats are cut into small pieces and seasoned with wine and vinegar, in addition of raisins and plums; served with *Felle di Pane* or slices of bread wet in meat broth.
- The cooking methods are well indicated, in addition to the normal baking, wood or charcoal cooking; a particularly cooking method, used in peasant cuisine, is indicated to place a terracotta pan on the embers, cover it with a lidl and place other embers on it, called: *Cooking over fire below and above.*
- In general, the use of spices, in various recipes included in the manuscript, is considerable and ubiquitous in food preparations; the use of *Green Moss* ,for example, was an edible spice that was frequently used in ancient kitchens for the green color and the aromas it gave to food. In addition to moss and black pepper are used, in the foods of the recipes: *Cloves, Nutmeg, Anise, Cumin, Coriander, Saffron, Ginger.*
- The use of sugar, in the dishes of the recipe book, is almost excessive and even the *cinnamon* sticks play a very recurrent presence; the fusion between ricotta, sugar and cinnamon powders is one of the most magical inventions of Sicilian cuisine, which finds direct application in: *Cannoli and Cassate.* The presence of dried fruit should not be underestimated in the confectionery compositions; of which Sicilian cuisine is prodigal: *Almonds, Pine nuts, Pistachios, Hazelnuts, Raisins.*

- Among the drinks to note the use of *Cooked Wine,* in cooking and medicine practise; there would then be to consider the use of *Waters* for healing and recreation of the sick and convalescents: *Licorice Water, Cinnamon Water, Coriander* Water and *Anise Water;* the latter would be eupeptic as it promotes the secretion of gastric juices, favoring digestion and appetite. Among these compositions is mentioned also a food suitable for convalescents, called: *Pan Lavato;* a preparation that dates back to Roman times and had been the favorite meal of the Emperor Augustus: it is bathed in toasted bread in very cold rose water, then the bread is squeezed, sweetened and soaked with wine in the cold seasons or with lemon or pomegranate juices on summer days.

- Relevant in the San Martino manuscript book is the number of sauces that refer to medieval cooking practices: the term *Salsa* comes from the Latin *Salsus,* that is salty. The binding elements of these sauces were toasted crushed almonds, egg yolks and vinegar dressings; these sauces were served cold, flavored with ground cinnamon and served separately from food. More than sauces, these were refreshments for the palate; for modern sauces, intended as a condiment to impinguare meat, we have to wait for the French and in particular the cook *Francois Pierre La Varenne* in the mid-seventeenth century.

- There is no shortage of soups and related tips for preparations, for example, for the soup of *Ova and Latte;* whose advice would be: *With diligence always stirring until quail.* About the soups, it would be enough to quote the Latin phrase to compose a soup of bread and wine: *Panem et Vinum, mistum in unum, quod Vulgater dicitur "Czuppa";* phrase taken from the *Declarus,*Latin-Sicilian vocabulary compiled in the year 1300 by *Angelo Senisio,* Abbot of the Monastery of San Martino delle Scale.

- Some compositions have been defined as *Signorili or for Aristrocrats* that is suitable for a noble cuisine: La *Oglia, La Torta di Acqua d'Angeli, La Sciroppata di Cotogne, the Latte Miele.*

    1. The first composition involves a rich preparation of peacock or poultry meats and meats of wild animals such as rabbit, cooked in a large pot with vegetables, dried fruits, cheeses and spices.
    2. *The Torta d'Acqua d'Angeli* would be a compound of poultry meats such as capons and pigeons seasoned with various elements, sugars and spices, firmed with eggs and locked in an *Alasagna,* that is, lasagna-type puff pastry, to then be cooked in the oven.
    3. *The Honey Milk,* finally, would refer to a False *Ricotta,* prepared with egg whites, crushed almonds, sugar and rose water; the mixture is processed until it takes on the consistency of fresh ricotta, which, to look really true, is served in a wood cone container.

- The San Martino manuscript still contains recipes of fifteen cakes and four pies. In the cakes we resort to layers, called *Alasagna* with seasonings of spices, pine nuts and raisins; therefore, the last layer of the alasagna will be greased with fat, sprayed with rose water, sugar and cinnamon. For pies it is recommended, so that the surfaces are well browned, to brush a solution with sugar and egg whites; type of icing that is used for biscuits; a culinary practice that, in modern cuisine, would refer to the pasta of timbales that is intimately sweetened.

- In the number one recipe of San Martino Manscript, we find the *Collorelle biscuits;* that, in Ragusa, they would be the *Cuddureddi cò Mustu;* that is, gnocchi or *damplings* cooked in grape juices; a dessert that was used to celebrate the harvest of grapes.

- The *Mustacciuoli* are indicated in the recipe n.30, in this case the almonds are the main ingredient, blanched and reduced to flour; which is sweetened and spiced with pepper and cinnamon; finally the mustacciuoli are cooked over low heat so as not to lose their whiteness.

- The recipes numbered 34 and 35 are dedicated to *Nucatoli,* which have been previously described. The traditional dough, in the manuscript recipe, would be based on almonds, hazelnuts, honey, sugar and egg white; the compounds will be enriched with nuts and dried figs.

- Recipe no. 33 concerns: *To Make The Bread of Spain:* in France known as *Bisquit de Roy or Pain de Savoye.* In Sicily the biscuits of sponge cake are also called: *Savoiardi or Ferringozzi.* The term sponge cake was born when a Spanish cook, in presenting the recipe; he titled it: *Pan De Espagna Es Ec Vizcocho Originario De Saboya;* in reality, therefore, the dessert should not be considered as a Spanish influence in Sicilian or peninsular cuisine; the actual name would be: *Pan Di Savoia.*

The first known recipe of this kind of sponge cake dates back to 1636 in the *Book of Letters and Various Secrets,* written by the aforementioned Florentine confecrionary chef Giovanni del Turco. The oldest presentation of the dessert is found in an amazing wedding banquet between Cosimo dei Medici and Maria Maddalena of *Austria* in 1608; the chronicles report that, on that occasion, were served: *Slices of spanish sponge cake De Saboya.*

Comparing now the recipe of the sponge cake n. 33 of our recipe book, with the one provided by the book of Del Turco; the composition of the Palermo monastery would be much softer than the Florentine recipe.

- The recipe n. 36 tells us: *To make a dish of Cassate di Ricotta,*in this composition is provided for the cooking in the oven of a crust of soft dough which, after the blind baking,will be filled with a mixture of ricotta, sugar and aromas; like the grated lemon peels.

   This recipe would correspond well to the *Cassate Ragusane;* whose composition also appears in the research of the aforementioned gastronomic writers: Carlo Nascia, Vincenzo Corrado and Vincenzo Agnoletti.

   — Prof. Rapisarda in the aforementioned writing: *A Baroque Sicilian Cookbook* presents us with three compositions related to recipes of fish cuisine, taken from different book authors:

   Trotis In Pastillo - Taken from: *Liber De Coquina* .

   Affare Postello De Trocte – Taken from: *Anonimo Meridionale.* -

   To make breaded mullet or Luvari – Taken from the Manuscript of San Martino.

What Rapisarda wants to demonstrate would be the similarity of these compositions that belong to various medieval and Renaissance recipes related to Sicilian cuisine; which will then give life to a culinary uniformity in modern Sicilian cuisine.

In the recipes of San Martino Book, the weights for the used ingredients are indicated not in the decimal system but in the local measures in force at that time:

1. Libra – Unit of weight equal to 300 grams
2. Roll – Unit of weight equal to 790 grams
3. Onza - Unit of weight rquivalent to the 12th part of the roll
4. Fourth - Unit of weight corresponding to 6.61 grams
5. Crock - Unit of rquivalent weight at 0.044 grams - For pediatric portions -
6. Jonta - Amount contained in the union of two hands

Certainly the given informations and the various compositions found in the Manuscript of San Martino delle Scale are to be considered a precious source on which to draw the different aspects and faces of our cuisine; which would be endowed with complexity and articulations; as well as rich in specialties and sceneries .

*   *   *

A separate speech would deserve our Sicilian dessert par excellence, that is: **The Sicilian Cassasta** that lends itself well to the above, requirements of our cuisine.

Studies to find the origins of this dessert are conflicting; the hypotheses would be:

- The Arab origin; supporting the derivation of the term cassata with: *Qas'A* or *Kas'At* – According to the research of the aforementioned scholar Michele *Amari*.
- Etymological origin in classical Roman cuisine for comparison with the Latin term: *Caseata*; from *Caseus,*that is cheese or cheese focaccia.

From recent research carried out by the aforementioned gastronome Mrs Anna Martellotti, regarding the Latin derivation; what is stated in the vocabulary of the Declarus is mentioned: *Cibus ex Pasta Panis Caseo Recens Conmixtus, Qui Dicitur: Cassata.*

Despite the wording reported seems clear and unquestionable; Mrs. Martellotti came to argue that the gastronomic etymology, conducted only in words, does not always come to truthful solutions.

In order to reach proper conclusions, due account must be taken of the ingredients used in the composition; in order to find historical references.

The elements to compose the *Sicilian Cassata* would be:

- *Sponge cake,* soaked in liqueur
- Filled with *Sweet Ricotta Cream,* with candied fruit and dark chocolate flakes
- An outer band of *Royal Pastry,* colored green
- A cover of *White Icing* adorned with ribbons of pumpkin and candied fruit.
  Taking due account of the above elements; Mrs. Martellotti found historical reference:
- In an Arab-Persian cookbook, written around 950, by *Ibn Al-Warraq* in the Iraqi capital of Baghdad.
- *Tabik,* written in Baghdad in 1226, which contains about 160 recipes
- *Maghreb recipe book,* which describes the cuisine from the African coasts to the Spanish ones of Andalusia; dated in the thirteenth century therefore contemporary to the aforementioned Frederick cookbooks.

In these recipe books we start from compositions such as pancakes covered with syrup; and then move on to the floured variants that look like soft cakes in which the tool *Qas'A* is used, from which the writer M. Amari derives the name of cassata: would be a large cylindrical container that would accommodate these floured cakes.

A composition of these cakes, took the name of *Isfunja or Isfunia;* that is, a spongy cake with the ability to soak or absorb liquids; this new pastry composition came to Sicily from the Arab cuisine of north-west Africa.

What we call sponge cake in the composition of sicilian cassata; it would actually be a Cake *of Spongy Pastry,* deriving from Arab confectionery; which will turn out to be sprayed with liquid and perfected with the addition of sweet fragments, such as: almonds, pistachios, walnuts, cinnamon spices or pieces of white sugar.

It would then be attributed to the Normans the use of liqueur or sweet wine, to soak the cake; instead of milk used in Arabic cuisine; causes the alcoholic restrictions imposed by the Islamic religion.

The foregoing would identify the origin of the first element of the Sicilian cassata; the sponge cake soaked in liqueur.

The second element that concerns the Sicilian cassata would be: The outer band of almond paste colored green; it would be a *Royal Paste* prepared with pistachios; which was available both in Norman cuisine with the term French of *Festicade,* whose corresponding Arabic term would be *Fustaqiya.*

The third element of the *White Glaze;* it was well known to Arab pastry chefs; according to what is derived from the aforementioned *Tabikh* recipe book.

The origin of the candied fruit, which are part of the decorations of the cassata, seems to come from a Norman legend, around the year 1000, when they, coming from Jerusalem, landed in Salerno freeing the city from the Saracens; the liberators received rich gifts from the population of Salerno, among which were paid homage to food preciousness, such as: sugars, almonds and walnuts.

These events are narrated by *Amato da Montecassino,* in the year 1080; although on the episode of the gifts of sugared almonds or candied fruit, used on that occasion, many gastronomes would express serious doubts.

The final element that concerns the filling of ricotta with flakes of fondant; clearly for these chocolate chips, we have to wait for Columbus to discover the Americas; it would therefore be a modern innovation of Sicilian pastry.

As for the Latin etymology of *Caesus or Caseada,* these compositions, of which in the recipe book of San Martino are mentioned in recipe no. 36, that of the crust of soft dough; they would present analogies with: cassate infornate, cassatelle pasqualine iblee, ricotta ravioli, molise casciatelli and compositions of savory cassate such as: *Casatiello Napoletano.*

* * *

The historical events, facing the first half of the twentieth century, were characterized by:

- The First World War, the fascist dictatorship and the Second World War.

It is well known that wars bring hunger and famine and our beautiful country was certainly not spared from the disastrous events of that time.

In 1925 the new fascist regime had, sought and obtained, wide consensus on the part of Italian intellectuals; most of them adhered to a *Manifesto* to express their union and express their support for the Mussolini regime.

Taking as a model the poet, vate and patriot *Gabriele D'Annunzio;* among the signatories of this manifesto there were the adhesions of the philosopher *Giovanni Gentile* and of the writers and poets: *Ungaretti, Pirandello, Marinetti, Curzio Malaparte, Ardengo Soffici, Papini, Prezzolini;* as well as animators and critics of literary magazines.

One of the few intellectuals not to adhere to fascism was the philosopher and economist: *Benedetto Croce,* who, however, being a national figure, was not persecuted by the regime.

It must be emphasized, on the merits, that the literary works of the aforementioned intellectuals were not affected by compromises of any kind on the part of the regime; as there was a clear detachment between the fascist convictions and the poetic and literary art of these intellectuals; who have had the privilege of being part of the rich twentieth-century literature that is indelible in our anthologies of Italian literature.

The philosopher Giovanni Gentile, born in Castelvetrano, as a good Sicilian was also interested in social policy; publishing in 1919 in Bologna, an essay entitled: *Il tramonto della Cultura Siciliana;* in which the author draws a not particularly enthusiastic picture of the social and cultural situation of the island of that time.
In this essay the philosopher takes his clue from the disappearance of the three nineteenth-century Sicilian writers:
Giuseppe Pitrè, Salvatore Salomone Marino and Di Marzo; highlighting the great void that was created by the lack of these scholars in the Sicilian literary world.

For the philosopher Gentile, Sicily had been seized, ousted from the modern, for its historical events and for its own geographical configuration; cultural life was asphyxiated and provincial and Sicilian society had been tamed by a baronial class that weighed on the popular mass, in the presence of a rudimentary bourgeoisie and economically, socially: *Immature.*

In 1937 Giovanni Gentile presented to Mussolini, at Palazzo Venezia, the *Treccani Italian Encyclopedia* consisting of 35 volumes in which they were treated: *Art, Language and Literature – Social Sciences and History – Technology and Applied Sciences – Natural and Mathematical Sciences – Sport and Leisure.*

Because of the adherence to post-fascism, that is, italian Social Republic; the philosopher and professor Giovanni Gentile was, in 1944, the object of an attack perpetrated against his person: who killed Giovanni Gentile, was not anti-fascism but the crass ignorance of those who acted; Because: *Ignorance denies philosophy and with it human knowledge.*

* * *

In the agricultural and food sector, starting from 1924, the so-called Battle of the Wheat began in our *country;* born from the will of the Mussolini Regime.

To carry on this battle, *Prof. Nazzareno Strampelli* was commissioned by the regime who, making use of the study of crosses between different varieties of wheat, experimented with hybrid seeds, which the Professor himself defined: *Seed Elected*.

The results obtained, in the food field, were excellent and the new wheat harvests allowed considerable increases in yields per hectare; with substantial benefits in the food availability of our country and of the countries that adopted new cultivars, based on Italian agricultural techniques.

Note: In Pianto e in Riso- Considerazioni Agro-Alimentari sulla Risicoltura – Available at: Amazon.It – Author: Franco Campo.

* * *

On November 15, 1930, after a banquet held at the Milanese restaurant *La Penna d'Oca;*the writer and poet Filippo Tommaso *Marinetti* officially launched the proclamation of *Futurist Cuisine;* whose intentions were to reform the diet of Italians; directed to the liberation of the obsessions of eating dry pasta: A food, according to Marinetti, with bad requirements that involved heaviness of the stomach, endowed with deceptive nutritional properties and that led, for those who ate it abundantly, negative effects connected with skepticism, pessimism, indolence and laziness.

The *anti-pasta speach* of the vate Marinetti had the social purpose of forging the character of the Italians not only towards nationalism or patriotism but to strengthen their souls, spirit and muscles - not the abdominal ones - in view of future war actions directed to the conquests of empires; in other words, the purpose was subtle: *Fascism needed daring fighters, human sacrifices, fearless heroes, Aiaxes of the modern age and not spaghetti eaters*

In order to denigrate the macaroni, so loved by Romans and Neapolitans, it was affirmed, according to a phantom research called *Cronaca dei Memorabilia by Dacovio Saraceno,* that this composition, composed with *Spelt flour,* at that time not so appreciated, came from the barbaric legacy of the Ostrogoths; as it appeared for the first time in Italy in the Veronese or Ravenna canteens of Theodoric around the end of the fifth century; cooked by Rotufo, personal cook of the Gothic and Ostrogoth prince and served boiled with onions, garlic and pumpkin pulp.

Due to the popularization of this dish by an Italian cook, Rotufo's assistant, the said *Macarono,* was disclosed in the popular canteens oin the regions of Veneto and Romagna.

With the end of the Middle Ages, always according to the research of the members of Futurist cuisine, *the miserable macaroni* would have been destined to vanish from the Italian Renaissance canteens; if it had not been for that rascal of *Pietro Aretino,* in the sixteenth century, who reintroduced them in the festive banquets of the Roman curies together with songs, dances and music by diners and festive women.

For the sake of chronicles these macaroni also recur in *the Decameron of Boccaccio,* seasoned with milk and pulp of bitter almonds and in the *Lustful Sonnets by Pietro Aretino;*the latter character, was very renowned, in the school desks, because of the ironic epigraph of Paolo *Giovio:*

- *Here lies the Aretin, a Tuscan poet, who said badly of each one, except for Christ, apologizing with the saying: I do not know him.*

There would then be yet another reference, less literary, because of the erotic paintings in the work of the Lustful Sonnets:

- *Of all, only the Aretino Pietro was saved with one hand forward and another on the back.*

The so-called *Linguistic Autarchy* was established in our country by the Futurists;thanks to the contributions of Marinetti himself, the Greek professor Ettore *Romagnoli* and the poet *Angelo Silvio Novaro* was founded: *the Accademia d'Italia;* whose main tasks were to modify the French or Albionic dictions or terms and to adapt them to the purity of the Italian lexicon.

Graphic, phonetic, semantic and periphrase adaptations were implemented in the context of gastronomic dictions; so that every single food, sauce, cream, dish, food or drink; had an Italian name.

Just as the autarkic fascist regime had arranged; the work of the academics led to the adaptation, in Italian, of about two thousand foreign dictions; here are some direct examples:

- *Cocktail:* Harlequin or Polybibite Drink – *Yoghurt:* Bulgarian Milk – *Bechamel:* White Sauce - *Caramel Mou:* Tender Candy - *Chateaubriand Steak:* Breton Steak - *Bar:* Here you drink - The *Maître d'Hotel:* it was called as: *Guidapalato* - for the *Sandwich* was found by D'Annunzio the term Of *Tramezzino* , while Marinetti wanted to call it: *Between the two.*

The Duce personally addressed to Marinetti the epithet: *To my dear friend of the first fascist hour, to the intrepid soldier whose indomitable passion for the Fatherland, was consecrated with blood.*

The periods of *infrancesimento* that characterized many Italian recipe books of the 700 and 800; followed the clear and precise project of Italian national cuisine recognized in the work of Pellegrino Artusi; destined to become, in those years, a classic of its kind.

The works and gastronomic research of the Futurists did not become extinct with the Accademia d'Italia; in 1931 the first Italian Gastronomic Guide was founded which presented a division of products and recipes according to their regional belonging; Italian cuisine was topographically pulverized for each individual province of Italy; in search, however non-existent, of a national cuisine of reference.

The futurist poet F.T. Marinetti volunteered for the Campaign of Russia, despite being 66 years of age; he managed to return alive to Italy; but Russia turned out, for him and for many like him, a fatal undertaking.

Now tired and ill, he settled in Bellagio on Lake of Como, where, shortly thereafter in December 1944, he died of a cardiovascular attack.

By Mussolini's will Marinetti's body received the solemn funeral honors of the State and even the New York Times, the day after his death, dedicated an article to *Doctor Marinetti, Italian Author, early associate of Mussolini.*

Futurist cuisine, apart from some success among the Milanese bourgeoisie and aristocracy; he did not find gastronomic results in the rest of Italy; it has been and still is the subject of studies, more by Foreign British and American scholars, rather than in the gastronomic philosophy of the motherland.

A cuisine, the futurist one, which presented excesses and gastronomic extravagances; it could not be accepted in particular in the popular traditions of the cuisine of Southern Italy or insular: let's imagine the farmer who eats mortadella with nougat or salami immersed in coffee flavored with cologne or pineapple with sardines or even pineapple juice with caviar eggs, chilli, cloves and all flavored with Strega: heavy alcohol liqueur.

The diet of fascism included: rice, legumes, oil and wine; while reducing the consumption of meat and pasta.

In addition, Italy should have applied an autarkic food sovereignty; minimise imports and rely exclusively on domestic products.

After the good omens of *the Battle of the Wheat;*in the decade related to the'30s, the diet was not sufficient for an excellent and healthy survival of the Italian population and food deprivation was felt more in the North than in the South; when a Friulian housewife was asked what were the favorite dishes of her cuisine; she replied that Friulian cuisine was composed of three dishes: *Polenta, polenta and polenta.*

The Duce would have preferred the Italian people to feed on fascist idealism but, as the Mayor of Monza said: *The stomach has no ideals; it is conservative when it is full, to become an anarchist if it remains empty.*

*   *   *

Another undesirable cultural event for the fascist dictatorship; it took place in August 1938 following the article published in an Italian newspaper, directed by *Telesio Interlandi,* born in Sicily in Chiaramonte Gulfi, entitled: La Difesa della *Razza.*

A few days later the *Manifesto* of the Race was issued by the fascist government; in whose points or codes it was stated: The population of *present-day in Italy is in the majority of Arian origin and its civilization is Aryan.*

There is a pure Italian Race, based on the purest blood kinship that unites today's Italians.

This ancient purity of blood is the greatest title of nobility of the Italian Nation.
Jews do not belong to the Italian race.
Even the Arab occupation of Sicily has left nothing but the memory of some names; and, after all, the assimilation process took place very fast in Italy.
The Jews represent the only population that has never assimilated in Italy; because it is made up of non-European racial elements; absolutely different from the elements that gave rise to the Italians.

Among the signatories of this Manifesto, there were various university professors in the faculties of Social and Scientific Sciences: Pathology, Anthropology, Neuropsychiatry, Pediatrics, Endocrinology, Zoology, Physiology, Demography.

The *Declaration of the Race* was approved by the Grand Council of Fascism *in* October 1938, and was considered the document that will start Jewish persecution; giving rise to anti-Semitism; although in Italy, fortunately, these provisions did not cause mass deportations; as, unfortunately, happened in Nazi Germany.

*   *   *

By September 1939, Hitler's Germany had already invaded Poland; and our *Dux Imperator, the man who never slept – the Duce works – the man who was always right, the earthly demigod;* he expressed that: *He could not stand with his hands at his waist; he needed only a few thousands dead, and then take a seat alongside Hitler, on the table of partitions;* although, in fact, we would have been content with little.

Unfortunately for Him and for so many innocent Italian soldiers and families, things went differently and badly; after July 1943 it was no longer known which way the Italians had to fight; who was a friend and who was the enemy: The Duce, the King, the Germans, the Americans, the British; the partisans, who in turn, distinguished themselves in the large ranks of: communists, liberals, monarchists, republicans, anarchists and so on.

In poetry *August 1943;* the poet *Salvatore Quasimodo,* born in Modica, Nobel Prize 1959, wrote:

- *Do not dig wells in the courtyards: The living are no longer thirsty. Do not touch the dead, so red, so swollen; Leave them in the land of their homes. The city is dead.... is dead.*

In another ode, with biblical references: When the Jews, deported into slavery in Babylon, refused to sing for their oppressors and hung on the branches of the willows the musical instruments with which they used to accompany their verses:

And how could we sing
with the foreign foot above the heart,

among the dead abandoned in the squares,
on the hard grass of ice,
to the lamb's lament of the children,
to the black scream of the mother
who went to meet his son
crucifix on telegraph pole.
To the fronds of the willows, by vote,
even our zithers were hanging,
they swayed slightly in the sad wind.

After these disconcerting and truthful verses; continue on further development of facts relating to the war in the years 1943-45; it would make no sense for our research.

* * *

At the end of the war everything was missing, everything had to be rebuilt, so there was no shortage of things to do.

In 1946 a strong economic aid was given to Italy by the American Nation with the *European Recovery Program plan;* which materialized in 1950 with the *Marshall Plan;* conceived and designed by *George Marshall,* Secretary of State of the American President Truman.

On June 2 of the same year, the *Italian Republic* was proclaimed, with a new *Constitution* and a new President of the Republic: *Luigi Einaudi;* prime minister was appointed *Alcide De Gasperi,* whose assistant was such a *Giulio Andreotti,* the man of the Italian future.

The Sicilian Special Statute, issued by Umberto II of Savoy on May 15, 1946, prior to the Constitution of the Italian Republic, gave life to the **Sicilian Region:** finally in Sicily we have a Constitutional *Parliament;* as it was converted into Constitutional Law in March 1948.

The Sicilians were granted the long-awaited *Special Autonomy;* to stop, with the laws, *the Sicilian independence of EVIS* – Ente Volontario Indipendenza Sicilia – and of the *MIS*
Sicilian Independent Movement; whose main exponent was the *AFA* parliamentarian – Andrea Finocchiaro Aprile – who in any case participated in the *Sicilian Constituent Assembly,*of June 2, 1946, on the same date on which the Italian Republic was proclaimed.

The legal structure of the *Special Statute of the Sicilian Region consisted* of *Five Titles* concerning: *Organs of the Region – Functions of the Regional Bodies – Jurisdictional Bodies – Police – Heritage and Finance.*

Article no. 17 of this Statute, relating to the *Title of the Functions of the Regional Bodies,* gave the Sicilian Region the power to issue laws concerning:

- *Communication and Transport – Hygiene and Health – Public Media and University Education Credit, Savings and Insurance Discipline – Social Legislation relating to Labour Relations and Social Assistance – Annonaria Policy – Recruitment of Public Services – Subjects involving Services of prevailing regional interest.*

In Italy there was a post-war global damage, calculated at 3,200 billion lire: particularly affected were the steel-industrial apparatus, the transport system including roads, ports, railways and homes; destroyed due to the various German and American bombings.

In the city's building apparatus there was often a lack of: running water, electricity, writing paper, wood or coal for cooking or heating.

*   *   *

In October 1944, after the fall of Fascism in Sicily and Southern Italy, in the Provisional Government of the South, he was appointed Minister of Agriculture: the Calabrian lawyer *Fausto Gullo,* who issued the famous decree n. 279 in which the distribution of uncultivated or poorly cultivated land to peasants or cooperatives of peasants; this decree was contemplated on the basis of long waited reform of agrarian pacts.

The hopes of the Sicilian *peasants* who had failed to *obtain* the coveted secular lands, neither under the dominion of the Bourbons, nor under the dominion of the Savoy or under the dominion of Mussolini; were rekindled, on the basis of the aforementioned ministerial decree that became a Sovereign *Act* in April 1946, bearing the signature of Umberto II of *Savoy* and the subsequent publication in the official gazette of the Kingdom of Italy.

The agrarian situation in Sicily, in the western part in particular, was still dominated by large land holdings and the Gullo decree was intended to break the centuries-old latifundium; cause of underdevelopment and poverty for farmers and agricultural laborers.
In other words, the Decree in question limited private property in relation to agricultural production.

There were attempts by peasant cooperatives who tried to take possession of some uncultivated land, planting red flags in the land as a sign of occupation of the soils.
The next day, these peasants found on the spot the carabinieri who forbade with weapons access to people and agricultural vehicles in the aforementioned lands, citing the peasants under accusation of violation of private property.

Committees of solidarity and assistance to the accused peasants were formed for this purpose, but the Gullo Decree could also have been called *the Null Decree,*because it did not produce any real, practical or legal effect of occupation of uncultivated lands.

In 1950 at the Sicilian Regional Assembly the law of the *Agrarian Reform* was approved, conforming to the directives of the Central Government of Rome; once again the opportunity to expropriate the uncultivated land to be granted to needy peasants was discussed in the Sicilian Assembly.

To this end, the Assembly appointed the Regional Deputy *Gioacchino Germanà of Lercara Friddi in* the province of Palermo, who had previously served in the ranks of the Independence Movement of *Finocchiaro Aprile* and after the dissolution of the independence party, had joined the ranks of the Italian Liberal Party whose political secretary, at the time, was the On *Olindo Malagodi.*

Germanà was called the Carabiniere of the *Agrarian Reform* for his dedication in finding the funds assigned by the Central Government, intended for the modernization of infrastructures, reclamation in the Sicilian agricultural sector that so needed roads, electricity and means to increase the annual production of crops and to improve the system of life in the work activities of farmers and laborers.

Apart from the renewal of agricultural structures and infrastructures in Sicily; at that time, as many as 12 thousand lots of uncultivated land were assigned to the peasants, taking them away from the landowners.

For these concessions, concerning the application of state laws aimed at the well-being of the Sicilian agricultural population, the politician Gioacchino Germanà suffered personal threats, was beaten, was expelled, by order of Malagodi, from his own party that was of clear bourgeois and anti-popular brand; but he, with strenuous courage and in the personal awareness of doing good and right to his land, managed to carry out, successfully, all the programs of agrarian reform.

Certainly having done his duty and for not having adhered to party compromises or accepted the rich proposals addressed to him by the counterparts; the political career of Joachim Germanà had no implications; so much so that, once he had completed the government programs, He retired from the scenes of politics.

Allow me, as evidence of the above, to transcribe an excerpt of the intervention that Gioacchino Germanà, as Councilor for Agriculture, addressed in October 1954 to the Sicilian Assembly:
Hon. The President, On.li Colleagues

*The historical fact is summed up in the joyful and solemn announcement that I have the honor and satisfaction to give you, namely that as many as **12 thousand peasants,**poor indeed destitute, have had the **Land** and already merge what can be called: The rural economy of tomorrow.*

This happened as a result of the implementation of the law of agrarian reform, decisively and inflexibly pursued by the Government, a law that for its political and human purposes to which it is inspired, does honor to our Assembly.

And allow me to send greetings and good wishes to these peasants on behalf of the Government and the Assembly, so that, in the satisfied need for work and justice, they may find that serenity of spirit and judgment, looking with confidence to their tomorrow.

The Municipality of the town of Lercara Friddi dedicated a statue depicting the bust to the memory of its valiant citizen; not the politicians but the Sicilian people recognized in Gioacchino Germanà their benefactor.

* * *

The Italian economy was entrusted to *the IRI – Istituto Ricostruzione Industriale –* already founded at the time of fascism; which had the arduous task of relaunching the Italian economy, during the phase of post-war reconstruction and the beginning of what would go down in history as the: *Economic Boom.*

The Italian development of this *Miracle* did not take place homogeneously in the various Italian regions; creating a dualism or an imbalance between the industrial North and the agricultural South.

One of the characteristics of this *Miracle* can be identified in the so-called: *Consumerism;* that is, the phenomenon of encouraging, to an increasing extent, the purchase of goods and services, provided by industrialized companies; through advertising messages, conveyed by RAI State Television and printed newspapers.

Economically, in order for consumerism to become effective as a production of goods and services, it would be considered necessary for consumer demand to be constantly sustained; a system that induces the State to intervene towards the policies of monetary expansion; which would constitute, in a broad sense, the creation of what is called: *Capitalist System or Capitalism.*

Starting from the second half of the '900, a series of profound changes caused by a greater economic availability; they have guaranteed the passage of the consumer society towards a modern-industrial diet. Similar availability has also resulted from the development of transport systems, the introduction of refrigerators and freezers and the opening of supermarkets with the display and availability of food from other regions; and then, with the passing of time, we moved on to globalized discoveries, such as: *Kebab, Sushi, Stir-fry, Curries.*

In some respects, it can be said that eating styles have greatly improved compared to the beginning of the last century; when the tables of the house or country were lacking in products necessary for a correct physical development of the organism.

In the past, a person's physical well-being was at risk for diseases, such as: *scurvy, rickets, goiter, pellagra* – for those who ate only polenta – *cretinism, chronic diarrhea.*

Nowadays, the excessive use of sugars, animal and vegetable fats, artificial additives to promote the preservation and aesthetic quality of industrial foods; exposes anyone to the risk of contracting diseases, such as: *Obesity, diabetes, hypertension, gastro-intestinal disorders.*

The food traditions of a nation or a region have been created and shaped by contacts between cultures that have met, developed, overlapped in a history made of customs, knowledge, specificity, shared experiences; which constitute the personal identity and the right to belong to this community.

* * *

Sicily is not a rich land but it is a lucky land because it has the richest, most varied and valuable heritage of typical products that, recently, are included in a food system, known as: **Mediterranean Diet;**and this recognition was, not surprisingly, attributed to the countries of the Mediterranean Basin; in November 2010, byUNESCO – United Nations*Educational, Scientific and Cultural Organisation* - as *Intangible Cultural Heritage.*

The eating habits of Sicily and the South Peninsular, have reached the optimum for a healthy diet and for the daily use of foods such as: *Olive Oil, Fruit and Vegetables, Cereals, Legumes and Fish.*
The prevalence of these foods, in Sicilian food customs, means that their association and integration with other plants; reduce the risk of so-called diseases of: *Well-being.*

The enhancement of the Mediterranean diet and the aforementioned awards must be attributed to the studies and food research conducted by the *American Doctor and Physiologist: Ancel Benjamin Kays – 1904, 2004 –* who recognized and consecrated the positive influence of the Mediterranean Diet as a prevention against cardiovascular diseases and pathologies; compared to the official data of the pathologies in the USA and North-European countries.
The basic ingredients of the Mediterranean diet found by American doctors, highlighting their dietary principles, would be found in the following elements:

- *Vegetables and Seasonal Fruits and Dried Fruits – Cereals, Legumes and Vegetables – Fish and Meat:* not in abundance – *Eggs and Cheeses:* without exaggerating – Olive *Oil:* to be used as seasoning and better if virgin or extra – *wine:* to be used in moderation during meals.

The food balance of these ingredients must consist of:

- *Carbohydrates* 55-60 percent
- *Fat* 30 percent
- *Protein* 10-15 percent

According to these guidelines, 60 percent of daily calories must come from carbohydrates; half of these carbohydrates must come from *cereal starches,* namely: *Bread and Pasta;* which are the basis of the diet for constant daily consumption; which contain carbohydrates and proteins; but it is not possible to consider them well-balanced elements due to the reduced content of Lipids, that is, fats: eating only bread or unseasy dough is not sufficient for proper human nutrition; the most common supplements are to be found in the union of the *Bread with companatico – cheese – and Pasta with condiments – tomato sauce –* in this way the quantitative and qualitative values of proteins and lipids are raised; comparable with the mentioned balance of the Mediterranean diet.

Legumes are also low in fat – except for soy and peanuts – but are rich in proteins, starches, and dietary fiber: for these characteristics they fit well into the diet in question.

Fruits and vegetables are linked not only to the presence of dietary fiber, mineral salts and vitamins; but also for different compounds with antioxidant activity; that is, chemical agents that slow down the oxidation produced by other substances.

Olive oil is the main source of fat in the Mediterranean diet; in which the most considered fatty acid is *Monounsaturated,* whose consumption reduces arteriosclerosis, cholesterol and cardiovascular diseases; unlike saturated fats of animal origin.

Small-scale fishing is widely carried out in the ports or inlets of the coastal strip; while the offshore one is carried out with fishing motorcycles in the ports located along the coast.

In *the Mare Nostrum* there are more than 30 thousand species of fish; some very valuable classes, others poorer but no less delicious on the palate: white fish, blue fish, molluscs, crustaceans, tuna, swordfish and invertebrates.

In Sicily, cattle and goat farms are carried out in the wild and semi-wild, in natural pastures, in arable land or in the woods.

The Sicilian cultivated areas consist of:

1. Dry surfaces, present in the internal area, with arable areas of cereals, leguminous crops, vegetables and dried fruits, such as: Almond, hazel and pistachio
2. Irrigated surfaces, present in the coastal strips, such as: Citrus fruits, vegetables and fresh fruit.
3. Also to be considered are the areas of cultivation with olive groves and vineyards; which can be part of both systems: dry or irrigated.

Ultimately, the *Mediterranean Diet* expresses, as a whole, a culture of food related to the attention of the genres and the qualities of the foods, attesting to the simplicity of the preparations that can be made:

1. On natural ingredients of vegetable origin - vegetables, legumes, cereals - or of animal origin - fish, game, milk, eggs -

2. On semi-processed ingredients, that is, those products that undergo manipulation, before being consumed, such as: Salt, spices, centrifuged foods

3. Based on the preparations of natural and semi-finished products; the finished dishes are composed, put in place following a specific recipe or making the best of it.

*　*　*

The planet is indifferent to human needs, so wrote the philosopher *Immanuel Kant* in 1700; humans are indifferent to the planet; so said the Swedish girl Greta *Thunberg,* ecologist and activist against the events of climate globalization; from these quotes it seems that the systems we have imposed on this planet and the systems that, in turn, the planet has imposed on us, are oriented by the regime of global indifference.

Consumerism has become global, therefore indifferent to the ancient eating habits of peoples, indifferent to the history and cultural traditions of the territory; in other words, human nutrition is now entirely controlled by a few and fierce multinational companies that tend to homologate food systems.

Flavors are increasingly standardized and some food traditions of basic or traditional recipes; they are no longer part of our knowledge and the cultural identity of people and places.

This indifference, now rooted, is denoted in the ways, rites and hearts of a globally urban society that no longer makes use of the principles of generosity, hospitality, mutual help, which was expressed in the rites of sharing bread together, of offering what little we have to those who have less than us.

The peasants and the offspring of peasats have become extinct; they were crude and illiterate, unkind and not very affable; but they were endowed with an almost childlike generosity towards the guests, the gifts of food, the comfort of a word, the benevolent smile of a housewitness, the mutual aid in the fields to collect the crops, the cooperation to take care of the animals or not to accumulate the rains in the roofs.
The children of the peasants have become workers, the children of the workers have become employees, the children of the employees have become doctors, and in this new and erudite *Silicon Valley,* many of these doctors are unemployed; living on the shoulders of their parents or grandparents.

The different behaviors resulting from the rapid and profound change in society, have changed lifestyles and also significantly affected food traditions; upsetting them under the pressure of a globalization implemented by business strategies and markets; dictated by a series of economic and social changes.

When on holidays or on the religious anniversaries of Christmas or Easter, I see young people who go to eat at MacDonald's; I feel saddened and I think: But these people will have a family, a mother who will have got up early to do the shopping, to cook roasts, to prepare sauces for the condiments of traditional festive dishes; how will these young people spend Easter without a cassatella, without a slice of breaded bread, without a glass of wine; without the smile of parents, the joy of siblings, the tenderness of grandparents.

Certainly I lived in a world that has now faded; I do not want to emphasize that traditional cuisine was far more genuine or better than the one that is prepared at this time; even if you can revive the flavors of the dishes; the peasant or bourgeois world that gave birth to them is now buried.

For us Sicilians we do not want to make a comparison between local foods and global foods; because, when the processes become too pushed, that need arises in us not to get lost; the nostalgia and melancholy make us remember the memories of those *Maccarruna in Ciazzisa, of the sauces, of the crazy waters, of the cottate of beans and why not; even for the scrambled eggs with fresh ricotta.*

True, there was in the 50s, a food inety; but we have overcome it; indeed, from this precariousness our mothers have created a model of cuisine, based on the techniques of simplicity; a gastronomic model that rank chefs try in vain to represent in their dishes so adorned with colorful sauces: simplicity in the kitchen is a difficult art to achieve; because with it you can reach the gastronomic spirituality

CAPITOLO III:
APPUNTI STORICO-GASTRONOMICI NEL TERRITORIO SICILIANO

LA MIA STORIA

PARAGRAFO I: CIVILTÀ GASTRONOMICA IBLEA

PARAGRAFO II: LA PERDUTA GIOVENTÙ

EPILOGO

CIVILTÀ GASTRONOMICA IBLEA

Lu Sabbatu si ciama allegra cori
miatu cu bedda l'havi la mugghieri
picchi' cu l'havi brutta, ci scura lu cori
e funnu di pararisu non ni viri.
Iu haiu na zita, ca si ciama: Nedda
bedda di facci ma senza murudda,
ci rissi: na ramu na vasatedda?
No – m'arispunniu – picchi' manciai cipudda.
Versi della canzone: *Ciuri, Ciuri*

During the WWII my father was *a Royal Sailor* in Cyrenaica, Lybia
In 1942 he was taken prisoner by the British and forced, along with thousands of Italian soldiers, to cross the desert with hunger and thirst; they arrived on the shores of the Mediterranean and were placed in the hold of a ship to be embarked towards the *White Cliffs of Dover*.
In his opinion: somewhere in England, my father spent the most beautiful period of his existence.

Back in Sicily, he married my mother in August 1946.

The two spouses, as children of two brothers, were also first cousins.
Shortly thereafter, my father's brother married my mother's sister; the two married couples moved to the paternal countryside located in *Contrada Mieta,*which could mean: *Quiet place* or could refer to the wheat harvests that were carried out in that place.

Our Mieta farm is accessible on the road from Ragusa towards the seaside of Marina; in the entrances of *Cimillà* or *Tribastone;* bordering the districts of *Magni' and Scifazzo;* it is located at the bottom of the valley where you can see on the horizon the road of *Malavita* and from the parts of the Malavita passed a railway line; which the peasants called: *U Treno di Ciccio Piecura;*and they based their schedules according to the sight of the passages of the locomotives and the littorine.
For completeness of topic; there was, in the city of Ragusa, a toy shopkeeper and among the merchandise of the store there were toy trains to entertain the children; the Ragusans compared the toy trains with the rail locomotive that traveled from Syracuse to Vizzini and Ragusa.

So my family came to be more united than ever together with that of the uncles; our geenertion were transformed into agricultural: we were direct farmers, breeders and peasants but without *a glimpse,* in the sense that we were not obtuse and our hands were not calloused.

Until the age of eight I was a guest of my paternal grandparents, in the house of Ragusa, located in Via Sirena, in the city district of *Ecce Homo.*

My childhood with my grandparents was not bad at all; grandfather Franco was a regular of *Caffè Mediterraneo;* he took me with him and we sat in the table occupied by the owner; Mr. Turiddu Tumino, who had been a builder and people had given him the nickname of: *Turi Papuri,*because he had made so much money to be able to full the holds of a steamship. While my grandfather argued with Mr. Tumino; I was served a cup of *Whipped Cream with chocolate vermicelli;* a welcome present from the owner, Mr Tumino himself .

Sometimes, grandfather Franco, took me to the main square *of Piazza San Giovanni at Caffè Italia;* where there were exposed in the counter many beautiful pastries such as *the Diplomats and Heads of Turk;*while in the ice cream shop was renowned: *La Cassata Semifreddo.*

Grandma Marietta was endowed with a ringing voice and often the cries were heard even in the neighboring areas, she reproached her husband because he always spent time outside the house instead of taking care of his wife and devoting himself to household chores: Let's imagine my grandfather washing dishes or passing the rag; when ever, not even for a dream.

My grandfather Franco gave to his wife the nickname of *Canaria* from a melancholic Neapolitan song: *Si, Tu si a Canaria, Tu si l'Ammore.*

Grandma Marietta did not devote herself too much to cooking, but she was a good cook; I remeber her breakfast: *The artichokes stuffed with a soft filling of cheese and breadcrumbs enriched with anchovies.*

After steaming the artochoke, the soft and stuffed leaves were dipped, one at a time, in a composition of oil and vinegar and the more the artichoke was browsed, the softer and tastier the leaves bicame; then there was the final bite, that is the stem of the *artichoke,* which properly cleaned of the skins, was *immersed in that uncompact solution of oil and vinegar:* the bite caused voluptuous chills, which migrated from the oral cavity into the inner parts of the body.

Then, grandmother Marietta, in the autumn months, prepared a truly *Sicilian Caponata:* the frying of vegetables in that huge pan and the noises of the thick oil of the lock, which attacked the segments of peppers, the diced eggplants, the circumferences of white onions and darkened the pieces of the beneficial garlic, the green olives previously crushed; the intense green of the capers collected in the valley; they were the chosen ingredients of this well-known composition in - *ajru-aruci* - sweet and sour flavors.

Towards the end of the cooking, in fact, the grandmother poured into the contents of the sprays of red vinegar, which had the power to make jump all the ingredients that melted evenly in the sour liquid, joined with the natural juices of the vegetables. The culinary use of sugars as a result of cooking, melted into those sauces, mixing the contents with complacency, had the effect of soothing the impetuosity sorrel; in the process of caramelization.

Another condiment was the oregano that was spread on the surfaces of the caponata, whose flakes lay down, as if to kiss that reddish sauce, caused by the sunny tomato extracts, which was ready to welcome him, like a tender lover, to receive the fragrances of country perfumes.

The stop of the caponata in the cooking pan that was properly covered, so that the luke worm ingredients and sauces could be more magnificent in flavors, colors, structures and join harmoniously as in a chorus of musical notes.

In this tenacious culinary composition, the magical touch was *the Shell of Basilicò* that she planted in the middle of the caponata, like a flower: In the Islamic religion it is believed that the green meadows and streams of clear waters, which will welcome the elects in Paradise, will smell intensely, emulating the scents of basil.

The recurring foods in the grandparents' house were broths:

- On Friday *Cod in Broth* because of the precepts of the Church that forbade the food use of meat for that day of the week and during the Lenten period. –

The preparation of this dish was simple: Compose a vegetable broth with garlic, diced tomato pachino and chopped parsley, pour a little olive oil, spice it with black pepper and cover everything abundantly with spring water or white wine.

When the broth is ready and you notice that the contents are a beautiful color, pleasing to the eye and on the palate; place the whole but gutted fish in the liquids of the broth and make them cook, with the liquids in motion, for 10-15 minutes, depending on their size.

Take out the fish from the broth, check the cooking and de-bone the cods.

Place the white fillets on a serving plates and sprinkle them at will with the cooking broth; the grandmother served cod *in Sciusceddu* - that is, by the breath - with slices of toasted bread.

Sunday lunch: *Meat Broth and Boiled Beef.*

As soon as the grandmother presented the veal bone at the table, my grandfather cut two slices of bread and on top of them he beat the bone to make sure that the marrow rested on top of the two slices that, so greased, were spiced with black pepper and seasoned with grated caciocavallo; these two slices were: One for me and one for my grandfather; while the grandmother abstained.

After this appetizing appetizer, Grandma presented the beef broth with the star-shaped pasta. The subsequent problem was that, after consuming half of the broth, the grandfather used to season the rest of his broth with chocolate; this custom provoked the regrets of Marietta but he did not worry so much: *I like my broth in this way* .

Grandma preferred boiled meat to broth more, with green sauce condiments, like *Bignè Piemontese.* Grandma's condiments were:*Chopped parsley, garlic, oil, capers and* a few red chili flakes.

*   *   *

In front of the grandparents' house there was the workshop of a blacksmith; *Don Pippinu* who worked in his forge blackened by the smoke of the forge. Once my grandmother commissioned him a grater and I personally saw how the work was carried out in the workshop that developed to the fire fed by the bellows; whose task was to shape and forge the hot iron with the gestures marked by the beating of the hammer on the anvil in which the ancient art of making tools and artifacts took place.

Don Pippino, after forging a thin slab of iron and having it properly curved, came to practice with an awl and the hammer the symmetrical holes on the grater, from these holes then sprouted, in the outer part of the slab, the pointed edges that will prove useful for grating the aged cheese; the making of the artifact turned out to be imperishable and again, this grater, it will be somewhere: *how nice it would be to see it again.*

The Sicilian handicrafts have remained authentic works of art that were made in the wrought iron balconies and in the gates of the houses or palaces of the two Ragusa; as well as the presence of architectural murals of imaginative or ghostly figures supporting the balconies; they are a constant theme of the late-Baroque style of priceless artistic heritage.
For historical and artistic duty, after the terrible earthquake or trembling of January 11, 1693 all of Eastern Sicily within a few years, changed its turn: The countries destroyed in the Val di Noto, adopted without reservation the architectural style to *the BAROQUE,* giving life to its important branch that will in fact be known as Sicilian *Baroque,* an architectural concentration that will be declared in 2002 by UNESCO as *a World Heritage Site.*

*   *   *

In the street adjacent to the Via Sirena there was the carpentry workshop of *Mastro Don Angelino,* equipped with pliers, pincers, drills, electric saws and tools suitable for seasoned woodworking; concerning the construction of household furniture such as: wardrobes, boards, windows, doors, chairs and headboards of beds.

He wore short pants and I the zuava pants, and together we ran through the narrow alleys surrounding to the Chambers of Ecce Homo church.
N'Zino, despite being older than me, couldn't catch me; his legs were slender and curved.
Then, I saw him panting, so I stopped running so that he could catch his breath.
I told him the exploits of the western movies that I had seen at the *Cinema Marino,* of how the *Indians of Crazy Horse* had rebelled and had attacked the fort of the soldiers in blue uniform that heroically defended themselves against the skirmishes of the savages: In reality the savages were not the Indians of the Crazy Horse tribe and the heroes were not, seems to me, the soldiers in the blue uniform.
N'Zino listened at my srories with his mouth open, He had never gone to a cinema; as he had not attended any school; he could not express himself well because he had a stuttering impidement speech.
N'Zino was hovering around the workshop of Mastro Angelino who made him occupied to smooth the wooden boards with a glass paper.

Sometimes I helped him in his task, because his body was slender and weak; and so do I discarded wooden planks and boards; so that the carpenter could give to N'zino a few pennies more.

Once, I accompanied him home and entered the room where his elderly parents lived.

They sat with the blankets turned over to warm their bodies,their arms and legs;

I remember the high ceiling of that room, where it had to be so cold; there was no greeting nor a word between me and his parents; sometimes silence speaks for itself; there is no words to express the hardships of poverty.

After I had accomplished the third year at infancy school; my parents, who had moved from the countryside to the sea, claimed thir son as if they had lost a postal package and then I abandoned the grandparents paternal house, the cups of whipped cream of the Mediterranean Cafe and I headed to the beaches.

I returned sporadically to the house in Via Sirena, I almost forgot about N'Zino, nor did I saw him hanging out in the carpenter's shop.

Years later, casually learned from a daily local newspaper that:

Mr. *Vincenzo Criscione of 20 years had passed away* .

After a moment of bewilderment, wondering who could have died at 20 years old ?

Christ, I said to myself, this is: *N'Zino.*

No one in the neighborhood gave any announcement of him,I presume the parents will have died before Him because they were elderly and N'Zino could have been taken into care in some Institute for the needy.

My friend went without possibly taking a bath in the sea, without having received a smile from a girl, without the comfort of a friend o relative and perhaps without any of those fucking things that life should have to pay homage to a young man in the prime of youth.

Goodbye, my dear friend, if I could go back I would liked to be by your side and tell you again the stories of the epic battles of the movies seen at Cinema Marino, to entertain you and your imagination to be the hero, like John Wayne was in his movies; because you have for sure been a hero in your brief life.

* * *

Among the delicacies of the foods of memory there is also the *Quince Jam.*

In the garden of the Mieta there was, among other things, a large quince tree and in the autumn, these large fruits were collected, to make jam.

My mother and my auntie first boiled these apples, then their pulp was joined with the same weight of sugar. Once the jam was made, the compost was arranged in ceramic containers of various shapes that were hollowed in the bases with abstract and baroque designs.

When the ceramic form was turned upside down on a plate; one could admire these ornate designs on the surface of the jam; it is no coincidence that our cuisine is part of the Baroque culture.

Then these compositions of quince came to the grandmother's house; which placed the jams in a wicker basket covered with a gauze cloth and placed them in the long balcony gallery overlooking the dead end court.
The aim was to dry the jams in the beneficial sun so that exposure to sunlight dried the jams even more, making the sugars emerge and make the composition even sweeter, more compact, and then be more pleasant on the palate.

When I lyed on the balcony I couldn't help but admire these forms of jam, so shiny, with those inviting designs; it seems that they were saying to me: *Take me, I am Yours.*
Taken by temptations, I lifted the veil and chose the shape of the smallest jam, so that the grandmother would not notice it; the one that had as its drawing the shape of a little fish swimming in concentric waves. I ate it hidden in small bites to be able to savor it in all its goodness.

Suddenly the grandmother arrived: *Ah -Tia, Vastasi* and headed towards me with her lips clenched and her hand raised; I curled up in fear; then: The *clenched lips turned into a smile and the hand,*which had been raised by mistake, became an affectionate hug.

An indelible event, of which grandmother Marietta was the protagonist; it was the fact that every Sunday morning she gave me castor oil to drink; I categorically refused to take that repulsive compound, also because there was no need for it.

One Sunday morning, she said to me: *Francuzzo, would you like a coffee?*
I had never had a coffee but I knew that adults appreciated a cup of coffee; I was excited by the proposal and accepted the offer.

That grany put castor oil inside the coffee; I also spat my soul out of the deep disgust of that concoction. After that purgative coffee, before he drank another, 40 years passed without being able to have a coffee; to the memory of castor oil.

However, I consider myself lucky; because think if my grandmother had put castor oil in wine; I would have become a teetotary and national oenology would be worth losing one of its admirers.

* * *

A recurring composition at the grandparents' house were the *Viscotta Scaurati,*also called: *Affuca Parrini;*which, however, were prepared by my mother on behalf of her mother in law: Marietta.

From the acquired data, the ingredients would be: *700 grams of durum wheat flour, 300 grams of Mallorcan flour, 8 eggs, 200 grams of sugar, 50 grams of suet and 10 grams of cumin or fennel or anise seeds.*

*Procedure: Use*the two flours and rub the suet with the flours so as to compose the bread crumbs. Combine the beaten eggs with sugar and fennel seeds that in Sicily are more available than cumin or anise and mix the mixture well.
Arrange the fattened flour from the sued to a basin and arrange the sugary eggs in the middle.
Work the dough for a long time, without using water, in order to obtain a smooth and compact mass.
At this point you could compose the biscuits, forming with the dough sticks that can be cut into cubes like taralli or to tracksed wheels, in the shape of glasses or giving a shape to them.
Once made the biscuits of various shapes; these should be *scaurati;* that is, immersed in boiling water, little by little, for about three minutes or until they sprout afloat from liquids.
Subsequently, the biscuits should be drained to slide away the superfluous liquids and when the biscuits are well dry, which would happen after several hours, you can put them in the pan and bake them over moderate heat for 30 minutes or over a stronger heat for 20 minutes.

Of this composition, I remember that my mother wet the mass of the dough with hot water and then beat it several times, working it on the work surface; it felt like a pugnacious fight between my mom and the dough, which lasted about 30 minutes, until it dried from the liquids.

After this intense one-on-one struggle with the dough, my mother composed the biscuits in its various forms and proceeded to bake them.

A characteristic of these biscuits was that they lasted over time, up to a month, without losing the flavors and characteristics; on the palate they were a bit hard and you could feel the flavors of the eggs and the fragrance of the fennel seeds.

Then there were the B*iscotti Savoiardi* that in Ragusa are called *Ferringozzi;* in which 12 eggs were separated, combining the yolks with 30 grams of sugar and beat with a whisk until a swollen, white and creamy mass was obtained; in which are incorporated, little by little, always mixing: 500 grams of flour and the egg whites of six eggs whipped until stiff.

Cover the baking trays with baking paper, arrange the mass of eggs and flour obtained in a *Poche Bag* and draw sticks on the baking paper; keeping them well away from each other; as once in the oven these will expand more than double.

Before baking for 20 minutes over medium heat, sprinkle these biscuits with icing sugar.

Due to the presence of eggs, *ferringozzi* were considered a nutritious and healthy biscuit, relatives of the sponge cake that they have previously met in the recipe book of San Martino.

∗　∗　∗

So at the tender age of eight, they transferred me from the hills to the sea; at the beach of *Mancina,* in the house of my maternal grandfather: Don *Giurginu Campo* who had been the Municipal Secretary of Mazzarelli, renowned, in his Office, for the beautiful calligraphy with which he drew up birth certificates, death certificates and marriage certificates.

People ironically recounted the fact that: a new husband was waiting for my grandfather to finish drawing up the marriage certificate, after a long hour of waiting, he told him: *Don Giurginu, cà mi spruggliarsi, pi' favuri* - he wanted to do quickly in filling out the said certificate so that the groom could free himself from marriage bureaucracies: to which my grandfather replied: *Nun ti staiu spruggliannu, ti staio imprugniannu:* that is, the act of marriage, which my grandfather was compiling, entailed for the groom the loss of individual freedoms and the beginning of marriage troubles.

Grandma *Ciccina* was very different from Grandma Marietta and I often couldn't understand her somewhat strange but certainly loving behaviors towards her first grandchild.

I attended the fourth and fifth grade in the Elementary School, just few steps away from our home, my instructor was Maestro Zisa.

At school, with the new classmates all older than me, it was a somewhat difficult start; in particular, I did not explain myself and did not understand the turmoil related to sex that was used in the classroom among schoolchildren.

Once, we were under Christmas, Maestro Zisa told us: *Those in the family who have the poverty card, can come to school on Christmas Eve to receive a free panettone.*

So I ran excitedly to my father and asked him: *Dad, do we have the poverty card?*
To my father's negative answer, I was very disappointed and asked myself: Why did you have to be poor to eat a panettone at Christmas?

When the lessons were over, we went to the refectory; in the hall of the school canteen there were tables in which above each table the cooks had arranged a soup bowl stuffed with pasta and beans with related spices, herbs and condiments; each table could accommodate twelve schoolchildren and the soup bowl, in fact, contained twelve abundant portions of pasta or soup.

On one occasion, of the twelve schoolchildren we had to eat at the same table; eight of them were missing because they were suffering from influenza that, at that time, was known, as: The *Asiatica*, very contagious but fortunately not deadly.
To be honest, it was a special lunch because, we four surviving students, put in the effort and ate all the soup that was intended for twelve.
Maestro Zisa met my father and describing my voracious appetites.

*   *   *

Grandma *Ciccina* was more a food *crammer than a cook;* she crammed, using coarse salt, in the appropriate capacious cylindrical containers, anchovy fillets and pork *lard cut into squares;* my first idea of cooking was to fry two eggs using pork lard instead of oil, it was a disaster.

In general, Grandma *Ciccina's* cuisine was more practical than exciting, devoted to saving; something that my father fully accepted the rules of economic moderation even if, being a little corpulent, he did not give up the abundance of food.

Once my dad had a culinary raptus and said to my mother: *Melina, prepare nu sfuogghiu of ricotta and sausizza, ca nu manciamu pi stasira.*

It was like music to my ears, finally it was my mother who set to work, this *Sfogliata* was a masterpiece of culinary art, which in my opinion, far surpassed the other compositions of *focacce and pies.*

It is necessary to fill a puff pastry discs with fresh but not watery ricotta cheese mixed with sausage, spiced with black pepper and fennel seeds.

The method of the puff pastry is peasant that my mother learned from *Auntie Rosina,* unmarried sister of grandfather Franco and grandfather Giorgio.

INGREDIENTS SFUOGGHIU OF RICOTTA

For the dough: Durum wheat flour 250 grams, Two whole eggs, yeast *-optional-* grams 5
Pork fats: 150 grams of suet, or *whatever sufficit,* dissolved.
For the filling: Ricotta grams 800, Sausage Ragusana grams 300

Procedure: Arrange the flour in a basin, insert the whole eggs in the middle and with a little warm water provide to form the dough; if you use yeasts: the dough must rest for at least 30 minutes. With the rolling pin compose a thin sheet, on which to apply throughout the surface, with a brush, the dissolved suet; now proceed to roll up the dough and at each face of the fold, spread the suet with the brush.

You should get a long strip of rolled dough, which should be completely sprayed with suement; roll up the strip again and flatten it with your hands, which should take the form of a dough, which must be left to rest, in a covered place, for at least an hour, so that the fat used is well absorbed into the dough.

After the period considered, the dough in question is cut into two parts, which will go with the *lasagnaturi* again stretched; so as to have two sheets: one for the base and one that will act as a lid. Place the cottage cheese on top of the base dough and arrange the crumbled sausage on top of the cottage cheese, you may be required to add more black pepper.

Arrange the second sheet on top of the filling and seal the internal contents well; joining with the fingers the two flaps of the sheets; what, in our area, is called: *Riefico Barocco.*

Place the sheet in a *baking board* and proceed to cooking, in a preheated oven, for 20 minutes over medium-high heat.

The flavors of this sheet were sublime, for those times; the sweetness and softness of ricotta were combined with the flavor of spicy sausage with fennel seeds; the crusts of puff pastry, then, crumbled with each bite, magnifying the contents in an amazing exhibition of composite tastes.

*   *   *

One of our family fortunes, in the seaside village of Mazzarelli, was that we had *Uncle Pinu Causarano,* brother of my grandmother *Ciccina,* who was afisherman by profession and had a fishing boat that could have been La *Provvidenza* like that of the *Malavoglia* of the Catania writer Giovanni Verga.

Uncle Pinu had a large family consisting of four sons and four daughters; the sons, when they were not embarked on merchant ships around the oceans, helped their father for the fishing of the place; which took place between the coasts of the sea stretches of *Mazarelli* up to that of *Marzamemi.*

Almost all the sunsets *Uncle Pinu* arrived on the shore, in the beach of the Mancina, to dry moor his boat in the sands and it was a party for everyone, to pull that boat to force to ensure the boat in a dry and safe place, away from the waves and tides.

One of his sons, on the shore, arranged the woods with fat under the boat to slide the bow towards the chosen place and the rest of the crew, that is, the four daughters, pulled the rope to which the bow was attached; to push it towards the shores.

When the work was completed, you could go home happy; because that evening, for dinner, there was fish soup, *with comb fish, onion fish, scorpionfish, sea cicadas;* and everything that would have composed a soup with heady flavors, even if there will be heads and bones; the sea soup remains one of the most delicious dishes of home cooking; my mother enjoyed it fully managing to chew the heads and then deposit bones and little vertibrae from the mouth in the dish.

Some funny and interesting considerations on the Neapolitan fish soup come from the essay by the Scottish writer *Norman Douglas;* who spent most of his life on the island of Capri, guest of the well-known architect and mayor of Capri in the '20s: *Edwin Cerio,* who had, in turn, as a guest also the Chilean poet Pablo *Neruda,* whose stay in Capri was represented in the cinematographic work: *Il Postino of 1994;* whose protagonist was the great and late comedian: *Massimo Troisi.*

What I will try to translate into Italian would be: *A last word about fish soup,* taken from the book: *The Land of the Sirens of 1911 – Author: Norman Douglas*

Italiano:	English:
Prendi fiato, soave fanciulla, nel mentre spiego al paziente lettore gli ingredienti della diabolica preparazione, conociuta come Zuppa di Pesce.	Take a break, gentle maiden, the while I explain to the patient reader the ingredients of the diabolical preparation known as zuppa di pesce.
Il guarracino, per esempio, è nero come la pece, un mostro marino lungo per un paio di pollici, un autentico sgorbio, con un profilo di tempi remoti e dai modi intollerabili, il cui unico riferimento sarebbe che il suo nome deriva dal greco Koraxinos – Korax..vorace.	The guarracino, for instance, is a pitch-black marine monstrosity, 1-2 in. long, a mere blot, with an Old Red Sandstone profile and insufferable manners, whose sole recommendation is that its name derived from koraxinos. - Korax... a raven.
Per lo scorfano, il suo nome risulta certamente onomatopoeico//esempio di onomatoepia è quando un treno viene chiamato: ciuff-ciuff// la sola differenza, da un punto di vista culinario, tra lo scorfano e un rospo, sarebbe che quest'ultimo possiede il doppio di carne nel suo corpo. L'aguglia è tutta coda e proboscide; un autentico incubo notturno-sottile come la grafite di una matita. Chi potrebbe credere che questo miserabile verme marino dalle pinne verdastre, che una persona ringrazierebbe per non essere servito a mensa, gli abitanti della Terra delle Sirene,//cioè napoletani e siciliani// hanno guerreggiato come nemici acerrimi?	As to the scorfano, its name is unquestionably onomatopoeic, to suggest the spitting-out of bones; the only difference, from a culinary point of view, between the scorfano and a toad being that the latter has twice as meat on it. The aguglia, again, is all tail and proboscis; the very nightmare of a fish – as thin a lead pencil. Who would believe that for this miserable sea-worm with verdigris-tinted spine, which an ordinary person would thank you for not setting on his table, the inhabitants of Siren land fought like fiends?
Il sangue dei loro più nobili soldati venne versato a difesa dei privileggi artificiosamene ottenuti tra i regnanti angioini ed aragonesi definendo I diritti di pesca delle aguglie; ed una parte di mare venne riconosciuta come " le acque delle agugliè' la quale venne posseduta, sin dai tempi di Murat, da una singola famiglia che la difese con le armi ed i tranelli. Tutti conoscono il totero o calamaro, una animata sacca di inchiostro dalle perverse tendenze, il quale nuota verso l'indietro in quanto tutte le altre creature vanno in avanti, le cui carni di gomma indiana possono risultare utili per ingannare la fame nelle isole deserte, da quando,	The blood of their noblest was shed in defense of previleges artfully wheedled out of Anjou and Aragoese kings defining the ius quoddam pescandi vulgariter dictum sopra le aguglie; that a certain tract of sea was known as the "aguglie water" and owned, up to the days of Murat, by a single family who defended it with guns and man-traps? And everybody knows the totero or squid, an animated ink-bag of perverse leanings, which swims backwards because all other creatures go forwards and whose india-rubber flesh might be useful for deluding hunger on desert islands, since, like American gum, you can chew it for months but never get it down.

come le gomme americane, possono essere masticate per mesi ma non vanno mai giù.

Queste, e cose come queste, galleggiano appena in un composto tiepido con olio irrancidito ed aglio insieme con pane tostato e stantio della scorsa settimana, con cozze decomposte e veli di cipolle, per conferire una parvenza di consistenza.

È per cose di questo genere che i napoletani venderebbero le loro donne?

Come questo miscuglio è incompatibile se si confrontasse con una bouillabaisse marsigliese.

Ma cosa ci si può aspettare considerando gli ingredienti? Scaglie dorate e verdi, e pinne dorsali ornate con elaborati disegni rococo, non soddisferanno un uomo affamato o un epicuro, e se i napoletani pagheranno somme di denaro per la vistosa prole ittica del Mediterraneo, questo viene solo a provare che essi mangiano con gli occhi, come bambini, che prefiriscono pessime caramelle rispetto alle buone. Questi pesci, del mare interno, hanno forme e colori, ma sono privi di gusti. Le loro carni sono flaccide, scriminzite e piene di ossicini ed in certi casi non hanno carni o polpe; con teste simili a dragoni ma senza corpo a esse attaccato; o corpi appiattiti adottando il principio del Magnum in Parvo -troppo nel poco-, presentando appena lo spessore di un foglio di carta tra la loro pelle e le lische; o una struttura serpentina, con occhi a fessura che ti guardano mentre provi a ricavarne un morso da questa rettile anatonia.

Non si trova un merluzzo, o un rombo, salmone, aringa nelle le due mila miglia tra Gibilterra e Gerusalemme; o se esite qualche specie non nè viene fuori.

'These, and such as they, float about in a lukewarm brew of rancid oil and garlic together with a few of last week's breadcrusts, decaying sea-shells and onion peels, to give it an air of consistency.

'This is the stuff for which Neapolitans sell their female relatives?

'How unfavourably this hotch-potch compares with the Marseillese bouillabaisse. But what can be expected, considering the ingredients? Green and golden scales, and dorsal fins embellished with elaborate rococo designs, will satisfy neither a hungry man nor an epicure, and if Neapolitans pay untold sums for the showy Mediterranean seaspawn it only proves that they eat with their eyes, like children, who prefer tawdry sweets to good ones. They have colour and shape, these fish of the inland sea, but not taste. Their flesh is either flabby and slimy and full of bones in unauthorised places or else they have no flesh at all – heads like Burmese dragons but no bodies attached to them; or bodies of flattened construction on the magnum in parvo principle, allowing of barely room for a sheet of paper between their skin and ribs; or a finless serpentine framework, with long-slit eyes that leer at you while you endeavour to scratch a morsel off the reptilian anatomy.

'There is not a cod, or turbot, or whiting or salmon, or herring in the two thousand miles between Gibraltar and Jerusalem; or if there is, it never comes out. Its haddocks taste as if they had fed on mouldy sea-weed and died from the effects of it; its lobsters have no claws; its oysters are bearded like pards; and as for its soles – I have yet to see one that measures more than 5 in. round the waist.

I loro merluzzi hanno il gusto come se avessero mangiato alghe marcite e sono morti per questi ingerimenti; le loro aragoste non hanno le chele, le ostriche sono barbose come mendicanti; e le loro sogliole non superano le dimensioni di cinque pollici nella vita. Il fatto è, quasi non esiste un pesce nel Mediterraneo che si puo. mangiare, e di consequenza: niente viene da niente. *La zuppa marsigliese è buona solamente perché viene cotta dai francesi.* *Ma, come quando un turco diventa furioso davanti alle teneri carni di pollo perché si sente privato dal piacere di masticarlo; cosi' il napoletano butterebbe dalla finestra una ottima zuppa di pesce: il masticare e lo sputacchiare fà parte del divertimento.*	*The fact is, there is hardly a fish in the Mediterranean worth eating, and therefore – ex nihilo nihil fit. Bouillabaise is only good because cooked by the French. But even as a Turk is furiouswith a tender chicken because it cheats him out of the pleasure of masticating, so the Neapolitan would throw a boneless zuppa di pesce out of the window: the splitting and spluttering is half the fun.*

On Sundays for lunch, in the house of Marina di Ragusa, we did not eat so badly; for the fact that my father went, around ten o'clock in the morning, to the Mazzarelli Recreational Club to play cards: *Scala Quaranta or Ramino* with the other meritorious members of the club; and most of the time, he was the winner of the competition; winning the stakes of 30 thousand lire, which were enough to visit the butcher or fishmonger.

Around noon usually he would come home with the shopping and my mom would happily get to work.

She had already prepared the sauces, Dad had bought the thin slices of beef and there would have been a pizzaiola lunch; Mamma Melina had the slices fried on both sides, then transformed them into rolls with the sticks of our caciocavallo made by my uncle *Ciccio*; attaching them with a toothpick inside the slices of beef.

The pizzaiola sauce was composed with fried garlic and peeled tomatoes, which did not have to cook for a long time but remain pulpy, enriched with capers and pieces of black olives and lots of oregano; salt and pepper seasoning.

At this point it was enough to put the rolls in the sauce still hot and cook everything for another five minutes so that the caciocavallo softened with the vapors of cooking and the sauce of the pizzaiola wrapped the meat in its aromas.

After Sunday lunch we went to bed to enjoy the afternoon siesta, to fall asleep softly after the libations magnified by the generous wine; which bring the satisfied body and the dormant spirit towards a well-deserved rest of the limbs; how to close oneself leaving the world outside, isolate with your one's ego, invoke calm, close your eyes as not to look at anyone, embrace yourself and let the imagination of our senses dictate our short dream.

The Amnesia of Awakening: *What Day Is It?... is it night or is it day? Is it late or early? Do I have to go to work? But, No – It seems to me that today is Sunday, I do not have to go anywhere and I stay in bed.*

*   *   *

I think that in Sicily there is no home canteen that has not been adorned with a plate of *Tuna with sauce* or prepared in other ways.

The *Mediterranean Bluefin Tuna* is used in the spring season when the tuna arrives from the Strait of Gibraltar along Sicily from Capo *Lilibeo to Capo Peloro* and then descend towards Capo *Passero;* in these places there were tuna traps: tuna fishing has been over the centuries an economic activity that has had a strong impact on the history and traditions of the island.

Let's see how you can compose the:

Tunnina Ammattunata or with Tomato Sauce

Find a slice of tuna of one kilo and put it in cold water for two hours; so that the slice can lose part of its blood, to become more digestible.

Dry the slice and cut it causing small openings in which you can insert strips of garlic and mint leaves and a pinch of salt

Brown briefly in vegetable oil, over medium-high heat, the tuna, so predisposed.

Prepare the sauce by frying the onion cut into strips in olive oil, add capers and pitted olives; proceed with the tomato paste and then dilute the compounds with copious sprinkles of dry white wine.

Add the browned tuna to the sauce and cook for 20 minutes over medium heat.

The trick now is to cool the dish; then take the bulk tuna and cut it into slices, serving it with the cooking sauce; as many diners prefer to enjoy this dish when the tuna is warm or even cold.

Tuna with sauce, in Palermo cuisine, can undergo the variation of using fresh peas - *Petit Pois* - instead of capers and olives.

Much used, in Sicilian cuisine, the *Ventresca del Tonno,* which would be the belly of the fish, which, cut into slices, you can compose another characteristic dish: *Tunnina with the Cipollata in Agro-dolce.*

A characteristic Sicilian sauce for grilled fish such as sardines, rich in Essential Fatty Acids -Omega 3- or any other grilled fish, would be the *Salmoriglio Sauce* which is composed of: *chopped garlic, mint or parsley leaves and thick olive oil;* the ingredients must be *enriched;*to which is added, by mixing the contents, with little hot water and lemon juice, always drop by drop; in other words, an *emulsion* should be created, which need to be spiced with fresh red or green chilli pepper and oregano.

The salmoriglio sauce, whose term comes from *Brine,* can be heated and kept in a hot water bath; to better preserve the organoleptic properties of the emulsion.

⋆   ⋆   ⋆

After elementary school I went to grammar school in Santa Croce Camerina, I was a listless student and was always sent back to September to repeat Latin and Drawing; used to spend my free time playing alone under the shadow of my carob tree in our large garden near the sea.
On top of that tree I dreamed of heroic deeds and faced all the enemies; my wooden sword was in the service of the King and the Dames; I fought against all the usurpers and had all the battles won: in real life, however, my battles have been always lost..

My hero was *Cirano di Bergerac,*which I had seen at the cinema of the Arena*Lalicata,*together with my grandmother *Ciccina.*I imitated Cyrano sword skills and deeds: *I defend, I pretend, and arrived at the end of the dispute: Je Touche – I touch-.*
In the final scene of the film, in the garden of the convent where the beautiful and beloved Rossana resided; the poet swordsman, who had been stunned in a cowardly attack, saw death appear; he faced her with a straight sword aattack: *Io Cyrano, astronomer, mathematician, man of arms and rhymes; I Cyrano that I have been everything and I have been in vain.*

Sometimes Grandfather Franco appeared for a visit and we hugged each other; he donated two thousand lire, bought for me an ice cream cup and told he was alaways waiting for me to be together.
Dear grandfather, I was his first and favorite grandson, who knows what he was expecting from me, I also disappointed his expectations.
On his deathbed he said to his *Canaria bird*: *You see, my dear, there is nothing in life; thank goodness I had fun.* Grandfather Franco had always been a libertine in spirit.

Now it happened that in the third year of grammar school, after having repeated the second grade, the school program of that time, provided for the study of the Latin classics, always standing above my carob tree, I got a Latin anthology and read the stories animatedly; the most fascinating was the plot of *Orpheus and Eurydice;*that of the sweet singer who descends to the underworld in search of his loving and lost Eurydice.

To be able to understand the classics well I had to know the Latin grammar and so, within a week, I learned the grammatical rules that I had not been able to learn in the past three years.

Despite my progress in Latin, there was no way to convince my prof.; in the versions in class I always took grades to be painful; I asked the professor why he gave me: *N.C.* – not classified – if there were no errors in the version? *Because you copied the version from your classmate,* he replied; while in fact it was my classmate who had copied from me.

Things that happen I have always been misunderstood.

My father saw me playing and reading classics on the carob tree and came, perhaps not wrongly, to the conclusion that I was if not stupid almost there; so at my age of 15, at the interest of my father, I was invited to find a job for myself; as I left the beaches of the Marina, I greeted my carob friend and promised that I would return to play again with trees of my youth garden; but my promise towards them was a rather vain promise.

*   *   *

In that of Santa Croce, however, I fell in love with the *Macallè di Ricotta* that were exhibited in every bar in the village; to be able to buy a *macallè* I spent the money that my father had given me to buy the bus ticket; therefore, I often traveled six kilometers of road on foot to be able to return home; but the *macallè* was appeciated with enjoyment of the senses and voracious lust.

Certainly in that of Santa Croce Camerina are renowned the *Dinners of St. Joseph,*as well as those of Gela or Salemi and also in the southern regions of Puglia and Abruzzo, the anniversary of March 19 in every year of grace, is magnificently celebrated with the preparation of canteens adorned with the paintings of the Saint and the Holy Family and the presentation of particularly genuine and traditional foods; such as the *Zeppole of San Giuseppe.*
The Sicilian canteens of San Giuseppe, called *Cene* show off characteristic sweets such as: *Cicirieddi, Mustazzola, Pignulate, Cannoli, Sfinci, orange and lemon fruit with their respective fruit jellies;* and a presentation of various forms of expertly decorated bread, among which *'u vastuni'* stands out and there will be no lack of symmetrical arrangement of flowers and lights in the table, together with rice *balls; cereals such as wheat, chickpeas or lentils; fennel and tomato vegetables;* everything is prepared to be distributed among guests, pilgrims and the needy; for that divine grace and for the generosity of those who have received it.

I could not indicate the origin of the name *Macallè;*if ever there had been an African relationship or if it had been some nostalgic legionary; who, having become a pastry chef, connected this dessert with the name of the Ethiopian capital.

Another term by which this composition is known, would be: *Il Cartoccio Siciliano.*

MACALLÈ DI RICOTTA

Ingredients for the Dough : 300 grams of double zero flour, 150 grams of warm milk,

7 grams of brewer's yeast, 30 grams of butter or lard

100 grams of granulated sugar, 1 whole egg, salt to .b.

Ingredients for the Filling: 500 grams of fresh ricotta, 250 grams of sugar

NB: With these ingredients you can compose 10 macallè

Miscellaneous : Seed oil for frying, granulated sugar for decorating.

Tools to be used : Aluminium cylinders, Baking paper

Procedure:

1. Mix sifted ricotta with sugar, to compose the filling
2. Compose a homogeneous dough with the ingredients indicated above.
3. Divide the dough into ten balls, which will rise.
4. Grease the aluminum cylinders, prepare a tray with ten individual triangles of baking paper.
5. Crush the balls, so that they can adhere to the length of the cylinders and join the edges of the dough around the cylinder.
6. Place each individual foil wrapped in the cylinder, above each individual triangle of baking paper, cover well and make the dough rise further; which should swell about twice the original size.
7. Heat the seed oil and when hot enough, fry the roll and also the paper attached to it, as as the effect of frying it will detach itself from the composition.
8. When the foil is believed to be golden enough, remove it from the oil and place it on absorbent paper to dry it

9. While the *Macallè* is still lukewarm, roll it in the sugar and slide the metal cylinder away.
10. Fill the roll from both side holes with the ricotta filling, possibly using a Sac a Poche.

*   *   *

Our activities, whatever the other stories were, basically concerned agriculture and cattle breeding in the Mieta countryside; that it was the kingdom of my uncles, while my parents loved it a little less and I too, when it came to work in the fields, I was not so enthusiastic,

At our farm there were happy moments and unhappy times; one of the latter were the crops and everything related to the wheat harvestall this involved work and physical effort from dawn to dusk.

At that time, in the Hyblaean countryside, there was a lack of light, water, toilets and showers.
If there had been hygiene checks, who knows how many houses would have been closed, including ours.

In the farmhouse of the Mieta there was a stone oven used for baking, a fire place where it was hanging from a pulley, the boiler saucepan which was used to cook the ricotta, the *tannures* that were the cooking points with wood fire; *the pantry* that contained the spices and herbs of common use.

In the adjacent room there was then the table for dining, equipped with two drawers in one there was the bread and in the other culteries, the *Mastreda* where cheddar, caciocavalli and toma cheeses were stored; the cabinet that contained in the lower part plates and in the up side there were glasses, bottles ofwine, jar of vinegar and the homemade rosolio liquor,

The rest of the building then extended around the closed court: the residential house, with living room and bedrooms; barns and haystacks with mezzanine; warehouses for foodstuffs; stables for oxen and horses; sheepfolds and chicken coop; the rural spaces were large, airy and capacious.

At the time of the harvests, the schools were closed, so all in the countryside.
Once the wheat was harvested, it was necessary to collect the sheaves of ears and piling them up to compose the bundles; which were tied with ropes and transported with monkey wagons in the field near the barnyard where it was necessary to set them up ; these bundles were placed one above the other to form stack pile , which rose upwards, so as to look like a skyscraper.
We began to prepare the threshing floor, that is, the place *where to pluck* the grain with three or four horses that were turned over to dash, first slowly and then with speed, over the wheat ears.
The horses driver, who was our apprentice *U Massa Vannuzzu*, held the strings of the horses and began to make them dance on the ears, to the sound of his songs.

At the end of each line of the song the farmer stretched the vowel by trailing it; to which the horse frightened by the cry became more obedients and galloped on the ears with greater determination.

Around the barnyard floor there were the *atturniaturi,* whose task was to push with the trident the ears that were at the edge inwards.

When the ears and the stem were well ground and the wheat grains were clearly visible; the *Spagliatura began;* that is, the procedure for separating the grain from the straw.

With the tridents the contents of the haying were thrown into the air and the wind carried the straw out of the hague; while the wheat grains rested in the perimeter.

This work was usually carried out in the late afternoon, when the breeze rose: *Maestro or Libeccio winds*

At the first light of dawn it was necessary to collect the straw that had piled up as a result of the spreading, placing it in special wide-meshed sheets and transporting them to the indoor haystacks and then, with my little brother and my cousin we had to stay in the haystack and dance on it so that the straw would pile up, occupying less space.

This work had to be done before the sun came out otherwise the movements of the straw would have caused dust which penetrated into clothes, nose, throat and everywhere: Do you imagine at five a.m. *doing somersaults?*

The wheat that remained in the hague was bagged and transported to the warehouse to be cleaned from the rest of the straw stems; through the sorting using sieves equipped with special meshes that, to facilitate the work, were attached with a rope to the ceiling of the warehouse .

Clearly it was necessary to start again as in the beginning, fulling the floor of the barnyard with new bundles of ears and repeating the work until the ears were all done.

Usually the harvested, began at the end of May with the harvests and ended in mid-August, the last act was the delivery of the wheat grains obtained that was deposited at the trusted mill that served as a bank; there were no Sunday rests, no commanded feasts that could interrupt or break the chain of work.

While if they had employed a threshing; with the use of machinery it would have been enough two days to collect the crops; the fact was that threshing cost money and we were devoted to savings.

In addition to the work of the crops there were also to carry out the normal tasks such as caring for the animals, proceeding with milking, leading the cows to pasture and cleaning the stables.

The peasant diet, in the hot summer months, consisted of a breakfast with bread and fruit such as prickly pears or table grapes; a lunch of dry pasta with tomato sauce and ricotta cheese and for dinner: short macaroni pasta with beans namely: *Pasta and Fasul;* this term reminds me of the American song: *That is love* interpreted by Dino Crocetti aka Dean *Martin;* friend of Frank Sinatra, Sammy Davis and Joe Bishop; that is the melodies of: *The Rat Pack* that came before the *Beatles.*

Here are some lyrical verses:

When the stars make you drool like a pasta e fasul

That's love

When the moon hits your eye like a big pizza pie,

that's love.

......

Scus-a-mi, but you see, back in old Napoli

.... You are in Love.

This song is the stereotype of us Italians, living abroad, who have fame as *Latin Lovers;*when I entered the Fiddler Pub in Aberdeen, the singer Mary, during the singing performance dedicated to me the notes of *That's Amore;* and love was.

At the Mieta the summer dinner was consumed in the farmyard towards dusk, in the dim light of the cart light and in the presence of the loving nocturnal butterfly; the insect was attracted to the light and began to make a thousand turns around the lumen; until, exhausted, he went to fall right inside the plate with the soup; but the farmer did not worry too much; with his fingers he grabbed the butterfly by the wings and deposited it on the ground; who knows if the butterfly ever survived the impact: *The more you will not go, loving butterfly*

PASTA AND BEANS *or* PASTA AND FASUL

The best time to enjoy fresh beans is from the end of June and throughout the summer.

The Borlotti, like many other species of beans, belong to the genus *Phaseolus Vulgaris;* the term *Phaseolus* would represent the forms of the small but fast boats used by the Phoenicians to sail the Mediterranean and carry out their trade.

Another family to which belong different categories of beans, coming from the East, would be the genus: *Vigna,* in fact have under this denomination: *V. Augularis, V. Mungo, V. Radiata, V. Umbellata and Vigna Anguiculata* to the latter category would belong the beans with black eye.

Ingredients:

for 4 people

- Carbohydrates: 300 grams of corallino or striped thimble pasta
- *Legumes:* 400 grams of fresh Borlotti beans
- *Vegetables:* Carrots, Celery, Tomato *concassè*, Onion, Garlic,
- *Meat:* Squares *of* crammed pork lard, engraved in slices, but attached to the skin
- Various: Olive oil, fresh or dried chili pepper, Bay olive, salt and pepper to .b.

Procedure:

1. Shell the tender beans, place them in a crock pan and cover them with salted water. Bring the contents to a boil, enter the onion cut into strips, the carrot into cubes and the celery in segments with the leaves. Lower the heat and cook over medium-low heat for about 60 minutes.

2. Prepare a quick sauté with olive oil, garlic teeth in strips, squares of lard, diced tomatoes, two bay leaves.
3. Pour the sauté into the beans, bring the contents to a boil.
4. Throw in the pasta and check the cooking water.
5. Proceed to dressing with chilli, addition of olive oil; eliminate the bay mad.
6. Check the cooking of the pasta, the softness of the beans and the condition of the juices of the soup that must be compact and dense.
7. Serve making sure that there is, in the plate for each diner the square of lard

*   *   *

There were those who for breakfast, instead of fruit, used to prepare a salad; when we talk about salads we think of tomato; while the most characteristic salad, in our Hyblaean land, was the *Piretto or lemon.*

This piretto or cedro lemon is a low-calorie winter citrus fruit, larger than lemon and with an idyllic scent; so much so that the German writer and playwright *Ian Wolfang Goethe of Weimar,* fascinated by the studies of Greco-Roman antiquity, expressed himself in the ode, The Land *of Lemons;* homage to the land of Sicily that he visited in April 1787:

Do you know the country where cedars bloom?
Golden oranges shine among the gloomy leaves.
A gentle breeze from the blue sky blows,
the myrtle is immobile, the laurel is high.
Do you know this land?
Over there, over there
With You, O my beloved, I would like to go.

These lemon cedars, in our area, are mainly used in homemade desserts, to compose jams, cedar creams type custards; or to compose sorbets or syrups; we can remember the *Cedrata di Modica* which would consist in cooking in honey, possibly thyme, the peel of the cedar grated together with the orange peels cut into strips.

Candied Cedar lemon jars are *renowned:* Remove the pulp and use the peel with the thin white part of the cedar. Soak the peel for three days, taking care to change the water every day.
Drain the peel and blanch it a little; then cool it in cold salted water.
Now cut it into strips and cook it in a saucepan with the same amount of granulated sugar and very little spring water. Cook, over low heat, the ingredients until the liquids dry and the peel of the cedar becomes crystal clear to the eye.
Store candied fruit in sterilized glass jars in the fridge.

However, let's see how to compose the *Cedar* Salad to be used for a capricious peasant breakfast: Scrape away a little peel from a large cedar and cut into slices or chunks the white part with the pulp; which will be spongy, then season with enough thick olive oil, a few tablespoons of spring water, with garlic slices and fresh parsley leaves, flakes of dried red chillie and sea salt. In this salad the dressings must be generous. The salad should be enjoyed with slices of bread cut at the moment, with thin strips of red onion and cubes of fresh cheese.

The cedar salad with the accompaniments described, will form a screaming breakfast; like the one that was eating *U Massa Vanni Cauraredda,*straddled above a wall holding a bowl of this salad and the accompaniments, alongside with a container of fresh water; passing by those parts, I asked him: *Massa Vanni what are you eating?* He replied: *So of whim.*

* * *

One of my coveted weekly tasks was to help my mom and auntie make bread at home every Saturday morning.
In Sicily the abundance of wheat has allowed the baking of *White Bread,* endowed with digestive and nutritional qualities, as well as distinguishable by particular fragrance; an art of which our bakers and our housewives have contributed decisively to create the cult of breadmaking in the intrinsic home traditions; unlike mounting peninsular sites when bread was made with millet, rye and even acorns: These were heavy breads that filled the stomach but of little nutritional value.

The favorable climate, the generous land and, modestly, the skill of the farmers, have allowed us to obtain from the raw material that is our wheat: Pasta and Bread, which are at the base of the pyramid in *the Mediterranean Dietetic Diet.*

How to make bread ragusan style?
Certainly in this regard there will be a wide gastronomic literature; for my part I can only point out my youthful memories based on the deeds, methods and stages of baking that were put in place in the paternal campaign of the Mieta, whose priestesses were my motherCarmela and my auntie Maria.

A first report concerns the use of the crescent to be combined with flour; the yeast was obtained by setting aside the bread dough used in the previous dough; that was the week before.
120 grams of natural yeast were used for every kilo of flour, i.e. *re-milled durum wheat semolina;* the water ratio was 50 cl for each kilo of flour.
Only salt had to be added.

Recipe for Ragusan home bread:

Re-milled durum wheat semolina Kilo 1
Natural growing g yeast gramme 120
Water cl 50
Sale quantu Sufficit

As soon as these elements were mixed, the dough was arranged in *the scaniaturi,* which was a square working surface, like a large table, in which you could trigger a board axis like a large rolling pin, called: *briuni.*
Then Carmela sat on this table where there was the dough to be kneaded and I moved the wooden plank, which was attached on he working surfice from top to bottom causing folds in the dough that was constantly stirred by my mother, so that the bends produced by the wooden plank worked the dough evenly.

After this work it was necessary to divide the dough into many loaves and compose, for each dough, a bread in the shape of: *Corona, Filone, Rosetta, Esse, Pagnotta, Treccia, Brioche, Mafalda.*
At this point the various loaves were made to rise, suitably covered by two blankets: one above and one below, the bread was actually put to bed, for at least 90 minutes so that it could rise well.
After the leavening time the bread was awakened with a stroke of the hand to ceck the state of lievitation occurred.

One could conclude the argument by saying that bread was baked in oven until it was cooked.

This was not the case as there was no conventional oven in which you just turn a crank or touch a button; it was necessary to burn the stone oven and prepare it to be able to accommodate the bread.

Burning the oven required time and constancy and certainly excellent wood; we had olive wood and carob wood available; the first was harder so it burned more slowly than the carob; then we needed the branches that is the various twigs that being fragile immediately caught fire creating the vamps that were necessary to bring the stone oven to an optimal temperature; this state was reached when the oven, once cleaned of the embers, appeared, on its sides and in the domed vault, of a pure white color and the base had to be shiny and bright.

Only if these events occurred, could the bread be put into the stone oven; placing directly the naked bread inside the oven; which was then closed with the appropriate lid called ' *la valatà* and in the base of the lid there was the burning embers so that cold air did not enter the oven during the baking process time.

While the bread was in the oven, a second bake was prepared: *I Scacci Inturciniati;* that is, the wrapped buns.

The term focaccia comes from the Latin *Panis Focacius,* that is: Bread on Fire.

Then my mother and my aunt, pulled from the dough of the bread a very thin sheet, whose surface was sprinkled with thick and tasty tomato sauce, flakes of aged caciocavallo and fresh basil leaves.

Two flaps of the dough were turned towards the center and again the spreading of tomato sauce on the surfaces of the flaps was practiced. Once this rectangle was obtained, other wrappings of the dough and other spreads of tomato sauce were practiced; to close everything in a shape of a well-sealed rectangle. With the same system they composed more focaccie with oil, fresh parsley and caciocavallo cheese.

So they had the red and the white focaccia, which were placed on the planks or baking trays and as soon as the bread came out of the oven, these were put inside, to cook beautifully in the remaining heat.

These *homemade focaccie* were a panacea, when, at any time, if anyone of the family was a little hungry, it was enough to open the drawer, cut a slice and enjoy it perhaps with half a glass of wine.

These turnovers focaccia are a characteristic of the Hyblaean peasant cuisine that, recently for their genuine workmanship and for the simple but characteristic flavor; have received gastronomic consensus and wider consumption in many backery shops of he City.

When it was time to take our bread out of the oven, I would use a wicker basket and my mother with the shovel, pulled out of the oven themagnificient cooked bread by placing it in the basket; at the finished work the bread was covered again to make it rest well.

These would have been the phases of the family bakery of the Mieta and I think they were common to the various bakeries that took place every Saturday morning in the Hyblaean territory.

Describing the smells of bread just out of the oven is something like rikindle dormant feelings, like living a love story, like a spring warmth; the smells were persistent throughout the day and raged through the farm house , leading and seducing our moods towards something indescribably close to the harmonies of life.

*   *   *

One of the happy moments in the Mieta was when the visits of friends or relatives, arrived to taste the hot ricotta soup; then in the room adjacent to the house a long dinner table was prepared that could accommodate up to twenty guests.

Now these live-ups take place in the countryside used for agri-tourism that has become a business; whereas before it was the farmer who received guests for free.

In our countryside ricotta was made twice a day.

To the freshly milked milk was added enzimes, which was a compound of sour milk preserved in a goat's gut, whose task was to solidify the milk.

Once solidified the milk was broken with hot water and everything was mixed with a wooden stick spatula - and then filtered: The solid part was the toma with which subsequently were composed cheeses such as provola, caciocavallo; the liquid part, that is the whey, was cooked together with milk, the ricotta cheese was composed; whose term, in fact, means: *Cooked twice.*

For this purpose the sauce boiler, that was located above the fireplace of the farmhouse, was filled with the obtained whey and the fire was set on usingas fuel wood branches, *zotte and saittuna.*

These *zotte* were the defications of the cows that gathered in the pasture fields, when these were solidified and dry, these defications were used as fuel, meanwhile the *saittuna* were seedlings of thorns that were used to make a final flush.

When the whey reaches a certain temperature it's necessary to add coarse salt and some milk; these were the ingredients for the ricotta; towards the end of cooking due to the final flush with the seedlings of thorns; the ricotta flakes began to emerge, from bottom to top, after that the flakes clummed into the surface of the boiler constituting a layer of ricotta with a thickness of about four fingers.

Then the *saucepan* was removed from the fire, using the pulley and placed on the ground, at this point my *uncle Ciccio* with a special tool, called *skimmer,* removed a small membrane of ricotta that had become dirty because of the fumes and began to arrange the ricotta with the whey in the various bowls of red terracotta.

On the lit ash of the same fireplace, where the ricotta was cooked, some sausage pork meat were arranged wrapped turned into straw paper sprayed with red wine; these savoury wraps were just buried inside the lit ashes and left to cook till will be ready.

Another job to entertain guests was *U pani cunzatu.*
The dough was previously composed with: Flour, oil, brewer's yeast, salt, milk and water; medium-sized round loaves were formed; during their lievitation, the oven was prepared and they were arranged in special trays and were baked at the same temperature as bread; but they baked faster than the bread of the house, because they were softer.
Once out of the oven, the loaves opened in half and were seasoned with thick olive oil, oregano, dried chili flakes and slices of fresh provola cheese .

The *savoury* bread was the appetizer, almost simultaneously the ricotta was served which was the main course.

In the bowls there was, together with the ricotta, the whey and the slices of bread ; then there were those who preferred it in this way, like soup; or those who preferred only ricotta, drained away the liquids and mixed the ricotta with the bread; there were also those who used sugar and black pepper condiments in the soup – De *gustibus* -.

The ricotta soup had the power to make flow into the souls of the guests, feelings of joy, of collective joy that led to talk about the strangest things as facts with a comic background with references also jokingly sexual and all those present participated in these bucolic celebrations; in which there was no particular recurrence such as birthdays, marriages or births; it was a spontaneous party created by spontaneous people, born from the randomness of a meeting between friends or relatives sitting in the same desco, with the same food and animated by a spirit of common cordiality; even dogs and cats, present under the table, participated in the party, waiting for some bite to be lovingly offered to them.

While enjoying the ricotta; from the fire place rose and spread, through the rooms of the house, the fumes and scents of the weapped sausage; as if that sausage meant to say: *I'm here too, don't abandon me.*

My *aunt Maria,*ran towords the fireplace and with a pliers unearthed these wrappers burned by the ashes; the straw paper had stuck to the casings of the sausage that had been beautifully cooked in that casing bathed in red wine and emanated unexplained scents.

The sausage meats, once discarded, were placed in a tray and brought to the table, as soon as these were touched by the prongs of the fork gushed out the dissolved fats and the tastes of the pressed and roasted meats produced effects of particular flavors; as if the ashes had infused the sausages with greater harmony making the meats more crispy and the spices more penetrating to the tastes of the palate.

*   *   *

After the ricotta festival it was a must to take a walk through the fields, the body felt a need to move towards the amenity of rural places in direct contact with nature; then, in the spring months, the locks and valleys of the Ragusa countryside were sprouting in new spontaneous herbs many of them were edible if not even of fine culinary workmanship.

One could make a classification of the spontaneous country herbs, which were collected in the fields by improvised botanists, lovers of nature and simple cuisine that is an integral part of the traditions of Hyblaean cuisine:

- *Cruciferous :* Turnips, Radishes, Rocket and Watercress
- *Chenopodiaceae:* Spinach and Chard
- *Liliaceae :* Asparagus, Leek, Shallot, Chives, Lampascioni
- *Composite :* Spiny Artichoke, Thistle, Endive, Cicoria
- *Umbellifere:* Parsley, Parsnip, Celery, Fennel, Dial
- *Labiatal :* Basil, Peppermint, Sage
- *Borage:* Borage or Uranie, with blue flowers
- *Capparidaceae:* Capers
- *Labiate :* Marjoram

Almost all these plants and herbs are present in the Hyblaean fields; in particular, the collectors were interested in:

1. *Lassini or Amaretti or Canuta Mustard*
2. *Spontaneous Cicoria, Piscialetto or Dandelion*
3. *Matalufi or Purrazzi or Asfodeli*
4. *Mustard herbs*

The culinary characteristics of these wild herbs, rich in vitamins and mineral salts, are, in general, a quick boiling – an entry and exit from boiling water – and passage in a pan with: Oil, garlic, lemon juice and red pepper flakes.

The cicoria can be used to compose a *Pesto:* frolling it with olive oil, blanched almonds, grated caciocavallo, clove of garlic and sea salt.

Spontaneous canuta mustard leaves have detoxifying and laxative functions, it also controls blood sugar and regulates the heartbeat; they can be used also for pasta or risotto or accompaniment for white meats.

The *matalufi or Asfodeli herbs* my favorites, are of sweetish taste; in which you have to eliminate the tuft or *gnummu* and obtain the inner stem that is soft; excellent as an accompaniment to red meats and in particular to season scruble eggs .

The *mustard leaves* thThat in Neapolitan dialect are called *Friarelli,* once boiled and well squeezed are seasoned with oil and red pepper, they are the ideal accompaniment for grilled pork sausages.

Furthermore wild asparagus can be found in the Hyblaean fields, although belonging to the *Acutifolius family,* has different characteristics from the common ones; equipped with a strong and inedible stem from which the sprouts of the stem are used in our cuisine.

Asparagus is also endowed with bitter tastes, so much so that my mother used to combine asparagus with some *asfodeli* stems to sweeten the compounds.

This delicious vegetable has multiple nutritional qualities and, as we know, has the power to improve kidney functions, accelerating diuresis.

The most characteristic method of cooking asparagus is to drown them; so that they can also be used as a condiment for pasta

Recipe Asparagus Affogati

First blanch them briefly, then fry with olive oil, clove of garlic, a tablespoon of tomato extract that is diluted with red wine drops and making everything simmer.

Care should be taken in this preparation, because the asparagus must not be watery scalded or overcooked.

If, then, you want to have a personal dinner; you can lay on the drowned asparagus, a poached egg cooked in a pan with the yolk still flickering.

Our mothers sent us to the fields to find asparagus; I left with my cousin Giorgio, wandering through the walls in the wild fields trying to find the stem of asparagus.

The fact was that while Giorgio was seriously engaged in the fateful search, myself after a while, abstained from it and my mind was absent from the task received as sat on the wall to contemplate the landscape ascetically.

When we returned to the farmhouse, my cousin had with him a nice bunch of asparagus and I held in my hands a few leaves of mint, which I had not been looking for but the mint itself had told me where it was because of the emanations of those characteristic pungent smells.

The bottom line was that all asparagus belonged to Giorgio because I had not been able to find even one. But when the asparagus omelette was made, with fresh eggs from the chicken coop, the booty was divided among all the members and bystanders of the family.

How good were the *eggs* of the Mieta. My mother composed the beaten eggs, mixing it with ricotta, grated caciocavallo and asparagus pins, spread the composition with salt and black pepper; forming an almost gelatinous union in which the colors of the red of the eggs, the whiteness of the ricotta and the intense green of the asparagus melted as in the palette of a painter.

For frying it was necessary to find the perfection of the oil temperature; if this is too hot it could cause burns in the components; an oil at a non-optimal temperature or low temperature would penetrate the mass by unduly aewing the ingredients.

After frying the bases, turn the omelette for a complete and uniform cooking; the contents must be removed by turning the pan upside down and depositing the non-amalgamated contents of the mass in a large dish; and then slide them back into the pan and complete the frying.
This work must be carried out with chronometric punctuality, not one minute more and not one minute less; the composition of the *frittata* and the softness of the composition depend on these elements.

*   *   *

In our farm and throughout the Hyblaean countryside were strictly observed the festive anniversaries such as the New Year's Eve and the commanded feasts, namely: Christmas, Easter and the anniversary of St. John the Baptist, protector of the city of Ragusa which is celebrated on August 29 of each year of grace; or Saint George who is the Saint protector of old Ragusa

The creative flair of the housewives exploded in the preparation of the dishes that were to enrich the festive tables; to satisfy and bring us humans being, closer each other with joyful souls, towards the anniversaries of religious events; to celebrate meant to love God and the Saints who had sacrificed themselves for us in divine glory.

In the countryside what little was available was combined with genuity and skillful manual skills of the housewives.

One of the recurring compositions during the celebrations was the: *Homemade Pasta:*

The Hyblaean recipe was:

- *500 grams of durum wheat flour*
- *Two whole eggs*
- *Warm salted water*

Once the dough has been composed and the consequent manipulation to make it homogeneous and malleable, it is necessary to obtain a sheet with a rolling pin and the shapes of the dough that you want to obtain depend on the thickness of the dough.

For *tagliatelle* it is necessary, for example, to pull a thin sheet and sprinkle a veil of flour on the sides of the dough; then fold the dough several times on itself for a width of about 6 cm.

Cut from the dough, lengthwise, strips of about 1 cm; taking care to cover the strips obtained with a napkin, to make them

From the same dough and with a thicker dough you can compose the domestic *macaroni* that were deposited in wicker baskets and placed on balconies and terraces covered with a veil of gauze.

The macaroni with tomato extract sauce and stews of pork or lamb, are a purely Sicilian dish in which different types of macaroni are used that have disparate names and denominations depending on the place and the forms attributed to them: *Ciazzisi, Ciazzisuotti, Maccarruna all'Uso, Maccarrunedda di Zita, Gnucchitti, Gnuocculu* and more *Cavatieddi, Causunedda* – purely Ragusan – *Pizzulatieddi, Incucciatieddi, Taccuna.*

Then there would be *the Lasagne* those with a wide dough that were used by the farmers on the occasion of the new year: *Annum Novum Faustum Felicem,* clearly did not refer to the year 2020.

The wide sheets with wavy edges, were boiled paying the utmost care that they did not break. After boiling they were seasoned with: *Ricotta, cheese and stew sauce;* and then be cooked in the oven.

These would be the: *Lasagne Cacate del Capo d'Anno,*used for the new year celebrations.

Despite my mnemonic efforts I do not remember if, in the hyblean countryside, there was a traditional course of meat or fish for Christmas dinner; I think unlike Easter foods; Christmas food was left to the inventiveness of home cooks.

For example, in Britain for Christmas lunch it is a must to cook baked turkey meats with *gravy sauce, roast potatoes, boiled vegetables and trimmings.*

The reason why turkey meat is used for Christmas, is inexplicable; as in Jesus' time there were no turkeys in Galilee or in Europe; the turkey was found as a result of the Columbian Exchange.

Returning to our parts, if there is no main course of Christmas tradition, it does not mean that at Christmas you do not eat; on the contrary, there would be: *The stuffed Ribs, La Turtera, the Tiano Stews, the Ravioli with Tomato Sauce* and there would be what we Ragusans call it: *Alliatina ..*

For the *Stuffed Pork Ribs,* these are large pork ribs with bone, which must be engraved in order to dig an inner bag that is filled with sautéed onion to which is added lean pork meat mixed with a little' suet. After a short cooking the filling can be mixed, with boiled and chopped egg yolks, with a whole raw egg and more breadcrumbs, grated cheese, salt and pepper.

The elements of this filling are inserted into the mentioned bag of the ribs that should be closed with a toothpick to avoid unpleasant spills. Once stuffed, the ribs should be covered with vegetable broth and baked until the broth evaporates. Before bringing them to the table you should make a short browning of the ribs in spicy red wine, to make them golden.

For *turtera,* is a characteristic dish of the cuisine of old Ragusa or South Ragusa, it is good to use minced lamb meat which, once salted and peppered, should be fried with suet and spiced with nutmeg, a few cloves and cinnamon powders; red wine can be used if the mixture is too dry.

Once the sauté is done, insert the grated caciocavallo cheese into the mixture. Now add some ricotta or pass it through a sieve, set aside two thirds and mix a third with an egg yolk.

Boil in vegetable broth the *Maccarruna, Causunedda or short pasta,* drain them al dente.
Wet the bottom of a baking tray with butter or suet and vegetable broth, place a layer of *causunedda* or short pasta previously boiled, place the fried and spicy lamb meat on top and follow a layer of ricotta. You should compose three layers and arrange the cottage cheese with the egg as the last compound. Sprinkle the surfaces of the turtera with ground cinnamon; slide a little broth along the circumferences of the tray and bake at 50 degrees for 20 or 25 minutes. Bring the *turtera* to the table in the same tray so as to preserve its warmth and aromas.

The *Tiano* would be the cooking vessel; a term that comes from the Arabic *Tajine;* which would be a terracotta or earthenware container, equipped with a lid, adaptable for cooking over high heat or in the oven. Clearly stews require slow cooking. To the sautéed onion, carrot and celery; segments of pork and veal meats are added; after the necessary browning, it is used the classic tomato paste mixture that will be diluted with red wine. Proceed the cooking of the ingredients over low heat; when it is considered appropriate, you can add segments of sausage meats to the *Tiano* and proceed to cooking always slowly, pouring red wine or broth if it should be considered necessary. Certainly in the composition of stews, the most renowned spices, such as: cumin or coriander, sage, bay leaves, oregano, juniper can be used.. When the meats are very tender and the sauces, the stew can be served accompanied with mashed potatoes and also as a condiment for pasta.

Although *Ravioli* are to be considered one of the pillars of Italian cuisine, it seems that the origin comes from the term French *Rauioles* and that they appeared in our country, as in the rest of Europe, around the fourteenth century; while in the South of France they existed previously.

In Sicilian home cooking it is difficult to find ravioli seasoned with meats or mushrooms or crustaceans; the filling of Sicilian homemade ravioli is composed of fresh ricotta and marjoram; a flavoring and mild spiced herb. The diatribe, about the filling of ravioli, would consist in whether we should add sugar to the ricotta or not. In my mom's kitchen she didn't put sugar in ravioli fillings but later my mom changed her mind.

Ravioli with tomato sauce or dressed with pork stew are one of the most delicious dishes of our cuisine.

Perhaps pork jelly has lost, in modern cuisine, its almost daily use of the post-war years; when it was considered, in winter, an inviting dish.

The process of composition required on the part of the housewives a complex culinary preparation due to the fact that: *nothing is thrown away from pork meats.*

In the gelatin aspic compositions were used the hidden parts of the pig such as: the head with ears, cheeks and muzzle and also the feet and shins.

These parts of the pig were soaked in hot water and then scraped with a knife to eliminate skin hair.

Nevertheless, some reddish hair remained attached to the skin but this was not a cause for concern on the part of the farmers.

Boil the parts of the pork in a large container, covering them with a composition of three quarters of water and one of vinegar, salt and lemon cut into slices; the cooking time of these parts, in general, must be at least two hours.

Once cooked, the meat must be boned and the pulps obtained must be arranged and wrapped in a cloth, giving them a shape of a large cylindrical sausage.

The cooking liquids were filtered and placed in a bucket. Once these liquids cooled, the fatty part that craped on the surfaces was eliminated.

Put the gelatinous liquids back on the fire to let them melt.

Carry out the cilindric shape of the meat and cut them into slices from the thickness of a finger.

Arrange three slices of meat for each single large and capacious dish and cover the meat with the broth obtained, place the red pepper flakes on top.

Allow the composition to cool so that gelatin is formed that will wrap the slices of mea

For the feast of St. John the Baptist and St. George protectors of the two Ragusa, the obligatory dish is the *Iadu cò Cinu,*that is the stuffed chicken or hen that the Romans, fond of stuffed foods, called: *Pullus Farsilis.*

The chicken had to be free-range or can be used a hen that had ceased to produce eggs; the fact that could give evidence to the saying: *Old hen makes good broth.*

The traditions of this dish include the division of the bird among the members of the family sitting at the same table:

One thigh belonged to the head of the family, that is, the father and the other thigh to the eldest son.

One wing to the mother and the other wing to the eldest daughter

The remaining parts were divided between family members and any guests

The *priest's morsel* was the neck of the hen. When the neck was pulled to the bird it was arranged upside down; so that the blood descended downwards, placing and stagnating in the neck of the poltry. As a result of boiling, the chicken's blood coagulated, clumsing around the vertebrae of the neck. This part of the bird was up to the grandfather in order to survive longer.

To the broth of chicken or pigeon the peasants also attributed therapeutic powers against diseases so apart from the use of celery and carrots, the broth was spiced with healing spices of cinnamon and nutmeg; so that the sick person found, with the ingestion of this dish, new vigors towards the coveted ricovery.

Since it was believed that if the sick person was healed it was the Patron Saint who performed the miracle; viceversa, in case of death it would have been the fault of the doctor; because of the lack of confidence that the peasants had in the science of Hippocrates.

In addition to the chicken broth clearly the wife of the sick person turned to the Saints for the speedy recovery of the relative; so it was necessary to light a lamp in the church, promise the ear pendants to the Vergin Mary and the braid of hair to Saint Sebastian and certainly to celebrate masses for the Holy Souls of Purgatory.

The recipe of *the Stuffed Chicken,* in the Hyblaean cuisine, is a masterpiece of Baroque art; when the kitchen fits well into the arts and creative structures of the place.

The success of the dish depends on the goodness of the filling, in which the chicken offal is used well cleaned and chopped that are combined in a sauté with oil and garlic and spices of nutmeg and cinnamon powders. When the heat is off, the sauté is mixed with fresh eggs, toasted bread crumbs and ground grains of black pepper, leaves of parsley and strips of seasoned caciocavallo.

At this point insert the filling into the sternum of the bird, making it adhere well in the interior; then take care to sew the cavity with needle and thread or to plug it in any way; for example by introducing a rectangle of aluminum foil internally.

The chicken is laid in a large pot with cold salted water, chunks of celery with leaves and carrots cut into cubes.

After boiling it is necessary to eliminate the foam that will form in the surfaces and proceed to complete cooking over medium heat, which can last up to two hours depending on the size of the chicken.

Once the bird is well cooked, to make it golden brown you could arrange it briefly to be cooked in the oven.

The savory broth can be used to compose an excellent first course using egg noodles or angel hair pasta.

Extract the filling that, during cooking, will be well composed and amalgamated; dissect the chicken into six or eight parts, divide the filling according to the parts of the chicken and distribute everything in the individual dishes or in a serving tray.

U Iaddu cò cinu in honor of the Patron Saint, can also be served with baked potatoes.

*   *   *

If the choices of the Christmas lunch could have been left to the free will of the housewives, the Easter Sunday lunch, in the Hyblaean countryside, would have been categorically orthodox: *Turciniuna of lamb entrails, breaded lamb and cassatelle of ricotta;* without lamb it was not Easter.

The family butcher was my *uncle Ciccio,*he said that, in sacrificing the aninals, he did not make them suffer; my father abstained from these practices and he did not eat lamb meat.

Fortunately, we did not use to kill suckling lambs but mature beasts.

Once our*Aunt Capece Minutolo* came to the farm to find tender lamb meat to make some pies and bring them to Naples, where she came from. My uncle was in town and the task of killing a young lamb was up to my father.

After we locked the mother sheep in the fold, we carried the lamb in our arms and placed it on a stone pavement.

The poor animal wriggled like crazy and my mom and I tried to keep him still.

We looked at my father, armed with a dagger and with his hands raised in the act of delivering the fatal blow; in that moment the lamb, I do not know why, stopped wriggling; there was a moment of total bewilderment.

Suddenly, my father throws the knife on the ground and emits a scream: *But,... Fuck off.* Then turning to my mother: you, tell your *auntie that she goes to buy it from a butcher shop, because I do not kill animals.*

That time I was really happy to bring the lamb back to the sheepfold where his mother Bianchina was waiting for him, emitting lyblaes that just seemed to be laments of call; the sheep ran to their little son and he immediately ceded on the udder to suck the mother's milk.

I am not a vegetarian but baby animals do not need to be killed; it is not true that their meats are better or more exquisite; at most a bit more tender but you can also do without it.

Better not to think about, but the Easter lamb pies were really good; it is believed that this culinary composition come from a Jewish colony that, apparently around the fifteenth century, had settled in the Hyblaean valley.

Finally to make *Impanata di Agnello* the lamb meats, including fats, are cut into cubes and were matured with olive oil, sea salt, black pepper, red pepper flakes, basil leaves and green garlic leaves or spring onions. The dough is like that of the bread previously described, possibly add a little fat to the dough such as olive oil, suet or butter; in order to make the dough more crumbly.

Pull two sheets with a rolling pin, which should not be so thin; one sheet will be used as a base and the other a little smaller as a lid cover.

Arrange the lamb meat on the base dough covering the surfaces abundantly, leaving only the thicknesses of the circumference free; then arrange the lid sheet and try to tightly join the two sheets operating what is called *riefico;* that is, turn and join the circumferences of the sheets with pinches.

Make with the cons of a fork some holes on the lid sheet, possibly brush the surface dough with egg yolk, to make it golden.

Once made, the lamb pies were placed in trays and baked in the well-arrenged stone oven; in a conventional oven the pies need to be baked at 200 degrees for at least 20 minutes.

As a result of cooking, the fats of the meat will melt by impregnating the basic dough, making it soft and appetizing.

Once the dough is well browned, even the meat inside will be well cooked.

This lamb pies are one of my favorite preparations and, once baked, I cut out the upper lid with scissors and present the pie well opened, placing on the cut sheet some lettuce salad seasoned with oil, salt and strips of aged cheese.

Animal entrails have always been a peasant dish; in the Middle Ages the four-legged animals belonged to the feudal lord, the two-legged ones belonged to the clerics and the farmer only the sardines or what remained of the animals, such as: leftovers and offal.

With regard to the latter; the internal parts of the lamb such as: Liver, lung, heart, the abdominal retina and the guts, are the parts used to compose the *Turciniuna,* an Easter dish of purely Sicilian and Ragusa tradition.

The offal of animals constituted in Sicily, especially in the city centers of Palermo and Catania, one of the dishes that at the time of today are called: *Street Food*.

A treaty should be made on this matter; in the city of Ragusa I remember only the peddler who sold the *Sanguinaccio or Sancielu;* that is the blood of the pig seasoned with cinnamon and chocolate, crammed into the large gut of the pig, boiled and kept warm.

The aforementioned entrails are thoroughly washed with coarse salt and lemon juice that acts as a sterilizer; lamb guts must be scraped and washed as above; the abdominal retina, called in dialect *Calia*, after being washed, is cut with scissors in the shape of a square.
Apart from the meats, which must be properly cut into non-tiny pieces, we need the strips of caciocavallo, salt, black pepper, fresh parsley and new onion stems that in the spring period is easy to find; can be used in this composition, along with meat and the already mentioned elements, also pins and stems of asparagus or asphodels tender stem..

For each individual roll, place the square of the retina on the working surface, place on top of the various pieces of meat, a stick of caciocavallo, the onion stem and everything else available; *seasoning* included. Tie the roll with the guts to prevent the retina from opening.
At this point the roll becomes *Turciniuni* because it is twisted around.

Before proceeding to frying, the *turciniuna* should be dipped in boiling water so that the meats heat up, losing blood and the elements join each other.
After the short boiling, the *turciniuna* should be fried in vegerable oil possibly; the duration of cooking depends on the size of the rolls; however, make sure that the turned meats are well cooked even if the surfaces of the retina will be slightly burned.

To complete the Easter review of the foods of the Hyblaean countryside, we can not do without the *Cassate di Ricotta* as those mentioned in the manuscript of San Martino delle Scale.

The dough of these *Cassatelle* is composed in incorporating and melting fats, such as suet or butter, in semolina flour: so in a kilo of flour we can use 100 grams of fat.

Arrange the flour, impregnated with fats, in a fountain and proceed, taking into account using a kilo of flour, to insert: 100 grams of sugar, three egg yolks, pinch of salt.

At this point if the dough should be hard; it can be soaked with water or Marsala wine and can be combined with grated lemon peels.

For the filling we certainly have the ricotta that must not be watery but well dry, which must be sifted to be combined with granulated sugar; in our case, we can use: 700 grams of ricotta with 500 grams of sugar; at this point the mixture can be garnished with chocolate chips.

Once we have obtained a soft and smooth dough, this is made to rest well covered; subsequently form round sheets, not very thin, with a diameter of 15-20 centimeters.

Raise the edges of the sheets to form a hem as high as the thickness of a finger and make sure that these edges remain straight, otherwise you should arrange the sheets in the freezer; to support these edges can be used the cutouts of the dough, forming cords that should be arranged inside the bases of the cassate.

Now practice with the thumb and index finger pinches in the hem, causing the folds that will give the *cassatelle* the classic shapes of fruit baskets.

Fill the *cassatelle,*almost to the edges, with the the ricotta cream and the flakes of dark chocolate.
In a normal kitchen oven the cassate should be baked for about 30 minutes at the optimum temperature of 180 degrees.
Once out of the oven, the surfaces of the cassate can be dusted with ground cinnamon.
To complete the topic, I personally insert a disk of almond paste or *Marzipan,* in the base of the sheets of the *cassatelle,*before filling them with ricotta cream.

This was the traditional Easter Sunday lunch: *Turciniuna, Impanata di agnello and Cassate;* made by the sicilian massaia or housewife for love, devotion and hunger in all the tables of the Hyblaean countryside.

Clearly the same foods could also be eaten for Easter Monday and the lamb pies, in particular, were used for the next two weeks after Easter; heating them in a bain-marie, that is, putting a little water and oil in a large pan, arrange the pie, cover with a lid and boil the liquids for a short time; which will make the breaded dough well soft and the internal meat will retain its flavors and aromas.

There were also occasions in Sicily to celebrate all the festivals and religious anniversaries with homemade sweets; such as: *Frittelle di San Martino, zeppole di San Giuseppe, mucatoli, cutumeddi, cuddureddi, fiscalora, pagnuccata, pignolata, impanatigni di Modica, amaretti al carob, cicirieddi al miele, crispelle di riso, nougat;*composition of sweet peaches, turkish heads, coffee cake, chocolate rice cake, sweet savoy, torta delizia, mandarin cake, royal almond biscuits, Sicilian cannoli - known and appreciated all over the world.

This list could last for a long time, occupying many spaces but to talk about it, even briefly, it would take another book. Certainly you can draw news and recipes of these characteristic sweeties of Sicily; reading, on the internet, the various cooking blogs.

I feel tenderness and pity, when on Easter Day, sorry if I repeat myself, I see people, especially young people who go to eat lunch at McDonald's; I wonder: *but how do you settle, on Easter Day, for a minute burger, a lick of ketchup and fries; and the waitresses of McDonald who tells you: Enjoy It.*

For those who have seen and experienced the Easter tables of Sicily it is impossible not to remember and try to reproduce the goodness of the foods of those tables: *The transcendescendality of gastronomy leads to the search for lost time.*

These foods represent the Hyblaean peasant civilization that has reigned for centuries.

* * *

A Christmas confection in my memory is the *Cubbaita,* of Arabic or, which in Ragusa is called: *Giuggiulena;* compote with sesame seeds, almonds, sugar and, if that were not enough, our honey.

The rhombus shape of *the giuggiulena* remind me of the bagpipes playerers who descended from the Hyblaean hills in the city streets to play the Christmas novenas, which lasted until 15 days after Christmas, that is, until January 9 when they played the last novena; in that dead end of the Via Sirena, under the long balcony sprinkled with flowers of my grandmother Marietta:

> *Chissa is the last nuvena*
> *Pani schittu and giurgiulena*

The music meant that the parties were over and with them also the stocks of delicious foods, we had to return to normal life that was not always lavish with delicacies and joys; when, for some families, they had left in fact in their pantries: a slice of bread and the last roar of the Christmas cake.

GUBBAITA OR GIUGGIULENA

Ingredients: A kilo of sesame that will be washed and dried in the oven over low heat without burning it. 600 grams of granulated sugar, 300 grams of Hyblaean honey, 500 grams of shelled, blanched and chopped almonds.

Procedure: In a large and capacious pan melt the sugar and honey, add the sesame seeds and insert the almonds into the mixture. Once the elements have come together, after short cooking; deposit the contents in a possibly of marble surfice, previously oiled. Wait for the mixture to cool a little down and smooth it out with a rolling pin, in order to obtain a well-compact square with the thickness of a finger. Now cut the *guggiulena* into diamonds shape. The confection will be crispy and certainly a little hard, but the taste of the sesame and almonds put togheter and cobined with honey is transcendental.

LA PERDUTA GIOVENTÙ

Trovare una mattina la via,
La pietra dove si volta.
una volta, una sola volta,
In un pugno di sillabe nude
Donarvi una leggenda che fu mia.

Da Suosoria, Collezione di Poesie, 1982
Autore: Gesualdo Bufalino

There are still present in my memory the images of *Massa Vannuzzu* when he sowed wheat in the field of *Fosso di Timpa della Mieta,* on an autumn day; taking from the saddle bag, which he carried over, the grain seeds to spread them evenly within the furrow path, throwing them in an oblique semicircle on one side first and then on the other; so that the distribution of the seeds could be regularly uniform. The transient and equal steps of the sower who at every right foot, spread a handful of wheat, from which the herbs, ears and seeds will be magically born: *The grace of God, food and human support.*

The land of The Harvest has been like a mother and a stepmother, the work of the fields although tiring and sometimes, let's face it, inhuman; has forged my soul and that of my two brothers towards that destiny to which each of us belongs.

* * *

The fishermen of Mazzarelli at dawn pushed their boats towards the waves that broked in the bows of the boats and the fishermen, with their bodies in the water and their soaked clothes, held with their hands firmly the planks of their boat to keep the bow straight, to prevent it from being overwhelmed by relentless waves.

The wives watched, with apprehension, their husbands fight against the breaks, until then the fisherman with a feline leap, mounted on the boat where the young son had previously taken his place to learn the hard trade of the sea; because a boat, a single wooden boat, 4 or 5 meters long, could have been the only good or the only source of living survival.

The hard job of the sea, where you can lose everything in a minute: life, the annexes and connected; because waves are not always placid or the wind always favourable.

Now in the weather forecast the storm surges are predictable for satellite images that reflect the approach of storms and hurricanes; in the past, it was more difficult to prevent the bad weather of the sea that was the cause of misfortune and mortality for sailors.

I have always admired, in the city of Catania, the iron statue of the *Malavoglia* that stands in the square named after the writer and verist author *Giovanni Verga*; where you can admire the boat called ' *The Providence* ' which is at the mercy of stormy waves: the old *'Ntoni* remains seated at the stern with his eyes lowered and his arms inert on his knees - He knows that there is nothing that can be done, meanwhile his son *Bastaniazzo* stands at the bow, with his arms raised and his body erected as if he wanted to face the God Neptune: a useless resistance, man can do nothing against nature; our God is the Universe and its laws are not always benevolent towards us humans.

*   *   *

In my now not short existence, I have returned few times to the Via Sirena and wandered through the adjacent narrow street or *vanelle* sorrounding the Ecce Homo Church; no longer as a resident but in the undeserved role of an *ex.*
I try to scrutinize the faces of those I meet, to remember or to be remembered, to exchange or reciprocate a smile or a past event; to find the lost time, as Marcel Proust did.

The *vanelle* are now silent, the stoned pavements have been covered with a mantle of pitch - black as the death - the roofs of the houses are covered with moss, the shutters lowered and hermetically closed; of the flowers and plants, which adorned windowsills and balconies, only the roots remain from which no more shoots will sprout.

- *Sunt Lacrimae Rerum, Mentem Mortalia Tangunt*

The tears of things that touch human feelings

- From*Virgil's Aeneid, 70-19ac*

Yet in those *vanelle* the popular life of the neighborhood took place, they were enlivened by the voices of the wives, by the cries of the street vendors, by the resounding workshops of artisans, by shops and shopkeepers, by the scents of a pastry cafe', by the fashions of the clothes displayed in the windows of the tailor's shop, by serenades to loving hearts, by love appointments, the songs of mothers, the cries of newborns and by the furies of us kids who imitated the deeds of the musketeers of Dumas.

The red dyed sunsets in the *vanelle* of the Ecce Homo, when the loudspeaker of the Church was heard reciting the Rosary and the Litany; then the pious women sat on the threshold of their homes with the rosary crown between their fingers; in the company of the daughters or granddaughters who they passed, on their white hairs, the narrow comb: a tribute to the grannies so that they could present themselves beautifully and attractive and they were pleased with these amorous practices addressed to their person.

These pious women, then, gave a smile and a wish to all passers-by and often they stopped to dialogue with them, they talked about household chores, the prices of fruits, the collection of crops or the state of health of family members, and more or less.

It was said that in Ragusa we all knew each other by name or by nickname.

Look out
to the balconies of the Via Sirena,
my fair women and
give a good-natured smile
to your unworthy villager.

I am one of yours, I still remember your names; we lived together the events, the stories, the rumors of the neighborhood, we shared the tribulations of life: rejoiced for the newlyweds and prayed, in the same altar, for the sick and convalescents; we wept for the dead and implored God for the salvation of our souls.

Come on, let's spread the white table cloth, the one with embroidered hems,then place those crispy wafers of vanilla cream non it: a single biscuit to be dragged into the world of my lost youth.

Let's Take from your neat pantry the little coffee cups with the golden edges, let's pour into the jagged small glasses the shining drops of the rosolio; tell me the funny stories of the kid called *Giufà* or tell me again the amazing deeds of the Paladins of King Charles The Great; repeat the sad verses: How the hero Orlando was betrayed or how for love he lost his mind .

YES, JUST YOU , My Fair Women,
because you have loved only one man;
defended, with the strength of your fists, the sacredness of the family;
accepted everything quietly, even
swallowing the bitterness of your own tears.

You have found the fortitude to take out the bread from your mouth,
and give it to others more in need;
You have untied with teeth the knots that others have fastened;
You that had suffered the lost war and even the peace in the coming time,
You that have faced the deprivations of life by digging with bare hands the land that was not yours .

Brides and mothers who have warmed your babies by attaching them to the soft breasts;
and then abandon the feathers of your bed, at the dawn of the day, because it was necessary to knead the bread to feed the old and young of the family.
Yes, you, Sicilian mothers and brides have been the angels who have erudited the arcane history of our peasant cuisine.

How nice it would be to meet again for just a single interminable moment and live it intensely, touch our land, the civilization of the customs that belonged to you and that you transmitted to us when, in our countryside, there was a lack of electricity, running water, no toilet, no television, no cars or telephone or radiators and all those things that are now called *Comforts;* in your time comforts were not means but human feelings.

EPILOGO

- *It is true that the Sicilies are many, we will never stop counting them.*
- *There is the green Sicily of the carob tree, the white one of the salt, the yellow one of the sulfur, the blonde one of the honey, the purple one of the lava.*
- *There is a Sicily that is mild until it seems stupid; a Sicily that is clever, dedicated to the most utilitarian practices of violence and fraud.*
- *There is Sicily 'Pigrà, a 'Freneticà, one that stretches itself in the anguish of the stuff, one that recites life like a Carnival script; one, finally, that is handed by a ridge of excess wind of dazzled delirium.*
- *So many Sicilies, why?*
- *Because Sicily has had the fate of being the hinge between the great Western culture and the temptations of the desert and the sun; between reason and magic, the times of feeling and of passion.*

- Prof. Gesualdo Bufalino, from Comiso

- Prof. Bufalino, endowed with a great humanistic and literary spirit, whom I had the immense pleasure of meeting personally and appreciating his installations and acute reflections; he could have moved and lived comfortably in Milan or Rome, Venice, Florence; or in any other city or district of the Peninsula; like many Sicilian writers did. He decided to remain in his hometown; not because Comiso is the most beautiful city in Italy but Comiso, which he called 'Città-Teatrò', was his homeland and the Comisani were and will be his fellow citizens: the writer identified himself as a Comisano, a legitimate son of our Sicily, whose history, customs, styles, idioms, aspirations, perplexities and anxieties he embraced with indoitable faith .

* * *

There would be one last line in the touching considerations of Dino Bufalino:

- *Understanding Sicily for a Sicilian means understand the ego, absolving or condemning himself.*

For my part, I have only tried to absolve myself towards the mistakes I have committed, the battles I have lost; to whom I disappointed, who or what I should have loved the most and did not.

* * *

One Sunday morning of that fateful 1987, after a murky rest, I rose in that of Punta Secca; the cottage was empty, I had lost my job and family: my wife had disappeared with another, taking away even our innocent two teenagers sons..

As chance would have it, I came across a magazine entitled: *Settembre in Cucina*, in which I read the recipe for spaghetti with tuna sauce.
I looked at the almost empty pantry where, who knows how long, they had been staying: a tuna box, a bag of spaghetti and a carton with tomato sauce.

I don't remember what made me cooking, as if fate moved my hand: I boiled the pasta and composed the tuna sauce, after assembling the elements, I sat down to the bare table; I try eating but tears came out.

That pasta and those tears had the power to crush bad thoughts from the mind; to the point that I promised myself to forget, not the children or my mother, but to shake a load of one hundred kilos related to a past that, for over a decade, weighed on my shoulders and that, from this moment on, I no longer had to give an account to any of my relatives, direct or acquired that they were, about the modus operandi regarding my future.

That food made me realize that I was a free spirit and as such make those decisions that I would have deemed appropriate and led me to create new resolutions that were to dedicate the rest of my life, no matter where or when and how: to food, cooking and the relevant gastronomic history.

I was aware that I would have to prepare a suitcase, put what I had left in it and head towards the unknown, venture towards a perigliosoful future on which I could rely only on my physical strength; meet new people, find remedies to survive, face fatigue and hardship, find the strength and courage with the determination not to succumb, to achieve specific goals and I was perfectly aware that it would not be easy to start weaving that canvas again at forty years of age among unknown people; that would turn out to be not complacent but, at the same time I was aware that human beings are not insensitive.

After various vicissitudes, such as spending sleepless nights at train stations or jumping from moving trains to not pay the ticket; I had the good fortune to be hired, on the occasion of the Tuscan harvest, in that of Pomino and later I found work as an agricultural worker in the Florentine Hills.

In those fertile countryside I met many unforgettable people and families who, on occasions, invited me to their canteens to divide the ribollita, the pappardelle with hare sauce, the rotisserie, the wild boar porchetta cooked by the foresters and consumed under the fragrant shadows of the fir trees.

I am surprised by the days of September 1987, spent in that of Pomino, among the rows of lush vineyards, to collect the precious grapes of: Pinot Grigio, Trebbiano, Cabernet Franc, Sangiovese, Malvasia; the joyful songs of the harvesting students, the spicy stories told by the housewives, the daring invitations to dinners and dances addressed to the harvesters; the shoreliness and availability of all those who participated in that harvest; they made me smile again, they spurred me towards the joy of being in a different world from the one in which I had lived for twenty years and it was like returning to be what I was: a Young boy born in the Hiblean countryside.

My closest friends, then, were the plants of the Florentine Hills, which I had in care for four years; vineyards that alleviated my loneliness and gave me the strength to lick my wounds to find inner peace; that nocturnal peace that took place in front of the volutes of the fumes of the fireplace, in my agricultural accomodation, with the embers of that beneficial fire I cooked pasta with the sauce of spicy Tuscan sausages and on Friday evening, to celebrate the weekend, grilling in the wings above those burning ashes, the Florentine steak, bought in the town of San Casciano.

How can I forget the beautiful Settimia, caregiver of the farm, who, during my stay, took care of me and looked after me like a mother, in the same way with which she looked after her own son Albano, my life-time friend.
The day I told her that I was leaving for Scotland, she imitated a smile, then turned her back and I realized that Settimia was in tears for my leaving: like a subdued emotion of a mother when her son moves away from the family.

It is true - In this world love and angels exist, friendship, generosity and respect are more available feelings, more frequent among simple people, troubled by fatigue and endowed with a big heart that is found in the countryside of Sicily or in those of Tuscany and certainly in all the districts of our Italian country.

They are not the false office colleagues, those who make friendship with the director manager to make a career; in the work of the fields you do not think about a career: *you just work*.

In the execution of handicrafts, such as cooking, it is not the director or the owner of the restaurant who gratifies the cooks; the skills, knowledge and, let's face it, the class of a cook, is noted in the goodness of the dish he has prepared and in the reception that this dish acquires from customers or guests.

In 1998 I wore the white jacket, I had become a professional cook in the Scottish city of Aberdeen; in 2006 a new restaurant called ' *Piccolo* ' was opened, of which I was the only cook; after a few months an article appeared for me unexpectedly in a Scottish newspaper: *Piccolo Restaurant, Hits High Notes for Foods*.

Ordinary people spoke well of the new restaurant, they appreciated my cuisine that was born from a passion for Sicily that, although geographically distant, had settled in my gastronomic feelings and adapted to a more international taste.

Other articles and interviews followed in the *magazines* of culinary fashions; which certainly made me so pleased; although the best compliments for me, were the spontaneous thanks of those who appreciated the hospitality and reception during the stay in the restaurant.

Well, after 40 years, I can at least say that I have kept the solemn promise of that unforgettable Sunday

This culinary research, on my land of Sicily, in which I intertwined stories, recipes and memories; it is an irrefutable proof that the determination and passion for the culinary art have not been extinguished; but these teachings of life have settled and rooted in my consciousness and I will carry them with me for as long as I have to live on this earthly life.

F. CAMPO
camporotondo1947@gmail.com

www.ingramcontent.com/pod-product-compliance
Lightning Source LLC
Chambersburg PA
CBHW041547120626
46551CB00002B/140